D0163051

TERRORNOMICS

Terrornomics

Edited by
SEAN S. COSTIGAN
Center for Security Studies, ETH Zurich, Switzerland

DAVID GOLD
Graduate Program in International Affairs, The New School, USA

ASHGATE

Published by
Ashgate Publishing Limited
Gower House
Croft Road
Aldershot
Hampshire GU11 3HR
England

Ashgate Publishing Company
Suite 420
101 Cherry Street
Burlington, VT 05401-4405
USA

Ashgate website: http://www.ashgate.com

British Library Cataloguing in Publication Data
Terrornomics
   1. Terrorism - Finance 2. Terrorism - Prevention
   I. Costigan, Sean S. II. Gold, David
   363.3'25

Library of Congress Cataloging-in-Publication Data
Terrornomics / edited by Sean S. Costigan and David Gold.
   p. cm.
  Includes index.
  ISBN-13: 978-0-7546-4995-3
  1. Terrorism--Finance. 2. Terrorism--Economic aspects. 3. Terrorism--Prevention. I. Costigan, Sean S. II. Gold, David.

   HV6431.T5544 2007
   363.325--dc22

                     2006034246

ISBN: 978-0-7546-4995-3

Printed and bound in Great Britain by TJ International Ltd, Padstow, Cornwall

Contents

Notes on Contributors

Katherine Barbieri is Associate Professor of Political Science at the University of South Carolina.

Frida Berrigan is Senior Research Associate with the Arms Trade Resource Center of the World Policy Institute at The New School.

Rico Carisch is a financial consultant and adviser to the United Nations.

Mark Edmond Clark is a military analyst and a foreign policy consultant.

Sean S. Costigan is Director for Strategic Initiatives, North America at the Center for Security Studies, ETH Zurich and co-chair of the Study Group on the Economics of Terrorism.

Rachel Ehrenfeld is the Director of the American Center for Democracy and the Center for the Study of Corruption and the Rule of Law.

Stephen E. Flynn is a former Commander in the US Coast Guard, and is Jeane J. Kirkpatrick Senior Fellow for National Security Studies at the Council on Foreign Relations.

David Gold is Associate Professor in International Affairs at The New School and co-chair of the Study Group on the Economics of Terrorism.

William D. Hartung is the President's Fellow at the World Policy Institute at The New School, Director of the Institute's Arms Trade Resource Center and co-chair of the Study Group on the Economics of Terrorism.

Michel Hess is Head of Studies and Training and directs the Master of Advanced Studies in Security Policy and Crisis Management program of the Swiss Federal Institute of Technology (ETH Zurich).

Russell D. Howard is Founding Director of the Jebsen Center for Counter-Terrorism Studies at The Fletcher School, Tufts University.

Gary Clyde Hufbauer is the Reginald Jones Senior Fellow at the Peterson Institute for International Economics.

Thomas Moll is a research assistant at the Peterson Institute for International Economics.

Loretta Napoleoni is an economist, journalist, and novelist. She has been researching terrorism since the 1980s.

Stacy Reiter Neal is a second-year MALD candidate at The Fletcher School at Tufts University, concentrating on non-governmental organization (NGO) management and migration studies.

Swapna Pathak is a PhD candidate at the University of South Carolina.

Rachel Stohl is a senior analyst at the Center for Defense Information and chairperson of the Small Arms Working Group.

Rockford Weitz is a PhD candidate at The Fletcher School concentrating on counter-terrorism.

Foreword

Show Me the Money

Brig. Gen. (ret.) Russell D. Howard

"Show me the money" is one of the most recognized catch-phrases of the last decade. First made famous in the 1996 Academy Award-nominated movie *Jerry McGuire* starring Tom Cruise, Cuba Gooding, Jr., and Renee Zellweger, the phrase has been widely used—some might say abused—within virtually all realms of society, from the political, social, and cultural to (not surprisingly) the economic.

"Show me the money" is an especially appropriate phrase to keep in mind when discussing and analyzing counter-terrorism efforts (although perhaps "Follow the money," a phrase made famous two decades earlier by the film *All the President's Men*, is more appropriate, if less contemporary). Eclipsed only by sophisticated communications monitoring capabilities, tracking terrorists' income, expenditures, and financial transfers is the most powerful mechanism in the intelligence arsenal for penetrating terrorist cells and organizations. This is particularly true for transnational, non-state actors such as Al Qaeda, who are not dependent on a state for operating capital, but instead have several independent income streams. It is also critically important for monitoring small terrorist cells that need only limited capital to fund their activities. When the recent investigation into the terrorist plot in the United Kingdom to destroy civilian airliners began, I suggested that, by "showing the money," investigators would get to the heart of the matter.

Terrornomics is an important and topical book that shows us the money, and much more besides. Contributors to *Terrornomics* are an eclectic group of academics, economists, and analysts from well-known think tanks, institutes, and universities specializing in security and terrorism studies. While their opinions and findings may differ at times, the authors of this comprehensive collection of original essays have the same purpose in mind: finding and defeating the terrorists that attacked the United States on 11 September 2001 and curtailing the threats posed by global terrorist groups.

At the Jebsen Center for Counter-Terrorism Studies at The Fletcher School of Law and Diplomacy at Tufts University, the overarching goal is to assist counter-terrorism professionals in their efforts to proactively counter terrorist threats today and in the future. To do this, the Center organizes its research efforts to further develop understanding and techniques for terrorist prediction, prevention, and preemption. Current prediction projects focus on knowledge management among counter-terrorism professionals and organizations, stress innovation as a key tool of counter-terrorism efforts, and seek to better calibrate knowledge management and counter-terrorism initiatives in general with the fluid and time-sensitive nature of the terrorist threat. Our research activities seek to provide long-term preventive diplomatic, economic, psychological, and military measures that could be taken to eliminate *causal* factors that prompt enemies to resort to terrorist activities.

The events of September 2001; the 2002 Bali, 2004 Madrid, and 2005 London bombings; the wars in Afghanistan and in Iraq; and the recent threat to destroy airliners flying to the United States—all accentuate the current hostile and perilous international security landscape, serving to keep us alert to the lessons learned from past tragedies and to changes in terrorist behavior and movements. *Terrornomics* will assist us all by analyzing the state of myriad fields related to money and terrorism, and by suggesting different policy and research pathways to combat it.

Because terrorist organizations must raise, move, and use money to exist and mount operations, aggressively pursuing terrorists on all financial fronts is an integral component of any counter-terrorism strategy. *Terrornomics* will be of great assistance to those employed in following this money. This book features contributions from a wide range of experts who offer a rich menu of cutting-edge economic and financial responses to the many facets of modern terrorism. The goal of this collection is to educate policy makers, academics, students, and concerned citizens about the critical economic and financial mechanisms that influence and fuel terrorist activity. Interdicting terrorists' means of financial support is one of the most—perhaps the most—important methods of defeating the terrorists who have declared war on civil society, modernity, and democracy. In this light, this volume will be of crucial interest to all those concerned with uncovering the financial flows that directly or indirectly result in terrorist attacks.

Acknowledgements

In our role as the editors of this volume, we are indebted to a great many people, particularly to the presenters at the Study Group on the Economics of Terrorism, in which forum most of these papers were initially presented, and to William Hartung, who co-chaired the study group with us during the 2005–06 academic year. The study group, which took place under the auspices of The New School's Graduate Program in International Affairs, was made possible through the support of the Center for Security Studies, ETH Zurich. Andreas Wenger, Director of the Center for Security Studies, ETH Zurich, and Victor Mauer, Deputy Director for Research, were supporters of this effort from the start, and their insights were invaluable. Our colleagues at The New School's Graduate Program in International Affairs, the World Policy Institute at The New School, the Center for Security Studies, and the International Relations and Security Network are owed an enormous debt of gratitude as well. Thanks in particular to Myriam Dunn, Michel Hess, Vivian Fritschi, Christopher Pallaris, Doron Zimmermann, Robin Williams, and Philip Akre. Alexandra Bell and Sarah Marusek were instrumental in managing the meetings and handling the many administrative details, among other critical tasks, including the glossary. This book would not have been possible without the incomparable editing and watchful eye of Dr Paul J. Erickson. He has the Midas touch. Our publisher at Ashgate, Kirstin Howgate, was quick to support this volume, and her sage advice made the timely crafting of it feasible. In addition, we would like to thank the members of the study group themselves for making the study group, and this book, possible.

Sean S. Costigan and David Gold

List of Abbreviations

Agricultural Development Bank of Afghanistan	ADB
Anti-Money Laundering	AML
Area Maritime Security Committee	AMSC
Armenian Secret Army for the Liberation of Armenia	ASALA
Asia-Pacific Economic Cooperation	APEC
Bank Secrecy Act	BSA
Basque Homeland and Freedom (Euskadi Ta Askatasuna)	ETA
Benevolence International Foundation	BIF
Bureau of Alcohol, Tobacco, and Firearms	BATF
Bureau of Industry and Security	BIS
Central Intelligence Agency	CIA
Combating the Financing of Terrorism	CFT
Commercial, off-the-shelf	COTS
Committee for Human Rights	CHR
Company Security Officer	CSO
Congressional Research Service	CRS
Container Security Initiative	CSI
Conventional Arms Transfer	CAT
Council on Foreign Relations	CFR
Countering of Financing for Terrorism	CFT
Counter-Terrorism Committee	CTC
Counter-Terrorism Committee Executive Directorate	CTED
Critical Infrastructure Protection Board	CIPB
Customs-Trade Partnership against Terrorism	C-TPAT
Cyber Incident Detection & Data Analysis Center	CIDDAC

Defense Threat Reduction Agency	DTRA
Demobilization, Disarmament, and Reconstruction	DDR
Ejercito de Liberacion Nacional	ELN
Executive Office for Terrorist Financing and Financial Crimes	EOTF/FC
FATF-style Regional Body	FSRB
Federal Bureau of Investigation	FBI
Financial Action Task Force	FATF
Financial Intelligence Units	FIU
Foreign Terrorist Organization	FTO
Improvised Explosive Device	IED
Instant Messenger	IM
Integrated Threat Assessment Centre	ITAC
International Action Network on Small Arms	IANSA
International Atomic Energy Agency	IAEA
International Consortium of Investigative Journalists	ICIJ
International Emergency Economic Powers Act	IEEPA
International Forest Monitor	IFM
International Islamic Relief Organization	IIRO
International Maritime Organization	IMO
International Monetary Fund	IMF
International Ship and Port Facility Security	ISPS
International Traffic in Arms Regulations	ITAR
Iran-Libya Sanctions Act	ILSA
Irish Northern Aid Committee	INAC
Irish Republican Army	IRA
Islamic Movement of Uzbekistan	IMU
Kababancola Mining Company	KMC
Kosovo Liberation Army	KLA or UCK
Kurdish Democratic Party of Iran	KDPI

Kurdistan Workers Party (Partiya Karkerên Kurdistan Workers Party)	PKK
Liberation Army of Presevo, Medvedja, and Bujanovac	UCPMB
Liberation Tigers of Tamil Eelam	LTTE
Man-portable air defense systems	MANPADS
Maritime Transportation Security Act	MTSA
Memorial Institute for the Prevention of Terrorism	MIPT
Middle East Newsline	MENL
Mujahedin-e Khalq	MEK
Muslim World League	MWL
National Council of Resistance	NCR
National Liberation Army	NLA
National Money Laundering Strategy	NMLS
National Union for the Total Independence of Angola	UNITA
Nuclear Non-Proliferation Treaty	NPT
Office of Foreign Assets Control	OFAC
Office of Weapons Removal and Abatement	WRA
Offshore Financial Center	OFC
Operation Green Quest	OGQ
Organization for Security and Cooperation in Europe	OSCE
Organization of American States	OAS
Palestine Liberation Organization	PLO
Partido Socialista Obrero Español	PSOE
Physical Security and Stockpile Management	PSSM
Politically Exposed Person	PEP
Proliferation Security Initiative	PSI
Provisional Irish Republican Army	PIRA
Revolutionary Armed Forces of Colombia	FARC
Revolutionary United Front	RUF
Secure and Facilitated International Travel Initiative	SAFTI

Terrornomics

Small arms and light weapons	SALW
Society for Worldwide Interbank Financial Telecommunication	SWIFT
Specially Designated Narcotics Trafficker	SDNT
Specially Designated Terrorist	SDT
Specially Designated Global Terrorist	SDGT
Supervisory Control and Data Acquisition	SCADA
Surface-to-Air Missile	SAM
Suspicious Activity Report	SAR
United Defense Forces of Colombia	AUC
United Nations Office on Drugs and Crime	UNODC
United Nations Security Council Resolution	UNSCR
United Self-Defense Forces of Colombia	AUC
United States Central Command	CENTCOM
United States Department of Homeland Security	DHS
United States Department of State	USDOS
United States Drug Enforcement Administration	DEA
United States Foreign Terrorist Asset Tracking Center	FTATC
United States Government Accountability Office	USGAO
Weapons of Mass Destruction	WMD
World Customs Organization	WCO
World Food Program	WFP
World Health Organization	WHO
World Trade Organization	WTO

Introduction

Sean S. Costigan

Today, no single issue dominates the global political landscape as completely as terrorism. Aware of their unique position in the newly unipolar world, terrorist leaders—Osama bin Laden foremost among them—have articulated a plan of attack that places economic warfare at the center of the new terrorist agenda. Governments have heightened the role of economic tools in their counter-terrorism policies while simultaneously maintaining an emphasis on the application of military force, or "hard power," even though such an approach often proves unnecessarily blunt, or in some cases is sorely inadequate. Given the complexity of the global threat posed by modern trans-national terrorist groups, combating terrorism with a mix of hard and "soft power" is more important than ever. The need for nuanced management and a full complement of choices in the policy toolkit is a pressing concern, one that a focus on military solutions largely ignores.

Recent economic efforts to combat terrorism have concentrated on denying terrorists access to financial resources and deterring states and groups from providing financial support to terrorists; they have also included the development of policies designed to discover and prevent terrorist acts. Tracking funding, closing off easy access to resources, physically hardening economically valuable targets such as power plants and industrial facilities, separating fact from fiction regarding terrorism's roots, understanding how terrorism itself can become a business, learning what costs the private and public sectors need to absorb, prioritizing risks, planning for continuity during emergencies as well as recovery after attacks—these are just some of the critical issues that require more extensive study if global terrorism is to be successfully relegated to the back burner of the world's security scene. Economic tools and policies—such as imposing sanctions against state sponsors of terrorism or monitoring financial transactions for suspicious signs—are not panaceas for what is clearly a complex and deeply rooted problem. Nonetheless, the development and rigorous use of such tools may dissuade plotters, uncover plans and, as has been seen, help in the apprehension and conviction of terrorists.

The twin goals of defending an individual nation's security and treating terrorism as a global problem that spans national and regional boundaries demand smart decision-making. Given that resources are finite—both for the terrorists and for those defending against them—not every potential target can or need be safeguarded with the same level of security. Thus, the task of prioritization becomes of paramount importance. To facilitate further study of the issues and to assist in such prioritization, the chapters in *Terrornomics* are arranged into the following sections: *Financing Terror* (Napoleoni, Ehrenfeld, Hess, and Clark); *Issues and Analyses* (Hartung and Berrigan, Stohl, Costigan, Weitz and Neal, and Barbieri and Pathak); and *Policies* (Carisch, Hufbauer and Moll, and Flynn). The chapters that compose *Financing Terror* examine the techniques employed by terrorists to raise money for their operations, including the sale of illegal drugs and the exploitation of charitable organizations. The chapters in the section *Issues and Analyses* deal with wide-ranging concerns including the weapons trade, cyber-terrorism, suicide bombing and knowledge sharing, and the costs of free trade. Finally, the chapters making up *Policies* serve to detail the range of policy options available to governments and institutions.

When Osama bin Laden suggested in 2004 that "bleeding America to the point of bankruptcy" was a goal of Al Qaeda, it was evident that he understood that the response to terrorist acts could be both costly and, perhaps, ultimately as damaging as the initial tally of lost lives and damaged infrastructure. However, while terrorists continue, as ever, to seek the biggest bang for their buck, derailing the US economy is a formidable task. According to the National Commission on Terrorist Attacks upon the United States (popularly known as the 9/11 Commission), the attacks against the World Trade Center and Pentagon cost somewhere between USD 400,000 and 500,000 to execute, plus the costs of training the 19 hijackers. Despite the deplorable human tragedy that unfolded on 9/11, as well as the destruction of the World Trade Center and the damage caused to the Pentagon, the overall effect of the attacks on the economy of the United States was marginal when looked at in the aggregate. In the introduction to *Resilient City*, Howard Chernick notes: "There is no question that in the short run the 9/11 attack was spectacularly successful. ... Despite the magnitude of the losses, the sheer size of New York's economy kept the effects relatively small as a fraction of total economic activity, and the flexibility of markets in New York has enabled the city to recover much of its economic vibrancy" (Chernick, 2005).

However, the costs of the war on terror are prodigious. There is debate on whether or not the war in Iraq should be considered to be part and parcel of the war on terror, but its tremendous costs are not to be denied. Depending on what variables one tallies—for example, healthcare costs for wounded veterans, lost productivity, equipment replacement, additional expenditures, and so on—the cumulative budget cost of the wars in Iraq and Afghanistan to the United States will easily go over USD 500 billion in 2007 (Belasco, 2006). The eminent economist Joseph Stiglitz has made the argument that the real cost of the war in Iraq alone is likely to be between USD 1 and 2 trillion, and perhaps more (Bilmes and Stiglitz, 2006). According to Gordon Adams, "Including all the funds Congress has voted this year, we will have spent $437 billion on Iraq, Afghanistan, and other parts of the war on terror since 2001—about $1,500 for every American" (Silverstein, 2006). As detailed by the Congressional Research Service, 73 percent of this USD 437 billion goes to the war in Iraq and 20 percent to the war in Afghanistan, while 6 percent is being used to enhance base security, with the remaining 1 percent having not been allocated (*ibid*). It is easy to imagine that it was figures such as these that Osama bin Laden had in mind when he announced that damaging the US economy was one of Al Qaeda's goals. Yet, just as terrorists are targeting the economies of Western nations, those nations are beginning to target the economies of global terror.

By tracing the dollars that support the terror networks, Loretta Napoleoni estimates that the new economy of terrorism has now grown, in both legal and illegal transactions, to rival the GDPs of large countries. As she points out, terrorist financing is a moving target, with new sources of revenue emerging all the time, and new tricks to preserve and direct the flow of money being invented constantly. In order for governments to successfully address the terrorist threat, they must consider the evolution of terrorist financing and develop better ways of predicting its next steps. Unilateral economic policies are not sufficient, and indeed, as Napoleoni contends, have simply forced shifts in terrorist finances and operations.

Michel Hess's research suggests that fund-raising through diaspora institutions and individuals is little understood, but is of enormous importance to combating terrorists worldwide. Hess notes that among the many difficulties of sorting good money from bad is the fact that financial support for terrorist activities can be generated both by legal and illegal diaspora sources, and is channeled through legitimate charities as well as shadowy front organizations. As Mark Clark's case study shows, the Iranian exile group MEK is but one terrorist organization that has proven its ability to draw on a diaspora community through both legal and illegal methods. The techniques he describes are likely similar to those used to extract support from other diaspora groups, and deserve more detailed scrutiny. Reiterating that root causes must be examined and treated in order to reduce terrorism, Hess states, "money is not the root cause of the terrorist scourge. While effective measures against the financing of terrorist acts and activities are important, they are not sufficient to eliminate the root causes of the problem: unsolved ethnic, political, religious, ideological, or socio-economic conflicts and disparities." Hess suggests that a certification regime for diaspora non-profit organizations would help confirm to donors that their contributions will not be used to support terrorist causes. Hess also stresses that counter-terrorism and intelligence agencies should focus on the small transfers of illegal money that make terrorist operations possible.

Illegal drugs play a significant role in funding terror. In 2003 the United Nations reported that the global illicit drug market was "estimated at USD $13 billion at the production level, at $94 billion at the wholesale level (taking seizures into account), and at $322 billion based on retail prices and taking seizures and other losses into account. This indicates that despite seizures and losses, the value of the drugs increase substantially as they move from producer to consumer" (UNODC, 2005, 127). Disturbingly, according to the United Nations Office on Drugs and Crime, Afghanistan's opium harvest in 2006 showed an increase of 59 percent over the previous year, meaning that Afghanistan in 2006 produced around 92 percent of the world's supply of opium (UNODC, 2006; Oliver, 2006). Much of the money generated by the production and sale of Afghan opium is funneled into terrorist hands, a fact that should serve as a powerful reminder of the dynamics and connections of the drug market. Rachel Ehrenfeld examines the nexus of organized crime, drugs, and terrorism, with an eye to explaining what distinguishes these endeavors from one another and what binds them together. She delves into case studies of the IRA, FARC, and Hezbollah, and considers the roots of "narco-terrorism," or terrorist acts carried out by groups that are directly or indirectly involved in cultivating, manufacturing, transporting, or distributing illicit drugs.[1] Ehrenfeld recommends implementing crop

---

1   The term *narco-terrorism* is generally applied to groups that use the drug trade to fund terrorism. However, it has also sometimes been used to refer to the phenomenon of increasingly close ties between powerful drug lords motivated by profit and terrorist groups with political agendas.

eradication programs and more stringent financial controls as ways to stem the flow of drug-generated dollars into terror networks, and offers pragmatic ways in which the United States can fight back—starting by identifying those who fund terror operations against the US and the West, and by being more vigilant about pursuing the terrorists' sources of funds, in particular the illegal drug trade.

Tracing the dollars behind terrorist networks is a key component of international counter-terrorism. As Rico Carisch states in his chapter, "The successful suppression of terrorism by discovering and tracking terrorists' sources of financing can result only once all the relevant political and bureaucratic processes are tuned to each other and cooperate fully." Carisch details how United Nations regulatory responses in the wake of 9/11 were hastily put together from bits and pieces of existing Security Council approaches, which included arms embargoes, economic sanctions, diplomatic restrictions, targeted financial sanctions, and individual travel bans. Despite this tendency toward ad hoc solutions, the United Nations remains a critical player in combating terrorism. Paul Allan Schott of the World Bank argues that the UN's role is significant for several reasons, including its broad membership, the active Global Program against Money Laundering (GPML), and its power to adopt treaties and conventions that become law in ratifying countries (Schott, 2003). A key element in the international fight against terrorism is the International Convention for the Suppression of the Financing of Terrorism, which was adopted in December 1999. The convention requires states to identify, detect, and freeze funds that are suspected of being used to support terrorist organizations, and to criminalize the funding of terrorist activities. This convention came into force in April 2002 with 112 countries ratifying it.

However, the concurrent debates on the viability and effectiveness of the United Nations have sapped much of the momentum of its counter-terrorism efforts. In his chapter "Institutionalized Responses to 9/11," Carisch criticizes the interagency process and lack of cooperation as the main culprits of 9/11. "As the 9/11 Commission made abundantly clear," Carisch writes, "the tragedies of 9/11 were made possible not because the perpetrators were unrecognized, but because no coordination of analysis and interdiction took place." Carisch—drawing on his expertise as a financial consultant specializing in compliance responses and security risks involving corporate networks, political power structures, and criminal and terrorist networks—posits that government agencies charged with fighting terrorism could learn much from the corporate world. Faced with the critical need to protect assets from terrorists, the private sector "needed to act fast and simply developed a prevention system on its own."

Understanding how governments spend money on counter-terrorism efforts is not without challenges. Looming largest among these difficulties is the fact that most of the world's governments do not transparently publish their defense, public safety, and civil protection budgets. Further confounding research efforts is the fact that few governments make budgetary distinctions between counter-terrorism and defense or policing efforts. Such caveats aside, researchers can use online and open sources to construct a general picture of how much money is being spent by the United States, Canada, some European governments, and other countries.

Canada began increasing its counter-terrorism spending prior to 9/11 after Ahmed Ressam, an Algerian living in Canada, was caught crossing on a ferry into Washington State with enough explosives to demolish a building. The so-called Millennium Plot, which ostensibly was a plan to attack Los Angeles International Airport on or about 1 January 2000, increased awareness of the porous border between Canada and the United States. Shortly thereafter, the Canadian government increased funding to the Royal Canadian Mounted Police and the CSIS (Canadian Security and Intelligence Service) by an additional CD 810 million, and provided an additional CD 371 million for the Immigration Department. According to Glen McGregor, "then-finance minister Paul Martin's first security budget, released three months after the World Trade Center and Pentagon attacks, contained $7.7 billion in new counter-terrorism spending. The government set aside $2.2 billion for air security alone, with cash for reinforced cockpit doors, new machines to detect bombs in airline luggage and the establishment of the Canadian Air Transport Security Authority" (McGregor, 2004).

European countries typically spend between 1 and 2 percent of their gross domestic product on public order and safety. An in-depth study by Gustav Lindstrom of the EU Institute for Security Studies revealed that in 2002 only the UK and Spain spent more than 2 percent of GDP on counter-terror-related activities (Lindstrom, 2004). It is critical to note that, in most European countries, the budgets for counter-terrorism are typically spread across several departments and agencies. The following, partial list, derived from a Congressional Research Service study, offers some insights into a few notable European countries' counter-terrorism efforts:

- France does not have a homeland security effort similar to that in the United States. In 2003, the French government allocated 52 million euros (through 2008) to combat chemical, biological, and nuclear threats.
- Germany similarly lacks a ministry for homeland security. Activities are coordinated at the federal and state government level, and detailed budgets are publicly available. In 2004, state ministers of the interior implemented significant changes, including a centralized database for collection and retrieval of all information regarding suspected Muslim terrorists, and a joint coordination and cooperation center to integrate state and federal prevention efforts.
- The United Kingdom has several departments responsible for counter-terrorism. According to Kristin Archick of the Congressional Research Service, spending on civil protection in the UK increased to USD 53 billion in 2005 from USD 40 billion in 2001 and total spending on counter-terrorism across departments will be over USD 3.6 billion in 2007–08 (Archick, 2006).
- Switzerland's counter-terrorism efforts are also spread across several departments. Doron Zimmermann, Senior Researcher at the Center for Security Studies ETH Zurich, notes that, "Counter-terrorism funding in Switzerland is not transparent to the public. The budget for CT endeavors is spread across at least three departments—Justice, Defense, and Foreign Affairs—and it is certainly accessible to members of the relevant parliamentary oversight

panels" (e-mail correspondence with the author, 10 December 2006).

The United States is a special case. Immediately after the attacks of 9/11, the government of the United States took an active role in changing its counter-terror and intelligence institutions, resulting in a dramatic restructuring. Most notably, the US created an entirely new cabinet-level organization, the Department of Homeland Security (DHS), with wide-ranging authority over commerce, travel, immigration, information sharing, and prevention. The US administration also created the Office of the Director of National Intelligence (DNI), which serves as the head of the intelligence community. The reorganization has been costly, and has both supporters and detractors. For the purposes of this book and future study, significant questions remain as to whether American citizens are receiving a level of security that is commensurate with the level of spending to date, and whether the DNI will be in a position, at some point in the near future, to have true coordination and command of the intelligence put at his disposal, by law. Regarding the costs of this reorganization, according to a recent report from Veronique de Rugy of the conservative think tank the American Enterprise Institute, total US government spending on homeland security will be at least USD 49.9 billion for FY 2006, roughly USD 450 per American household (de Rugy, 2005). Furthermore, such financial resources are not always allocated transparently, making it that much harder to judge effectiveness. It is of utmost importance that budgets are made transparent to policy makers. As David Gold contends, "The US should establish greater spending and administrative discipline over the government agencies most responsible for combating terrorist activities. Such discipline should start with Congress, which has the constitutional authority to authorize and oversee spending but which must first discipline itself" (Gold, 2006).

The Washington-based Homeland Security Research Corporation estimates that worldwide annual counter-terrorism spending will reach USD 350 billion by 2010, with 36 percent of that figure spent by the United States alone. Yet, as several chapters in this volume point out, in many instances the critical work of identifying key potential targets in the United States and building appropriate defenses has yet to be done. As both Stephen Flynn and Rachel Ehrenfeld state, more than five years after 9/11, the United States is still exceedingly vulnerable to terrorist attack. As Flynn notes in his chapter, "The United States has been living on borrowed time—and squandering it. In the four years since the 9/11 attacks on New York and Washington, the Bush Administration has chosen to emphasize the use of military operations overseas over an effort to reduce America's vulnerability to catastrophic terrorist attacks at home."

On the whole, critical infrastructures continue to be susceptible to attack, and ports are particularly vulnerable. In the United States, private industry bears the brunt of security costs, even though industry's interests may be different from the government's. In their chapter, Katherine Barbieri and Swapna Pathak outline the divergence in priorities between operators and users of ports and the US government, highlighting the vulnerabilities that may result. As Barbieri and Pathak state: "The key concern of business is not an attack, but faster turn-around time at customs and at ports. Given the firms' priorities of cutting costs and the tendency to view a terrorist attack as highly improbable, the majority of small businesses are unlikely to want to increase security. Large businesses and vessel owners may be the exception. The problem is that much of the responsibility for security falls on the shoulders of private security firms." In another area that is largely the responsibility of the private sector in the United States, computer networks—though they have not yet been targeted by terrorists—remain by and large as open to attack today as they were before 9/11. My chapter on cyber-terrorism details the hype, costs, and potential risks associated with this threat. In addition, through examining trends in cyber-crime and in how terrorists are using information technologies, and what has been done to date to curtail such behaviors, the chapter concludes that both government and the private sector need to do a much better job of securing the critical infrastructures on which our lives and livelihoods increasingly depend. As Stephen Flynn notes, "Today's terrorist masterminds know that the main benefit of attacks on critical infrastructure is not the immediate damage they inflict, but the collateral consequences of eroding the public's trust in services on which it depends." With regard to cyber-crime and cyber-terrorism, furthering international cooperation is a key step in preventing the next generation of terrorists from using information technologies both as weapons and force multipliers, since insufficient mutual aid and limited enforcement regimes in many regions of the world currently allow criminals the space to work with relative impunity and at little risk to themselves. Port security should likewise receive further attention, and policy makers should examine the risks associated with leaving security decisions primarily in the hands of actors in the private sector, who are more interested in lowering costs than in maximizing security. Securing critical infrastructures from the disruptions that could be caused by terrorists should be a high priority.

Increasing knowledge on how governments fight terrorism is critical if a truly international and successful counter-terror effort is to be maintained. Sanctions are only one tool that requires an international stance. Though the use of economic sanctions in the twentieth century has not revealed a multitude of instances where foreign policy goals have been achieved solely through their use, sanctions can play an important role in counter-terrorist policies. As Gary Hufbauer and Thomas Moll put it in their chapter, "Economic sanctions, in particular, have routinely foreshadowed or accompanied broader war efforts. What sets the campaign against international terrorism apart from other wars is the emphasis on economic tools." The supporting role of sanctions in the financial struggle to limit terrorist groups' support originated in the Clinton Administration, and has been reinforced by the current Bush Administration. While Hufbauer and Moll note that economic sanctions have rarely worked on their own—and are particularly difficult to impose on trans-national, non-state actors such as Al Qaeda—they do not discount the use of economic sanctions in the campaign against terror. As in the case of Libya, sanctioning states that support terrorists can work. In addition, Hufbauer and Moll note that the United States has realized the need to recalibrate its arsenal of economic weapons, having realized that "confronting the new terrorist enemy has required the mixing of sanctions strategies according to their intended target: nation-state or terrorist group."

Weapons, particularly small arms, play an important role in supporting terrorist activities. Frida Berrigan and William Hartung detail their dual role in international terrorism. Weapons serve both as the tools with which terrorists perpetrate violent acts and as a source of money, generating revenue through arms trafficking. Berrigan and Hartung note that, "in the current period it is possible for these organizations to become virtually self-financing, or to find their own sources of armaments without any significant help from governments." Small arms and light weapons, as Rachel Stohl notes in her chapter, are the ideal tools for terrorists. For example, as evidenced by several near catastrophes in the past few years, Man-Portable Air Defense Systems (MANPADS) that have fallen into terrorist hands are a known threat to civilian airliners. As Stohl notes, "the linkages between small arms and terrorism have been clearly articulated by the United States government in three distinct areas: policies on MANPADS, policies on arms exports, and official policy statements on the illicit trade in small arms." Understanding the linkages and the shifts in arms procurement and financing are critical to helping curtail terrorism.

Modern terrorism is a complex phenomenon, and the heads of terrorist organizations are often acutely aware of trends in policy and law enforcement. The most savvy of these leaders have shown themselves capable of readily meeting the need to adopt and transmit new skills and practices in order to better ply their deadly trade. It is now often observed that Al Qaeda is a network-based organization, one that is in search of new ways of doing business. Along those lines, as Rockford Weitz and Stacy Reiter Neal point out, "to realize its full potential, a network-based terrorist organization must develop the capability to identify potential new technologies, weapons, or know-how successfully employed by individual terrorist nodes, and evaluate them for wider use and exploitation by other terrorist nodes across its network." They posit that, in order to understand the challenges and opportunities facing Al Qaeda, one should consider their efforts through the lens of the Technology Adoption Life Cycle, particularly as Al Qaeda attempts to furnish other terrorist groups with new skills and best practices. Weitz and Neal speculate that Al Qaeda is a network trying to maximize its opportunities in the same way that a successful business enterprise would, and that the ability to predict Al Qaeda's use of new technologies, weapons, and methods will be instrumental in preventing Al Qaeda from becoming more lethal and effective.

Terrorism is not truly an "ism" in the popular sense; it is a tactic, not an ideology. While politically useful after the tragedies of 9/11, declaring war on a tactic has not helped define the nature of the threats, nor has it clarified what measures can be taken to diminish them. It is clear that military power—which has been critical in unseating terrorists from a position of security in Afghanistan—is not the only solution. Terrorism is not a problem that only occurs in some other land. Criminal investigative and human intelligence efforts will remain key methods in the struggle to deter and preempt terrorists, and ought to be given substantial support. Economic and financial efforts, such as those mentioned in this volume, are equally necessary endeavors. Continued study of the relationships between terrorism, diaspora communities, the weapons trade, cyber-crime, and drug trafficking will help foster new approaches and techniques to combat and minimize terrorism.

References

Archick, Kristin (2006), "European Approaches to Homeland Security and Counterterrorism," Report 33573 (Washington, DC: Library of Congress, Congressional Research Service) (6 December); at <http://www.fas.org/sgp/crs/homesec/RL33573.pdf>

Belasco, Amy (2006), "The Cost of Iraq, Afghanistan and Other Global War on Terror Operations Since 9/11," Report 33110 (Washington, DC: Library of Congress, Congressional Research Service) (16 June); at <http://www.fas.org/sgp/crs/natsec/RL33110.pdf#search=%22%24437%20billion%20afghanistan%22>

Bilmes, Linda and Stiglitz, Joseph (2006), "The Economic Costs of the Iraq War: An Appraisal Three Years After the Beginning of the Conflict," NBER Working Paper No. 12054 (Cambridge, MA: National Bureau of Economic Research); at <www.nber.org/papers/w12054>

Chernick, Howard, ed. (2005), *Resilient City: The Economic Impact of 9/11* (New York: Russell Sage Foundation).

de Rugy, Veronique (2005), "What Does Homeland Security Spending Buy?" AEI Working Paper No. 107 (Washington, DC: American Enterprise Institute); at <http://www.aei.org/publications/pubID.21483/pub_detail.asp>

Gold, David (2006), "Is the War on Terror Worth It?" Security Policy Working Group (Amherst, MA: The Proteus Fund); at <http://www.proteusfund.org/spwg/pdfs/Is%20The%20War%20On%20Terror%20Worth%20It.pdf>

Lindstrom, Gustav (2004), "Protecting the European Homeland," Chaillot Paper No. 69 (Paris: Institute for Security Studies); at <http://www.iss-eu.org/chaillot/chai69.pdf>

McGregor, Glen (2004), "Cash Alone Can't Terror-Proof Canada," *The Vancouver Sun* (15 December).

Oliver, Mark (2006), "UN Urges NATO Crackdown on Afghan Opium," *Guardian Unlimited* (12 September); at <http://www.guardian.co.uk/afghanistan/story/0,,1870814,00.html>

Schott, Paul Allan (2003), "Reference Guide to Anti-Money Laundering and Combating the Financing of Terrorism" (Washington, DC: The World Bank); at <http:// www1.worldbank.org/finance/html/amlcft/referenceguide.htm>

Silverstein, Ken (2006), "Six Questions for Gordon Adams on the Real Cost of the War on Terror," *Harper's Magazine* (3 August); at <http://harpers.org/sb-six-questions-for-gordon-adams-1154646051.html>

United Nations Office on Drugs and Crime (UNODC) (2005), *World Drug Report 2005* (Vienna: UNODC).

United Nations Office on Drugs and Crime (2006), "Afghan opium cultivation soars 59 percent in 2006, UNODC survey shows," UNODC Press Release (2 September); at <http://www.unodc.org/unodc/press_release_2006_09_01.html>

PART 1
Financing Terror

Chapter 1

The Evolution of Terrorist Financing Since 9/11: How the New Generation of Jihadists Fund Themselves

Loretta Napoleoni

Jihadist terrorist financing is a dynamic phenomenon; indeed, it is the most challenging aspect of modern terrorism. So far, these terror groups have shown a remarkable ability to mutate their funding mechanisms in response to anti-terrorism legislation, to the extent that such measures are often obsolete even before they are introduced. To defeat terrorism, it is imperative that governments develop the capability to predict the next mutations in its financial structures. To succeed, this strategy requires an in-depth comprehension of how terrorist financing has evolved to date, leading to a better understanding of its continued evolution.

The Bush Administration's response to 9/11, and the US-led war in Iraq, have triggered major metamorphoses in the financing of the jihadist movement in Europe and the Middle East, as shown by the subsequent investigations of the Madrid and London train bombings. Far from curbing the growth of Islamist terror, the "war on terror" activated a new network of loosely connected, home-grown, self-funded jihadist cells.[a] Their main inspirational leader was the legendary terror guru Abu Musab al Zarqawi. Ironically, his myth was largely created on 5 February 2003 by Colin Powell, who, to justify America's preemptive strike in Iraq, presented al Zarqawi to the UN Security Council as the link between Saddam Hussein and Al Qaeda. Far from being a go-between, al Zarqawi was not even a member of Al Qaeda (Casadei, 2005). A skillful leader, he exploited the mythology that the United States manufactured around him, as well as the war in Iraq, to turn the battered Al Qaeda—a small trans-national armed organization, embattled in its stronghold in Afghanistan—into a global anti-imperialist ideology—that is, Al Qaedism (Napoleoni, 2005). European counter-terrorism intelligence concurs that today Al Qaedism, a synonym for the global jihadist movement, is the driving force behind new, self-funded terror networks that are emerging in Europe and the Middle East.

This chapter analyzes the impact of counter-terrorism policies—among which I include the Patriot Act and the war in Iraq—on the financial structure of European terror networks. It argues that such policies, far from defeating jihadist activities, have ended up bolstering them. In response to such measures, the financial systems supporting terror groups have been skillfully restructured, the main changes being the decentralization of funding activity in Europe and in the Middle East and the declining cost of terrorist attacks.

Post-9/11 Policies to Counter Terrorism Financing

Prior to the events of 9/11, the GDP of the New Economy of Terror—money generated by all armed terror organizations around the world—was USD 500 billion (Napoleoni, 2004). The primary currency used within the terror economy was the US dollar, and the most common denomination was the 100 dollar note. This calculation included wealth generated by all armed organizations as well as the economies of state-shells, regions that are controlled by armed groups and warlords (for example, Eastern Congo).

One-third of the "GDP" of the New Economy of Terror was generated by legitimate businesses, ranging from donations from businessmen to salaries received by members of armed organizations. Two-thirds came from criminal and illegal activities, and was mostly laundered into US dollars, much of it in the United States. The most important source of revenues for armed terror organizations was, and still is, narcotics smuggling. Al Qaeda's finances represented a very small fraction of the New Economy of Terror.

Following 9/11, the main policy steps taken to counter terrorism financing were the establishment of "terror lists," the passage of the Patriot Act, the destruction of the Taliban regime in Afghanistan, and the invasion of Iraq. None of these legislative or military measures were part of a multilateral response to 9/11; instead, they were the result of the United States' decision to take the lead in all aspects of the war on terror, including countering terrorist financing. To gain an idea of how unsuccessful such policies have been, it is sufficient to mention that only USD 200 million of terrorist funds have been frozen around the world to date. Conservative estimates of the growth of the New Economy of Terror since 9/11 range from 4 to 6 percent.

The terror lists—registers of people and companies suspected of bankrolling terror organizations—failed to curb terror financing primarily because they were not implemented globally. Several countries, including France, did not participate in the lists because of the illegality under their constitutions of blacklisting people purely based on suspicion; other nations were forced to back off after being taken to court by people whose names appeared on the lists (as in the case of three Somalis employed by *Al Barakat* in Sweden). Some other countries simply did not comply with the lists (for example, Malaysia and Saudi Arabia). To date, a comprehensive global list compiled from all the extant national lists does not exist.

The Patriot Act was approved in October 2001 by the US Congress. Among its many provisions, it made money laundering in the US and using US currency much more difficult. US banks and US-registered foreign banks were prevented from doing business with offshore shell banks. At the same time, the Patriot Act imposed tougher controls inside the United States; today, for example, it is not as easy as it was before 9/11 to open a US bank account. In addition, it allowed US monetary authorities to monitor dollar transactions anywhere in the world. It is a criminal offense for a US bank or a US-registered foreign bank not to alert the authorities of any suspicious transactions in US dollars.

The Patriot Act, however, did not address the problems of terrorist funding generated by legitimate businesses or money laundered outside the United States. The law blocked the entry of dirty money into the US via offshore facilities purely because it was in effect only in the United States. Therefore, it simply shifted the epicenter of global money laundering from the US to Europe, which to date still lacks comprehensive anti-money laundering legislation. Since 9/11, Europe has become the most important international hub for the criminal, illegal, and terror economy, and the Euro has become the currency of preference for conducting most money laundering activities. Thus, the Patriot Act ended up causing damage to Europe without reducing the financing of terrorism worldwide.

Restructuring of Jihadist Finances

Ironically, unilateral counter-terrorism policies laid the groundwork for the rise of the European funding networks and the decentralization of the financing of jihadist groups. Until 9/11, Europe was simply an operational base for Al Qaeda—a place to gather funds and to recruit fighters for deployment in distant conflicts, for example, Afghanistan, Kosovo, or Sudan. Today, Europe is a target of self-funded, home-grown jihadist armed groups.

The metamorphosis of the European funding networks was triggered by legislation such as the terror lists, which aimed at freezing the assets of Al Qaeda's sponsors. In the aftermath of 9/11, money held in the United States by Al Qaeda's sponsors quickly exited the US and was converted into Euros. The main destinations were Europe and the Middle East. By the end of 2001, as much as USD 200 billion of Saudi money had left the US In August 2002, the filing of a lawsuit by relatives of some victims of 9/11 against several members of the Saudi elite, the government of Sudan, and a number of Gulf banks and charities accused of having funded Al Qaeda prompted another capital flight of USD 200 billion worth of Arab assets held in the United States. The bulk of the money was reinvested in Europe in equities, bonds, and real estate. Overall, Saudi financiers are believed to have had about USD 750 billion invested in the United States ("Saudi Investors," 2002). According to the United Nations, Saudi funds converted into Euro investments wound up supporting Islamist terror groups in the Muslim world and in Europe (UN Security Council, 2003).

In Europe, Al Qaeda's financiers used their funds to strengthen the mosque network, a web of radical preachers and recruiters who, before 9/11, had provided human and financial resources to radical Muslims fighting in Kashmir, Chechnya, Bosnia, and so on. In an intercepted conversation from inside the Milan mosque of Via Quaranta, recorded by Italian magistrates, an unidentified Arab visitor said to the imam: "The thread begins in Saudi Arabia. Do not even worry about money because Saudi Arabia's money is your money" (see "Targets Inside Cities," at <www. siteinstitute.org>).

Italian authorities are adamant that, since 9/11, Arab terror sponsors have also provided funds for the recruitment and indoctrination of European suicide bombers deployed in Iraq and Palestine, most of them recruited through the European mosque network ("Police 'Pounce'," 2003). In April 2003, two British suicide bombers staged suicide attacks in Tel Aviv. They were members of the London-based group Al Majahurun, and frequented radical mosques in London. In 2004, Jean-Louis

Bruguiere, the French anti-terrorism investigative magistrate, admitted that since the summer of 2003 dozens of new European recruits had reached Iraq (Bruguiere, 2003).

Funds from traditional sponsors of Al Qaeda became seed money for the development of a European network of recruiters, while the notoriety of mythical figures such as al Zarqawi became a powerful advertising tool among young Muslims. In the Mediterranean basin, al Zarqawi's media-manufactured international profile facilitated the work of a handful of close lieutenants, such as "Mullah Fouad"—also known as "The Gatekeeper of Iraq"—responsible for supplying European suicide bombers to Iraq (Barnett, Burke and Smith, 2004). Born Mohammed Majid, Mullah Fouad is an Iraqi Kurdish member of Ansar al-Islam, the Islamist terror group from Iraqi Kurdistan founded in September 2001 and loosely linked to Al Qaeda. Before fleeing to Syria in 2003, he resided in Parma for several years. He was granted asylum by the Italian authorities because he had been persecuted by Saddam Hussein. Until the summer of 2005, when he was arrested in Syria, "The Gatekeeper of Iraq" supervised the smuggling of European suicide bombers into Iraq ("Tentacle of Terror," 2004).

At the end of 2005, a new series of arrests of suspected terrorists in Spain, Germany, France, and the Netherlands confirmed the presence of a terrorist network in Europe that recruits suicide bombers and fighters for the war in Iraq. In June 2005, Spanish authorities broke up a web of jihadists that recruited radical Islamists to fight in Iraq, arresting 16 people—11 of them suspected of having ties to al Zarqawi's terrorist network. According to Magnus Norell of the Swedish Defense Research Agency, in Europe there has been a rise "in both the number of recruits and the number of people returning home to develop networks and patiently plan for attacks" (author's interview with Magnus Norell).

A major departure from pre-9/11 recruitment methodologies has been the inclusion of women among suicide bombers. In the fall of 2005, Muriel Degauque, a 38-year-old Belgian woman who had converted to Islam, carried out a suicide mission in Baghdad. Degauque was born in the southern Belgian town of Charleroi, married a Moroccan, and converted to an extreme form of Islam. She traveled to Morocco with her husband and became radicalized. According to Marc Ginsberg, former US Ambassador to Morocco, "Moroccans, who are inspired by the Takfiri movement, are behind many averted terrorist plots against Europe. … Takfiris are especially dangerous in Europe because they adopt a Western lifestyle (i.e., Western dress, no beards) to assimilate into European society, thereby making it difficult for law enforcement to track them. Takfiri recruit women and use petty crime and drug trafficking to fund their operations" ("Tentacle of Terror," 2004).

Degauque's documents show that she traveled with her husband to Iraq. On 9 November 2005, she blew herself up in a car bomb attack on a US military convoy, killing (according to conflicting reports) either only herself or six people. Her Belgian passport was nearby. Her husband was killed by American troops in a separate incident. Both husband and wife were deployed by al Zarqawi's jihadist group, a fact that confirmed that the Jordanian-born terror leader had tapped into the European jihadist network. Al Zarqawi was a strong supporter of radical Salafism, of which the Takfiri movement is a branch. Belgian investigators have revealed that wives of several Islamist detainees in Belgium are ready to commit suicide attacks (Joannou, 2005).

It is unquestionable that the war in Iraq, and not al Zarqawi's association with Al Qaeda, turned Europe into a rich recruiting field for Al Qaedism. Until November 2004, when Osama bin Laden finally welcomed the Jordanian into Al Qaeda as the representative of the organization in Iraq, al Zarqawi's network was only loosely connected to Al Qaeda. Ironically, the main link was the myth created around the man himself by the US administration and the legends disseminated by the international media.

Until the Madrid bombing, counter-terrorism intelligence services underestimated the role of the mosque network in supplying suicide bombers as well as financial support for Al Qaeda and its offspring. Spanish counter-terrorism officers claimed that some European mosques are "havens for Al Qaeda planning and fund-raising" (Mackay, 2004). In the spring of 2004, Spanish magistrates discovered that a Spanish cell, called the "Soldiers of Allah," which started in Madrid's Abu Bakr mosque in 1994, had provided support and money to the Hamburg cell which participated in the 9/11 attacks (Mackay, 2004).

The primary channels that terror sponsors use to move seed money within Europe are shell banks and offshore facilities. Unlike in the United States, in Europe banks are still free to do business with such financial entities. Italian magistrates investigating the Milan mosque in Via Quaranta, for example, discovered that the cell received funds, denominated in Euros, from Arab sponsors via British offshore accounts ("Tentacle of Terror," 2004; "Connection Europa," 2005). Once terror money has successfully entered the European banking system, it can be wired and withdrawn anywhere. Members of terror groups operating in Europe use ATM machines, as the 9/11 hijackers did, to access the cash made available by their sponsors. Those who participated in the Bali, Istanbul, and Madrid attacks also used ATM machines (*ibid*). In addition, Islamist groups rely on couriers and the *hawala* system to transfer money and gold to Europe. A courier delivered USD 50,000 of the USD 150,000 used to fund the November 2003 bombing in Istanbul; the balance was provided to the terrorist cell by funds already in Turkey (cited in Brookes, 2003).

Legitimate businesses play an increasingly important role in European jihadist financing. Funds gathered by the mosque network, for example, often stem from legitimate activities; this is clean money, legally earned, which is then diverted to fund terror groups. European members of Islamist armed organizations often have legitimate jobs. In Spain and in Italy, many of them work as mechanics and waiters to support themselves and reduce the financial burden on the organization.

Nevertheless, illegitimate activities still represent the bulk of the funding sources for European jihadist terrorism efforts. Global terror financing still originates from criminal and illegal activities, which range from petty crime to large-scale fraud (Napoleoni, 2004). "For people who have no link with Al Qaeda, people who never traveled to the camps, and that after 9/11 felt compelled to join in the fight, it is easier to fund themselves with criminal activities than to get in touch with Al Qaeda and ask for money" (author's interview with an Italian magistrate). Farid Belaribi, an Algerian immigrant jailed in England in the summer of 2003, helped raise USD 250,000 through an international fraud network. He admitted to having defrauded banks and credit card companies (Walls, 2003). Credit card fraud is often conducted with skimming devices—a technique used to copy credit card numbers. In the case of Belaribi, these skimmed numbers were used throughout Europe and in Dubai. In 2002, credit card losses due to fraud in the EU alone amounted to USD 424 million ("Credit Card Fraud," *Evening Gazette*, Essex, 2 July 2003). Experts maintain that this money bankrolls crime and terrorism. Finally, the European networks also fund themselves by trafficking drugs, as the investigation into the Madrid bombing proved (Fuchs, 2003). Armed groups continue to rob banks and kidnap people to fund their activities. For example, in the spring of 2006, Al Qaeda operatives carried out a bank robbery in Pakistan which netted USD 12 million.

The Decentralization of Jihadist Financing

The terrorist funding network in Europe is in constant evolution. While there is sufficient evidence that jihadist European terror groups benefited directly from funds originating in Saudi Arabia and the Gulf, there is no evidence that Al Qaeda played any role in the restructuring of jihadist finances and in the birth of the European network. Both were spontaneous phenomena, structural mutations triggered by the war on terror.

The destruction of the Taliban regime dramatically altered the financial role of Al Qaeda. By the beginning of 2002, the armed organization's global financial structure had vanished. Gone, too, was the complex network of investments and sponsors, whose primary aim had been to bankroll training camps in Afghanistan where Muslim warriors were forged for eventual deployment wherever they were needed—Kashmir, Chechnya, or Kosovo, as well as New York City. 9/11 was the last trans-national attack carried out by an armed terror organization to date. It was also the last attack plotted, planned, and fully funded by Al Qaeda. All subsequent bombings were self-funded by home-grown groups. In the first Bali bombing, where Al Qaeda participated as a financial partner, the money had been transferred before September 2001.

The disintegration of Al Qaeda, which had only ever been a small trans-national armed organization, gave birth to a much more dangerous phenomenon: Al Qaedism, a new, global, anti-imperialist ideology that is not reliant on a central source of funding. Al Qaedism is the powerful phoenix born from the ashes of Al Qaeda and nurtured by the war in Iraq. Its icon was the US-manufactured myth of Abu Musab al Zarqawi. Until recently a living legend, al Zarqawi's terrorist activity in Iraq was skillfully exploited by the jihadist movement to spread this new doctrine. Today, the new creed is in the hands of Osama bin Laden and his lieutenant, Ayman al Zawahiri, who are using the mythical figure of al Zarqawi, the super-martyr, as a potent recruitment and inspirational tool. The new leadership will affect the next mutation of the network. It is likely that bin Laden will try to re-centralize the web of jihadists and use the European financial network to stage another spectacular attack inside the US.

The epicenter of Al Qaedism is Europe and the Middle East; its architects were Al Qaeda's traditional sponsors. By March 2003, seed money had been disbursed in

Europe; therefore, when the invasion of Iraq started, the European network began evolving, assuming a novel structure with regard to Al Qaeda. Home-grown groups blossomed everywhere. Some have become financially independent, with some outside encouragement; others have done so spontaneously. All European attacks, including the brutal killing of Theo Van Gogh in Amsterdam and several foiled attacks—for example, the 2006 Sarajevo bombing plotted by a Danish jihadist cell— are the work of home-grown, self-funded groups operating under the ideological umbrella of Al Qaedism. Within this new European network, therefore, Al Qaeda only played a marginal role. European Islamist armed groups, while inspired by bin Laden and the 9/11 attacks, have never been directly tied to the man or his organization.

While before 9/11 the world faced a small, highly integrated, trans-national organization, today the web of jihadist armed groups resembles a cluster of decentralized, loosely connected and often self-financed networks. This phenomenon could be described as the privatization of terrorist financing within the globalization of terrorism masterminded by the old Al Qaeda.

The new generation of terrorists is ideologically driven and more brutal than the previous one. "European counterterrorism officials stress that there is a new, more dangerous generation of Islamic extremists, younger and more radical than their forbears," reads a December 2005 report from the Transnational Threats Project of the Center for Strategic and International Studies, in Washington, DC Finally, as with most global systems, Islamist terror presents an inverse correlation between size and cohesion.

Al Qaedism is the offspring of two enemies, a grotesque union. While the war on terror prompted a major metamorphosis within the jihadist movement, the desire of radical Islamist groups to emulate the attacks of 9/11, coupled with the pressures exerted by counter-terror measures, such as the war in Iraq, fuelled the jihadist network's transformation. Counter-terror measures have been, and are still, perceived by Muslims, including European-born Muslims, as hegemonic and anti-Muslim. This explains why Europe has seen the spontaneous emergence of home-grown jihadist groups whose members have not been trained in Islamist camps in Afghanistan or Sudan (Graff, 2004).

The US-led war on terror pushed Europe to the forefront of the conflict. While Al Qaeda's primary enemy was the United States (and, to a lesser extent, the Saudi regime), European jihadist groups have focused their fight inside the Old World and linked it to the war in Iraq. In a chilling video recorded before the 7 July 2005 transit bombings in London, one of the perpetrators justified his decision to become a suicide bomber to avenge US forces' killings of Iraqis. A year later, another video released the day before the anniversary of the London attack, known as the "Al Qaeda Testament," warned of new attacks in Europe.

European cities are today primary targets, as proved by the Madrid and London bombings, and clearly articulated by the jihadist leadership in many statements. "Strikes within cities are a type of military diplomacy," stated *Al Battar*, Al Qaeda's online magazine, after the attack in Madrid. "This type of attack is often written with blood, embellished with body parts and perfumed with gunpowder" (Northeast Intelligence Network, 2004). The document is a chilling reminder of the reasons why, since the tragic events of 9/11, the incidence of terror attacks in Muslim and Western cities has continued. "Strikes bear a political meaning related to the conflict in ideology. They are considered a message sent to multiple parties, thus choosing the targets is done with extreme precision" (*ibid*). Most European intelligence services are adamant that several attacks are currently in the pipeline. After the Madrid bombings, even European politicians admitted that the danger was very serious, and the July 2005 attacks in London demonstrated that existing counter-terrorism measures are insufficient to prevent repeated attacks on mass transit targets.

The European terror campaign has completely different aims from Al Qaeda's pre- 9/11 terror strategy. Its aim is to terrorize European populations and force them to put pressure on their politicians to abandon an increasingly unpopular war in Iraq. This strategy has already proved successful, as shown by the outcome of the 2004 Madrid bombing. Occurring shortly before elections in Spain, the attack may have provided the margin of victory for the *Partido Socialista Obrero Español* (PSOE), which pursued a policy of disengagement from Iraq. The November 2003 car bomb attacks in Istanbul similarly reinforced Turkey's reluctance to back the war in Iraq. Paradoxically, attacks in Europe and against European interests in the Middle East, as well as the kidnapping and beheading of European nationals, strengthen a growing anti-American sentiment among the European population. People see these actions as a confirmation that Europe should not be involved in what is perceived as an American crusade. This perception originated from the unwillingness of the Bush Administration in 2002–03 to carry on the fight against terror under the umbrella of the UN and by its determination to go to war with Iraq, a country with no direct link with Al Qaeda or the Islamist terror system. Anti-Americanism in Europe is clearly linked with the war in Iraq (Donovan, 2003).

Cost–Benefit Analysis of Terrorist Attacks

The success of the decentralization of terrorist financing is linked to the methodology of the attacks conducted in Europe and the Middle East; they are all replicas of the 9/11 attacks—that is, suicide missions. Clearly, 9/11 is the template. What has changed is the scale, because the main constraint is financial. Home-grown groups— some of which we should call "improvised terrorists" (for example, two of the London bombers were recruited and indoctrinated in less than a year)—have access to a limited amount of funds. They have no connection to Al Qaeda's financiers or the world of crime; therefore, they are forced to rely upon money gathered through a network of friends and family as well as their own savings. Self-funding via legitimate businesses is their main source of funding.

Against this background, self-funding has been successful because, since 9/11, the unit cost of terror attacks has declined sharply. The execution of the attacks on the World Trade Center and the Pentagon cost USD 500,000. In contrast, the plotting and execution of the Madrid train bombings cost USD 10,000, and the 7 July suicide missions in London cost less than USD 8,000. The killing of Theo Van Gogh in Holland probably cost less than USD 100, but the impact has been enormous, shifting the previously tolerant attitudes of many Dutch people to intolerance towards ethnic and religious minorities.

Today, Al Qaedism is engaging the West in a fierce ideological battle, a clash between two visions of the world, reminiscent of the struggle between capitalism and communism during the Cold War. Militarily, the new conflict is an example of asymmetrical warfare, involving guerrilla and terrorist tactics against the strongest army in the world, that of the United States. The economic and financial disparities between the two opponents are also enormous. Yet, on the cost side, the gap is closing. The cost–benefit analysis of terrorist attacks carried out before and after 9/11 shows alarming signs that, as times goes by, jihadist terrorism is becoming less costly and more effective. The opposite is true for the war on terror; witness the tragic example of New Orleans, a city decimated by flooding because, since 2003, funds authorized for the Southeast Louisiana Urban Flood Control Project had been diverted to pay for the war in Iraq. This is a crucial factor. The Cold War ended in victory for the West because the prolonged confrontation bankrupted the Soviet Union and not, as Osama bin Laden claims, because the Red Army in Afghanistan was defeated by US- and Saudi-sponsored *mujahedin*.

The most recent UN report on sanctions against the Taliban and Al Qaeda stated that, while the November 1998 twin truck bombings of the US embassies in Kenya and Tanzania cost Al Qaeda less than USD 50,000, the attacks of 9/11 cost ten times as much (Report on Sanctions against the Taliban and Al Qaeda, United Nations, 2005). This simple fact does not imply that terror activity became less cost-effective over this time-span; in fact, the opposite is true. Two hundred and thirty-one people died in the two embassy bombings, while almost 3,000 died in the attacks on New York and Washington. The cost of reconstruction of the US embassies was a tiny fraction of the USD 2 trillion of estimated losses and reconstruction costs resulting from 9/11.

While 9/11 may still be the most cost-effective terror operation in history, it is not a benchmark for current jihadist activity, because it was a trans-national attack. Trans-national attacks imply cross-border movements of people and money; therefore, they are, by their very nature, more expensive than national terror operations. As discussed above, since 9/11, the disintegration of Al Qaeda and its mutation into a less structured global anti-imperialist ideology has altered the global terror landscape, a change that is today characterized by the activity of small, national, underground armed organizations. Under the banner of Al Qaedism, these home-grown groups have funded, planned, organized, and executed all post-9/11 terrorist attacks.

Of all post-9/11 operations, only the Bali bombing, in October 2002, was partly funded by Al Qaeda. The cost, estimated at USD 50,000, is the highest to date for a domestic terrorist operation. The human and economic cost for Indonesia was enormous: 202 people, many of whom were tourists, died inside the Bali nightclub; the Indonesian stock market crashed, and the Bali tourist economy, which contributed about 5 percent of the country's GDP, came to a halt. Overall, the attack resulted in a 2 percent drop in Indonesian GDP for 2002.

The next major terrorist attack came in November 2003, in Istanbul; it cost less than USD 40,000, and was a small-scale replica of 9/11. Four suicide truck bombings hit four different targets, killing 62 people. The consequences for the

Turkish economy were very serious: the attack reversed the country's slow economic recovery, and caused an outflow of Western invested capital. The attack was funded locally, so it cost Al Qaeda nothing, yet it was praised by Osama bin Laden and is regarded as part of the overall conflict between the West and Al Qaedism.

Economically and financially, the transition from Al Qaeda to Al Qaedism has dramatically lowered the cost of terrorism. Not only are national attacks cheaper to execute than trans-national attacks but, by not requiring cross-border movements of people and funds, they are harder to track via the money trail. This explains the difficulties that the British authorities have encountered in retracing the activities of the July 2005 London suicide bombers.

The 2005 UN report on sanctions against the Taliban and Al Qaeda confirms that the transformation of Al Qaeda into a "loose network of affiliated underground groups," which operate largely independently against local targets of their own choosing, using limited resources, actually makes central flows of money less relevant (Report on Sanctions against the Taliban and Al Qaeda, United Nations, 2005). It also stresses that the UN sanctions have been ineffective, because they have addressed a set of circumstances that no longer apply.

The failure of the UN sanctions contributed to the declining cost of terrorism as shown by the comparison of the expenditures involved in the Madrid, London, and Sharm el Skeikh bombings. The Madrid bombings killed 191 people and cost as little as USD 10,000; the London and Sharm el Skeikh attacks killed 55 and 88 people respectively, and cost significantly less than this amount. All these operations were carried out by local underground groups willing to emulate 9/11; the script is identical, but the scale is much smaller, adapted to the modest finances available to the groups. Yet their socio-economic impact is enormous.

The most cost effective of these "local" attacks may well have been those of London and Sharm el Skeikh. It appears that a third or more of London's annual USD 18 billion revenues from tourism alone was lost in 2005. In the United Kingdom, the cost of lost business, reconstruction, insurance, and security will run into several billion dollars. The Sharm el Skeikh bombing inflicted proportionately even more damage on Egypt's much smaller economy, which relies heavily upon an annual USD 10 billion in tourism receipts.

The operational costs of terrorist activity are also falling in Iraq. In November 2005, Osama bin Laden estimated that the weekly cost of al Zarqawi's insurgency was as little as USD 250,000. In sharp contrast, the cost of the war for American troops is rising. According to the last official figures, the American taxpayer has so far sustained a weekly cost of almost USD 1 billion (Napoleoni, 2005).

Al Zarqawi's low operating costs were mainly due to two factors: the ready availability of cheap weapons, ammunition, and explosives inside Iraq; and the declining cost of suicide missions. While in the past suicide bombers had to be indoctrinated and forged, and their families financially compensated, today they are independently indoctrinated and self-funded, and their families are often kept in the dark about the operations. The cost of suicide missions has never been so low; in Iraq it is essentially equivalent to the sum of the costs of the explosives and transportation to the targets.

Conclusion

The war on terror, coupled with tougher, less tolerant legislation in the West, has been instrumental in the formation of a jihadist terror network. The war facilitated the transition of the battered Al Qaeda organization into the global ideological movement of Al Qaedism. Images of the Iraq invasion and coalition troops traveled across the world, fuelling deep-rooted feelings of solidarity and humiliation among Muslims. Less tolerant legislation in Europe, coupled with the presence of European troops in Iraq, gave birth to an anti-European sentiment among radical Muslims, many of them born in Europe.

The restructuring of jihadist finances and the decentralization of these terror groups' funding activities is the direct consequence of counter-terrorist measures, such as the Patriot Act and the war in Iraq. These measures facilitated the transition of Europe and the Middle East from serving as bases for recruitment and fund-raising into becoming targets of jihadist terrorism. The Madrid and London bombing attacks brought global terror home to the Europeans. These attacks were directly linked to the US-led war in Iraq, and brought into focus the tragic consequences for Europe of the decision of certain countries to back a preemptive strike in Iraq.

Home-grown, self-funded jihadist groups are today operating in Europe under the umbrella of a new anti-imperialist ideology: Al Qaedism. After 9/11, these groups have used terror financiers' seed money, which landed in Europe after the introduction of the Patriot Act, to start their activities. They are primarily motivated by the war in Iraq. Unlike Al Qaeda, their primary target is not the United States but Europe. Today, these groups need very little money to carry out attacks inside European cities—so little that they can easily self-fund their activities.

The lesson to be learned from the fiasco of counter-terrorism measures is that terrorist financing is a highly dynamic phenomenon, in constant evolution. It is the new scenario described in this chapter and the next mutation in jihadist finances that European efforts at countering terror financing should address. A successful strategy will need to focus on the leadership of Osama bin Laden and its impact on the financial structure of the European network.

References

Barnett, A., Burke, J. and Smith, Z. (2004), "Terror Cells Regroup and Now They Target Europe," *Observer* (UK) (11 January).

Brookes, P. (2003), "Al Qaeda's Cash," *The New York Post* (29 December).

Bruguiere, J. (2003), "Terrorism after the War in Iraq," US–France Analysis Series (Washington, DC: The Brookings Institution).

Casadei, R. (2005), "Connection Europa," *Tempi* 10:6 (3 February).

"Connection Europa: Rubrica Terrorismo" (2005), *Tempi* 6.

Donovan, J. (2003), "U.S.: New Surveys Show Anti-Americanism Growing Stronger," Radio Free Europe/Radio Liberty (9 June).

Fuchs, D. (2003), "Spain Gives Details on Terror Cell," *International Herald Tribune* (15 April).

Graff, J. (2004), "Terror's Tracks," *Time Europe* (19 April).

Joannou, E. (2005), "Wives of Islamists Detained in Belgium 'Ready to be Suicide Bombers,'" *Middle East Times* (2 December).

Mackay, N. (2004), "Was it ETA or Al Qaeda? The Confusion over what was Behind the Madrid Bombing Obscures Intelligence Predictions of an Enhanced Terror Threat," *The Sunday Herald* (Scotland) (14 March).

Napoleoni, L. (2004), *Terror Incorporated* (New York: Seven Stories Press).

Napoleoni, L. (2005), *Insurgent Iraq: al Zarqawi and the New Generation* (New York: Seven Stories Press).

Northeast Intelligence Network (March 2004), "Al Battar Training Camp," at <www.homelandsecurityus.com>

"Police 'Pounce' on Al-Qaeda Cell" (2003), BBC News/Europe (28 November); at <http://news.bbc.co.uk/1/low/world/europe/3245470.stm>

"Saudi Investors Pull out of United States" (2002), BBC News (21 August); at <www.news.bbc.co.uk.>

"Tentacle of Terror: Ansar al-Islam Goes International, Causing Tremors" (2004), *Daily Star* (Beirut) (17 January).

UN Security Council, Monitoring Group Established Pursuant to Resolution 1363 [2001] (2003), Report S/2003/1070 (2 December); at <www.un.org>

Walls, J. (2003), "Man Jailed for Raising Terrorism Funds," The Press Association Limited (10 July).

Appendix

The international community needs urgently to address terrorist financing as a fundamentally new problem that requires new solutions. The international community should not divert existing resources from organized crime, and in this context we propose a series of interlinked measures that will prevent the further degradation of democratic rule, while offering the best possible chance of disrupting or preventing efforts by terrorist organizations to utilize their financial and economic resources.

We recognize that terrorist finance is not to be confused with financial criminality, typically associated with offshore tax havens and tax evasion. While recognizing that terrorists have become remarkably innovative in the way they handle, distribute, and conceal their financial arrangements, with much of their activity taking place in the informal sector, we are aware that they make extensive use of formal financial institutions in both the East and the West.

Second, we believe strongly in an international and multilateral approach to this problem. Ad hoc arrangements made by individual states are not enough to combat this extremely serious threat. We are very conscious of the fact that prevention requires forward-looking measures and extensive sharing of information.

Our proposal encompasses three components: the creation of an independent terrorist finance centre mandated under Chapter 7 of the UN Charter, whose aim would be the collection, analysis, and dissemination of information on the ways in which terrorists acquire and use their access to financial resources; the creation of a judicial review process to put onto a legal footing the anti-terrorist measures already taken by the international community; and the creation of forward compliance mechanisms as a means to institutionalize measures to prevent the spread of terrorist activity.

Chapter 2

Funding Evil: How Terrorism is Financed and the Nexus of Terrorist and Criminal Organizations

Rachel Ehrenfeld

The escalation in terrorist activities since the attacks on the United States in September 2001 demands infinite amounts of readily available cash. Supplying funds for terrorist groups is still regarded by many interested parties as constituting a form of "political support." This creates a situation in which legitimate "clean" money is contributed to further criminal or terrorist activities. These funds, however, do not satisfy all the needs of any expanding terrorist group, and most engage in criminal activities to generate the funds necessary for their activities. That is where the connections between terrorist groups and criminal organizations occur. The following is an overview of how these links operate.

By 14 June 2006, according to the White House, "Over 400 individuals and entities have been designated pursuant to Executive Order 13224, resulting in nearly $150 million in frozen assets and millions more blocked in transit or seized at borders" (The White House, 2005). Judging by the increase in the number of terrorist organizations and activities worldwide since 9/11, the United States' success at cutting off financial flows to terrorist groups, despite spending billions of dollars on prevention, is below par. Indeed, the performance of the rest of the world's wealthiest countries is not much better. Russia's Interior Minister Rashid Nurgaliyev stated on 16 June 2006, during the G-8 law enforcement officials' meeting in Moscow: "Our countries need a renewed and more effective anti-crime and anti-terrorist strategy" (Associated Press, 17 June 2006). Recognizing the radicalization of and cooperation between terrorist and trans-national criminal groups, the participants vowed to increase their level of cooperation and step up efforts to develop more effective means to deal with these threats.

There are experts who claim that terrorist activities do not require large amounts of money—that when you "kill one, [you] frighten ten thousand," as the old Chinese proverb suggests. In fact, individual terrorist acts do not cost much; the attack on the World Trade Center is estimated to have cost only USD 500,000 (Beckett, 2002). However, the maintenance and expansion of terrorist bases require constant infusions of large amounts of money.

An expanding terror network also needs funds to spread its ideology, and to support a variety of activities, such as:

- Recruitment
- Training camps and bases
- Housing and food

- Equipment, explosives, conventional and unconventional weapons
- Forged identity and travel documents
- Intelligence gathering
- Communications among organizational components
- Bribery
- Day-to-day maintenance expenses for members awaiting commands to launch operations (Middle East Newsline (MENL), 20 January 2003).

Terrorist groups also require money for electronic communication, television, radio, print media, videos, and paid demonstrations to foment hatred against their targeted enemies. Funding is needed to maintain the families of terrorists, including those deployed as "sleepers"—operatives who live undercover and do not support their dependents—as well as to compensate families of terrorists who are captured or killed. Taking all that into account, the total cost of maintaining the global Islamist terror network is estimated to be in the billions of dollars each year. To sustain these operations, sophisticated and multifaceted worldwide funding networks have been developed over the past three decades. Funding sources for terrorism include:

- Governments such as Saudi Arabia, Iran, Syria, and the Palestinian Authority
- Charitable organizations, which the Saudi government now calls "multilateral organizations," such as the Muslim World League (MWL) and the International Islamic Relief Organization (IIRO) (see <http://suekelly.house.gov/terrorfinanceforum.asp>)
- Legitimate businesses operating as fronts
- The exploitation of financial markets, especially unregulated commodity markets
- International trade, which converts cash into precious commodities such as diamonds and gold.

Funding also comes from a wide range of criminal activities, such as:

- Extortion and protection rackets
- Smuggling
- Kidnapping
- Prostitution rings and human trafficking
- Credit card fraud and identity theft
- Counterfeiting currencies and pharmaceuticals, cigarettes, alcohol, and other goods
- Pirating of videos, compact discs, tapes, and computer software.

A major source of funding for terrorist organizations comes from trade in illegal drugs such as heroin, hashish, cocaine, and methamphetamines (Ehrenfeld, 1992, 159–210; Bodansky, 1999, 315; Hutchinson, 2002). The 9/11 Commission report identified Saudi charities and individuals as the major sponsors of Al Qaeda, but ignored Al Qaeda's revenues from criminal activities, and said nothing about the huge profits obtained by Al Qaeda from the illegal drug trade (9/11 Commission,

2004; MENL, 20 January 2003). Moreover, despite mountains of evidence regarding Saudi funding of Al Qaeda prior to the attacks on 9/11, the Commission concluded: "We have not been able to determine the origin of the money used for the 9/11 attacks. Al Qaeda had many sources of funding and a pre-9/11 annual budget estimated at $30 million. If a particular source of funds had dried up, Al Qaeda could easily have found enough money elsewhere to fund the attack" (9/11 Commission, 2004).

Narco-terrorism

"Terrorism and drugs go together like rats and the bubonic plague," said former US Attorney General John Ashcroft. "They thrive in the same conditions, support each other, and feed off each other" (Ashcroft, 2002). In 2002, only 12 of the 36 groups on the US Department of State's Foreign Terrorist Organizations list had been identified as being involved in drug trafficking.[1] In October 2002, a Colombian courier for the Revolutionary Armed Forces of Colombia (FARC), which is funded mostly by profits from drug trafficking, was arrested in the US for having attempted to transport 182,000 Euros into the country; the money was confiscated. In another case, US law enforcement derailed an Al Qaeda plot to exchange "9,000 assault weapons, such as AK-47 rifles, sub-machine guns and sniper rifles; 300 pistols; rocket-propelled grenade launchers; 300,000 grenades; shoulder-fired anti-aircraft missiles and 60 million rounds of ammunition," for USD 25 million in cash and cocaine (Carr, 2002). Attorney General Ashcroft stated that the "toxic combination of drugs and terrorism" threatens US national security (*ibid*).

The connections between terrorist groups and international criminal organizations are complex, linking money, geography, politics, arms, and tactics to create a mutually beneficial relationship. This nexus yields hundreds of billions of dollars in revenues worldwide—in 1992 alone, close to USD 1 trillion (Ehrenfeld, 1992, xvi). A decade later, given substantial increases in drug consumption, US experts estimated the profits to be as high as USD 2 trillion per year.[2] "It's so important for

---

1   The US Department of State's *Patterns of Global Terrorism 2002* listed the following groups as being involved in drug trafficking: Abu Sayyaf, ETA, Hezbollah, IMU, KPP, LTTE, ENL, PIJ, Al Qaeda, FARC, Shining Path, and AUC. See US Department of State, 2003, iii–xiii, 155–6.

2   The State Department's Bureau of International Narcotics Matters (INL) estimates that the production of 1 kilo of cocaine costs about USD 3,000. The wholesale price for the same kilo is USD 20,000, and street dealers pay USD 250,000 for the uncut cocaine. The State Department figures for the street value of cocaine in the year 2000 was USD 10 billion per metric ton. Cocaine production takes as long as it takes for the leaves to grow, and in Latin America they grow fast; in Colombia, Peru, and Bolivia, the cultivation is practically limitless. The estimate is that at least 800 metric tons of cocaine are produced in Colombia annually. Opium is cultivated twice a year in Asia and the Middle East, and at least three to four times a year in Mexico and Colombia. Four hundred to 500 metric tons of heroin are produced in Afghanistan every year; approximately 180 are produced in Burma, and 7 in Mexico. According to an interview with John Walters, the White House drug czar, Colombia produced at least 16 metric tons of heroin in 2001, but only 12 metric tons in 2002 (see Robles, 2003). The production of heroin is more expensive than cocaine. In 2000, the estimated cost

Americans to know that the traffic in drugs finances the work of terror, sustaining terrorists," said President George W. Bush. "Terrorists use drug profits to fund their cells to commit acts of murder" (Bush, 2001).

There are no other commodities on the market today with as high and rapid a return on investment as illegal drugs. The drug trade is also a triple-pronged weapon that helps terrorists to:

* Finance their activities
* Undermine targeted countries politically and economically, and create crises in public health
* Recruit new members by citing drug use as an example of Western social degeneration and arguing that such corrupt societies must be destroyed.

Global Terror

Before 9/11, terrorist groups most often attacked relatively small, select targets—political figures, military installations, airliners, and multinational corporations—using conventional weapons of low lethality to achieve clearly defined goals that advanced their ideological or political objectives. Even though today's terrorists still target political leaders—for example, three failed attempts in 1995 to assassinate Egypt's President Hosni Mubarak, and the IRA's attempts to blow up 10 Downing Street in the early 1990s—they appear to prefer mass attacks on random civilians, with the explicit intent of inflicting as much damage and death as possible, and gaining the maximum amount of international visibility. Osama bin Laden publicly declared his policy of targeting civilians in his February 1998 *fatwa*. He said that any Muslim striving for God's rewards should "kill the Americans and plunder their money, wherever and whenever they find it" (World Islamic Front, 1998).

Most modern international terrorist organizations were initially trained, sponsored, and supported by the Soviet Union and its surrogates to help expand Marxism and Leninism (*Sovetskaya*, 1979, 7: 493; Pope, 1987; Suvorov, 1983, 1210). To them, Communist domination meant the absence of national boundaries and the presence of a globalized Communist world order. According to the *Soviet Military Encyclopedia*, their objective was to conduct unconventional warfare to subvert and destabilize the targeted nations. The Soviets trained the PLO and various nationalist groups in guerrilla and terror techniques, and then used those groups to expand Soviet influence.

The Soviet Bloc continued to train PLO terrorists in countries as diverse as Cuba, Vietnam, South Africa, Bulgaria, and Hungary, until the Soviet Union's demise in 1991. All terrorists who were schooled by the Soviets or their allies received Marxist/Leninist indoctrination as part of their training.[3] Such indoctrination was

---

of production was about USD 4,000 to 5,000 per kilo. That kilo sold for USD 250–300,000 on the street. The 500 metric tons of heroin produced in Afghanistan in the year 2000 are said to have generated at least USD 30 billion on the street.

3   *Sovetskaya*, 1979, 7: 493; Pope, 1987; Suvorov, 1983, 1210. In addition, see Russian texts of the *Soviet Military Encyclopedia Dictionary* of 1986, wherein the definition of

also part of the training provided by the PLO in Lebanon (with the assistance of the Eastern Bloc) to terrorists from all over the world. In addition to training Middle Eastern terrorists, these camps also trained recruits from many different parts of the world, including Holland, Turkey, Japan, and Ireland. Instructors working for the PLO included East Germans, Hungarians, Bulgarians, and Russians. Eastern Bloc countries supplied material support, including weapons and tanks (Israeli, 1983, 33–168). The PLO oversaw these camps until it was expelled from Lebanon in 1982. Since then, Hezbollah in Lebanon, supported by Iran and Syria, has taken over the training of terrorists in Lebanon and Syria, including members of Al Qaeda and Hamas. In addition, Islamist jihadis have received advanced training in Afghanistan, the Balkans, Chechnya, Iraq, and the Palestinian territories.

The Soviets specifically linked drugs and terrorism as part of their strategy. The *Soviet Military Encyclopedia*, in its 1979 edition, provides a list of "measures to be used in peacetime" to promote Soviet foreign policy objectives. These measures include the use of "poisons and narcotics" as weapons against the West (*Sovetskaya*, 1979, 7: 493; Pope, 1987; Suvorov, 1983, 1210). Involvement in illicit drug trafficking grew among terrorist organizations like the Revolutionary Armed Forces of Colombia (FARC), the PLO in the Middle East, the Liberation Tigers of Tamil Eelam (LTTE) in Sri Lanka, and the Provisional Irish Republican Army (PIRA) in Ireland, as well as trans-national terrorist and criminal organizations operating and cooperating in and from the Indian sub-continent, and laundering their profits in Dubai (South Asia Intelligence Review, 2002).[4] Their growing involvement in the illicit drug trade reinforced alliances and intensified cooperation between nationalistic and international terrorist groups and criminal organizations.

In fact, terror groups that were trained by the Soviets and their surrogates all seem to have adopted this strategy. For example, Antonio Farach, a Nicaraguan diplomat and former member of the Sandinista regime, explained how the Sandinistas trafficked in drugs:

> In the first place, drugs did not remain in Nicaragua; the drugs were destined for the United States. Our youth would not be harmed, but rather the youth of our enemies. Therefore, the drugs were used as a political weapon against the U.S. The drug trafficking [provided] a very good economic benefit, which we needed for our revolution. We wanted to provide food for our people with the suffering and death of the youth of the U.S. (Farach, 1983, 48).

The PLO turned to international drug trafficking and criminal activities in order to generate money as it began to globalize in the late 1960s. Documents discovered in Lebanon in 1982, following the expulsion of the group, expose in minute detail how the PLO committed itself even in its earliest days "to alliances on the international

---

"special reconnaissance" remains the same. This information was also verified by consulting with experts on Soviet strategy, among them Dr Leon Goure from SAIC, Maclean, Virginia, December 1989.

4   According to US intelligence sources, Afghani and Lebanese heroin growers and producers were instrumental in Colombia's heroin production, instructing them how to grow and refine heroin.

scene" and to using all means possible to generate funds, including drug trafficking, to strengthen the organization, until it would be able to exert enough pressure "to bring about international measures, and especially UN resolutions ... which will tighten the isolation of the Zionist and the American enemy" (quoted in Israeli, 1983, 18).

The Legacy of Narco-terrorism

Some Islamist terrorist organizations received early exposure to the Soviet drug-trafficking doctrine, and most currently depend upon revenues from illegal drugs—especially Afghan heroin sales—as their major source of funding. As of 2006, Afghanistan was producing 90 percent of the world's opium supply, up from 70 percent of the opium that was sold worldwide before 2001, according to the US Drug Enforcement Administration (DEA, 2001). What this 2001 report failed to mention is the fact that Al Qaeda benefited from the revenues generated by this trade.

The current increase of violence in Afghanistan and the resurgence of the Taliban are fueled by Afghanistan's ever-increasing opium production. The United Nations Office on Drugs and Crime (UNODC) reported on 2 September 2006 of a 60 percent increase in opium production in Afghanistan. Earlier that year, US Defense Secretary Donald Rumsfeld noted: "I do worry that the funds that come from the sale of those products [illegal drugs] could conceivably end up adversely affecting the democratic process in the country ... and you have people like the Taliban that it gives them an opportunity to fund their efforts in various ways" (McKeeby, 2006). He added that the United States had evidence that the Taliban extorted "protection" money from local Afghan drug dealers ("Rumsfeld: Afghanistan Drug Trade May Help Fuel Taliban Resurgence," Associated Press, 10 July 2006). Indeed, the Taliban had a long history of engaging in such criminal activities.

Despite the visible evidence of this illegal trade, the International Monetary Fund (IMF) estimates that, in 2005, opium accounted only for 38 percent of Afghanistan's GDP, which they calculate at USD 7.1 billion (IMF, 2006a). However, the IMF points out that this figure excludes illegal drugs (IMF, 2006b). The Central Intelligence Agency (CIA), in June 2006, still posted an estimated 2004 GDP for Afghanistan of USD 21.5 billion, a third of it from opium (CIA, 2006). Yet another estimate, this from USAID, gives Afghan opium production credit for making up about 60 percent of the economy (USAID, 2006). The cost of these drugs to the US economy in 2002 alone has been estimated at USD 180.9 billion (NDIC, 2006).

The discrepancy in the estimates is mind-boggling, considering the technological capacity that exists among law enforcement agencies to monitor both heroin and cocaine production. Moreover, the growing availability of illicit drugs has reduced prices all over the world (Debussman, 2006; Kurtz-Phelan, 2005). In June 2006, a kilo of cocaine was worth from USD 20 to 25,000, and a kilo of heroin was worth from USD 60 to 80,000 on the street in New York City, according to law enforcement officials. A gram of Asian heroin cost USD 90 to 100, while a gram of South American heroin cost USD 200 to 350, and a gram of cocaine only USD 22 to 25.

The growing availability, lower prices, and higher purity of drugs available in the marketplace have dramatically increased overdose incidents (Johnson, 2006). Yet, despite this upswing, and the general acknowledgement that illicit drugs fund terrorism, neither governments worldwide nor international organizations seem able and/or willing to deal with the problem.

From Afghanistan, opium, morphine base, and heroin move to expanding international consumer markets through various routes:

- To Europe through Pakistan and Turkey or the Balkans
- To the United States through Pakistan via the port of Karachi
- To Moscow through Pakistan, Central Asia, and Chechnya
- To Europe through the Central Asian republics to Moscow, and from there by air to Iraq.

Drug trafficking has its own logic. It seems that some of these circuitous routes are used because they are profitable. Apparently, because of various factors, the risk is less and the profit is greater to move drugs and other illegal commodities through Moscow instead of, say, Berlin.

Another transport route to Europe passes through Pakistan, and from there to the Gulf States, Saudi Arabia, Egypt, and Lebanon.[5] All the countries through which the opiates are transferred are also affected by the growing number of people who are exposed and become addicted, and by the destabilizing effects of illegal profits on the economy and of growing criminal activity.

Many terrorist groups benefit from the trade in heroin, cocaine, methamphetamines, and hashish. The last overview available includes: the Revolutionary Armed Forces of Colombia (FARC); the National Liberation Army (ELN), also in Colombia; the United Self-Defense Forces of Colombia (AUC); the Shining Path; Hezbollah; the National Movement for the Liberation of Kosovo, the Kosovo Liberation Army (KLA or UCK) and the National Liberation Army (UCK or OHA) in Macedonia; the Liberation Army of Presevo, Medvedja, and Bujanovac (UCPMB); the Islamic Movement of Uzbekistan (IMU); and the Abu Sayyaf Group in the Philippines.

Hezbollah's *modus operandi* is a perfect example of the dual identity of Islamic radical organizations that publicly identify themselves as "political" entities—but are in fact designated as Foreign Terrorist Organizations by the US State Department— and their less known, but equally detrimental, criminal activities (McCraw, 2003). To maintain and expand its political-social activities in the Shi'ite community in Lebanon and elsewhere, Hezbollah needs large sums of money (Ehrenfeld, 2006). The USD 100 million to 120 million it is said to receive annually from Iran, and the weapons and supplies it takes in from Tehran and Damascus, are just a drop in Hezbollah's bucket. Where did Hezbollah's funds come from? By the mid-1980s, Shi'ite Hezbollah loyalists in Western Europe had quietly and effectively infiltrated local Muslim communities with the subversive aim of converting them to

---

5   The different routes of illicit drug trafficking around the world, including the movement of heroin from Afghanistan to its destined markets, are detailed in Library of Congress, 2002; and Molyneux, 2002.

Ayatollah Khomeini's version of Islam, and of eventually gaining control over those communities. Countless legal and quasi-legal institutions—including religious, cultural, and economic groups—were established to conceal these dormant Hezbollah networks; to finance their activities; to serve as a source for future recruitment of European-based terrorists; and to provide financial support for their operations.

Hezbollah's support comes from both legitimate and illegal resources (Karmon, 2003). The legitimate channel includes charitable organizations operating worldwide, donations from individuals, and proceeds from legitimate businesses. Drug trafficking is a major money-maker for Hezbollah, endorsed by the mullahs through a special *fatwa*. In addition to the production and trade of heroin in the Middle East and cocaine in and from South America, Hezbollah facilitates, for a fee, the trafficking of other drug smuggling networks. It cooperates, for example, with the Revolutionary Armed Forces of Colombia (FARC), the National Liberation Army (ELN) in Colombia and the "Abadan drug ring," a long-established Iranian drug network, allowing them to use the Hezbollah-controlled drug routes in Lebanon to transport heroin and opium from Iran and Afghanistan to Europe and North Africa.

Hezbollah's other illegal sources of funding include money laundering; illegal arms trading and smuggling; counterfeiting and selling currency (US dollar "super notes") and goods (designer clothing and accessories); piracy of compact discs and DVDs; trafficking in humans; and conducting elaborate import-export schemes with traders from India and Hong Kong to Ivory Coast, Belgium, and South and Central America. Hezbollah also extorts "donations" from Shi'ites, especially Lebanese immigrants in South and North America, under the threat of physical harm or death.

Hezbollah operatives also generate huge profits from the theft and resale of stolen vehicles and baby formula; credit card, welfare, social security, marriage, healthcare, and insurance fraud; forgery of passports, drivers' licenses, and other forms of identification; arson; robbery; food coupon fraud; telecommunications fraud, such as selling long-distance telephone access through fraudulently obtained services; and cloning the identification of cellular phone subscribers.

The magnitude of Hezbollah's criminal operations serves not only to reap huge profits—estimated at USD 6 billion in 2001, thus enabling it to buy its way into the Lebanese parliament and government—but also facilitates Hezbollah's infiltration of their targeted countries, weakening these states' economies while furthering Hezbollah's terrorist agenda. Hezbollah documents captured in Lebanon by the Israeli Army during the July/August 2006 confrontation with Hezbollah demonstrate that the terrorists provided drugs to Israeli criminals to collect intelligence in Israel (Intelligence and Terrorism Information Center, 2006). Considering Hezbollah's wide range of criminal activities, it should also be identified and designated as a global criminal organization as well as a terrorist organization.

From Drugs to Dollars

In January 2002, as part of the US Drug Enforcement Administration's "Operation Mountain Express," members of a Hezbollah drug ring were captured by US and Canadian law enforcement agencies. This action resulted in the arrests of 300 people who had been selling methamphetamine in Detroit, Cleveland, Chicago, Phoenix, Los Angeles, San Francisco, and elsewhere. The DEA also seized USD 16 million in currency; eight real estate properties; 160 cars; 181 pounds of methamphetamine; 30 tons of pseudoephedrine; and nine methamphetamine laboratories.

According to the DEA, a significant portion of the revenues from selling the drugs had been sent to the Middle East to support Hezbollah, Hamas, and Al Qaeda terror operations. Some of the money had simply been carried to the Middle East in cash; the rest of the money had been laundered and then transferred to the Middle East via banks or informal money transfer channels (DEA, 2002; CBSNews.com, 2002).

The Money Laundering Control Act of 1986 defines the crime of *money laundering* as an illegal act in which a person:

> ... knowing that the property involved in a financial transaction represents the proceeds of some form of unlawful activity, ... conduct[s] or attempt[s] to conduct such a financial transaction which in fact involved the proceeds of a specified unlawful activity with the intent to:

- Promote the carrying on of specified unlawful activity;
- Conceal or disguise the nature, location, source, ownership or control of the proceeds of the specified unlawful activity; or
- Avoid a transaction report requirement under state or federal law (Bosworth-Davis and Saltmarsh, 1994, 113).

The former managing director of the International Monetary Fund (IMF), Michel Camdessus, has estimated that the global volume of laundered money in 1999 amounted to between 2 and 5 percent of the world's combined gross domestic product—or approximately USD 1.8 trillion. By April 2006, the IMF's *World Economic Outlook* estimate of the size of the world economy was USD 65.174 trillion, of which at least USD 3.25 trillion consisted of laundered funds (IMF, 2006c). These estimates, however, do not take into account the huge volume of legitimate funds appropriated by charities and businesses that is funneled to terrorist organizations.

Most money laundering operations are conducted through unregulated financial centers known as Offshore Financial Centers (OFCs). According to the IMF's February 2006 progress report, "Offshore Financial Centers: The Assessment Program," the total assets deposited in "offshore" domiciles are unknown (IMF, Monetary and Financial Systems Department, 2006).

After the 9/11 attacks, the international community established reporting guidelines for OFCs. However, monitoring compliance is "coordinated with mutual evaluations of anti-money laundering and combating the financing of terrorism

(AML/CFT) arrangements by the Financial Action Task Force (FATF) and FATF-style regional bodies (FSRBs)" (*ibid*). In other words, monitoring is voluntary, and its complexity renders the process meaningless.

These tax havens do not require either the owners of the accounts or the beneficiaries of the transactions to disclose their identities; nor do they require reports on any transactions, regardless of size. The OFC guidelines lack effective means of monitoring cross-border currency movements or the maintenance of financial records.[6]

OFCs include shell banks and shell companies—fictitious corporations that are created to conceal the identities of their owners, whose names never appear on the registration papers. Only the names of the local representatives or the "nominees" are listed.[7] The company's activities are couched in obscure and vague terms that satisfy lenient and permissive local requirements. Once money is safely deposited in such a "corporate" account, it can easily be transferred.

Another way to launder money is simply to convert cash into money orders. Despite tightening controls on banks and wire transfers in the US, money launderers can still buy money orders in small denominations and transfer them, often under the guise of sending support to their families, as countless immigrants in the US do legitimately every day.

Terrorists and other criminals often call upon members of legitimate professions, such as accountants and lawyers, to help move and hide their money. "Money laundering is now an extremely lucrative criminal enterprise in its own right," stated the US Senate Committee on Government Affairs at a 1985 hearing:

> The Treasury's investigations have uncovered members of an emerging criminal class—professional money launderers that aid and abet other criminals through financial activities. … They are accountants, attorneys, money brokers, and members of other legitimate professions. They need not become involved with the underlying criminal activity except to conceal and transfer the proceeds that result from it. They are drawn to their illicit activity for the same reason that drug trafficking attracts new criminals to replace those who are convicted and imprisoned—greed. Money laundering, for them, is an easy route to almost limitless wealth (quoted in Bosworth-Davis and Saltmarsh, 1994, 53).

The "Super Hawala"

Terrorists also clandestinely transfer money through the *hawala*, an informal exchange system in which payments are delivered without money actually being moved. Say you wish to transfer USD 20,000 to your friend in Karachi. Since you

---

6   The term *offshore center* usually refers to: (1) a jurisdiction that has a relatively large number of financial institutions engaged primarily in business with nonresidents; (2) a financial system with external assets and liabilities out of proportion to domestic financial intermediation designed to finance domestic economies; and, most popularly, (3) a center that provides some or all of the following services: low or zero taxation, moderate or light financial regulation, banking secrecy, and anonymity. See IMF, Monetary and Exchange Affairs Department, 2000.

7   Nominees, for example, can be local lawyers in offshore centers like the Bahamas or the Cayman Islands who register the corporation.

conduct business both here and in Karachi, you give your USD 20,000 to someone in the US, and that person arranges with a business contact in Karachi to give USD 20,000—or its equivalent—to your friend. No physical financial instrument ever leaves the US, yet the funds are delivered. The process is totally untraceable.

There are even official *hawaladars* who conduct *hawala* transactions for a fee of 1 percent. The advantages of transferring money through the *hawala,* according to the US government's 2002 *National Money Laundering Strategy*, are the low overhead, the integration with existing business activities, and the ability to avoid taxation and foreign exchange regulations. A *hawala* transaction is often completed more rapidly than international wire transfers that involve corresponding banks. For customers in the US who do not have a social security number or adequate identification, opening a bank account can be problematic. But the *hawaladar* requires only the customer's cash and some link to establish trust, usually one based on a cultural or ethnic relationship. The *Money Laundering Strategy* continues: "The anonymity and lack of paper trail also hide the remittance from the scrutiny of tax authorities. Lastly, some areas of the world are poorly served by traditional financial institutions, while the *hawaladar* may offer a viable alternative" (US Departments of the Treasury and Justice, 2002, 22). For terrorists, there could hardly be a system that is faster or more discreet.

Technology has enabled an even greater "super *hawala*" system to arise— one devoid of the ethnic or personal components that infuse traditional *hawala* transactions. Although the Bank Secrecy Act requires financial institutions to file reports and record transactions, improvements in technology permit "peer-to-peer" transactions to take place even without financial institutions. As the *Money Laundering Strategy* states, "Internet money transfers and new payment technologies such as 'e-cash,' electronic purses, and smart-cards based electronic payment systems, make it more difficult for law enforcement to trace money laundering activity, and easier for money launderers to use, move, and store their funds. These faceless transactions and the greater anonymity they may afford pose new challenges to law enforcement that must be addressed" (*ibid*, 47).

Attempts to Stop Money Laundering

How well does the US government do at stopping terrorist money? Not very. To trace money (or commodities) that fund terrorism, the government tends to rely on sophisticated technologies such as special computer programs to detect suspicious transactions. However, since money is often provided to terrorists through legitimate businesses and institutions, such as non-governmental organizations or even international aid organizations, and through various charities, no amount of technology can detect where each dollar goes.[8] Money is interchangeable; when

---

8   Funds provided by international organizations such as the United Nations and the European Union sometimes, as in the Palestinian territories, wind up in the hands of members of terrorist organizations—for example, EU funds given to the Palestinian Authority were used to pay the salaries of members of the al-Aqsa Martyrs Brigade.

there is a mix of legitimate and illegitimate funds, how can anyone identify which dollar came from where?

On 26 October 2001, when it had become apparent that the laws that were in place before 9/11 were not sufficient to stop the flow of money to criminals and terrorists, and on the premise that terrorists would not be able to operate without money, the US Congress enacted the USA PATRIOT Act.[9] The new act better enabled the US government to identify suspicious transactions, trace transfers of funds, and stop the laundering of money. As part of this effort, the US Treasury Department also established Operation Green Quest (OGQ)—a "multi-agency terrorist financing task force" that focuses on promoting coordination among all US law enforcement agencies in "identifying, disrupting, and dismantling the financial infrastructures and sources of terrorist funding."[10]

Additionally, in July 2002, the US government put into place its *National Money Laundering Strategy* (NMLS) to "deny terrorist groups access to the international financial system, to impair the ability of terrorists to raise funds, and to expose, isolate, and incapacitate the financial networks of terrorists" (US Departments of the Treasury and Justice, 2002, 4). Also, the United Nations Security Council adopted Resolutions 1373 and 1390, requiring member nations to join the US in its effort to disrupt terrorist financing. And US Government Executive Order 13244 was put in place to "block property and prohibit transactions with persons who commit, threaten to commit, or support terrorism."

In March 2003, to better coordinate the government's efforts to stop the flow of money to terrorists at home and abroad, the US Department of the Treasury established a new Executive Office for Terrorist Financing and Financial Crimes (EOTF/FC) (US Department of the Treasury, 2003).

Nevertheless, although 166 countries had blocking orders in force, by April 2003 only USD 124 million in assets had been frozen—USD 88 million overseas and 36 million in the US.[11] According to frustrated US intelligence sources, despite cooperation agreements, some European countries unfroze or released some of the

---

9   *Uniting and Strengthening America by Providing Appropriate Tools Required to Intercept and Obstruct Terrorism (USA PATRIOT Act) Act of 2001*, US Public Law 107-56, 26 October 2001. "The USA PATRIOT Act contains sweeping provisions to our anti-money laundering and anti-terrorist financing regime that dramatically enhanced Treasury's ability to combat the financing of terrorism and money laundering. These provisions reflect the important principles of (1) enhancing transparency in financial transactions; (2) protecting the international gateways to the U.S. financial system; and (3) increasing the vigilance of all our financial institutions that are themselves the gatekeepers of the financial system." (US Department of the Treasury, 2002, 10).

10   US Department of the Treasury, Customs Service, 2001. OGQ was announced on 25 October 2001. The agencies involved are: the US Customs Service; the IRS; the Secret Service; the Bureau of Alcohol, Tobacco, and Firearms; the Office of Foreign Assets Control; the Financial Crimes Enforcement Network; the FBI; the Postal Inspection Service; the Naval Criminal Investigative Service; and the Department of Justice.

11   US Department of State, 2003. However, then-Secretary of State Colin Powell, in his press conference to release this report, stated that "since 9/11, more than $134 million of terrorist assets have been frozen."

assets on the grounds that the US did not provide the requisite information to warrant the seizure. Moreover, a US request to freeze Hezbollah's assets was refused outright by Syria and Lebanon, who claimed that Hezbollah is "a resistance group and not a terrorist organization" ("Lebanon Refuses to Back U.S. Stance on Hezbollah," IslamOnline.net, 7 November 2001).

Anti-money laundering laws, like any other laws, are effective only when they are implemented. Unfortunately, there seems to be little political will to apply and enforce existing laws—often because of stated "other political priorities" that come between the laws and their implementation. As for wire transfers, following the revelation in the *Los Angeles Times* on 23 June 2006 about government tracking of money transfers, Western Union and other wire transfer agencies came under attack for blocking or delaying money transfers from or to individuals with Middle Eastern-sounding names.

Indeed, technological surveillance of financial transactions has yielded some positive results. However, most information received by US intelligence agencies about funds belonging to terrorist organizations has come from human sources, and not from the highly sophisticated electronic surveillance technology upon which US intelligence is so reliant. Those methods prove to be helpful *after* a terrorist incident, when the authorities conduct their investigations. Clearly, what is needed is a better way to identify the people who deposit the money and then to intercept it before it reaches the terrorists.

Legitimate Fronts

Terrorist groups have established legitimate businesses that serve as covers for their illegal activities, provide employment to their members, generate additional income, and serve as ideal vehicles to launder money. Money made through drug trafficking might be invested in farmland in South America, prime real estate in London, or hedge funds in the US Perfect laundering vehicles are cash-and-carry businesses such as pizzerias and car washes—how can an investigator prove that any part of the profits was not generated by the legitimate business, since almost all the transactions are in cash? Since the money is either laundered before it is invested or made legitimate afterwards, its use in capitalizing legal enterprises makes it difficult to trace.

Moreover, the ability to integrate illegal funds into legitimate businesses helps provide those businesses with unlimited sources of money. This not only weakens the ability of genuinely legitimate businesses—which lack illicit financial backing— to compete, but also severely undermines the economies in which they operate.

A recent example of a legitimate business that has been accused of serving as a front for terrorist activities is Ptech, a computer software company in Quincy, Massachusetts (see op-ed in *The Washington Times*, 15 January 2006). Ptech, which is privately held, uses artificial intelligence to provide organizations with a blueprint of their operations and tools to analyze their data.[12] Ptech was raided by US federal agents on 6 December 2002. Apparently, a secret owner of the company was Yassin al-Qadi, a Saudi millionaire. After 9/11, al-Qadi was listed on the United States Treasury Department's Specially Designated Global Terrorist Entity list for allegedly funneling millions of dollars to Al Qaeda through the Muwafaq Foundation, a Saudi charity that he headed. Federal agents involved in the case anonymously voiced their concern not only that Ptech was suspected of being a front for Al Qaeda, but that it was also using the software it had supplied to the government agencies for which it did work to access government data. Moreover, if the allegations against Ptech prove true, there is room for concern about Ptech's involvement in designing the Rocky Flats nuclear plant near Denver for the Department of Energy (Hosenball, 2002). Following the burst of negative publicity, Ptech was renamed GoAgile.

Osama bin Laden's own legitimate front businesses were first established in Sudan in 1983.[13] His investments included peanut and sunflower farms; a bakery; a furniture company; International al-Ikhlar Company, which produced honey and sweets; Bank of Zoological Resource, a cattle-breeding operation; and the Laden International import/export company. In 1996, bin Laden was expelled from Sudan under extreme pressure from the US and Saudi Arabia, and the Sudanese President Omar al-Bashir announced that his businesses had been liquidated, but as late as 2001 his holdings in the Sudan were still estimated at about USD 30 million (Willman, 2001). Other Al Qaeda investments included an ostrich farm and shrimp boats in Kenya, agricultural holdings in Tajikistan (Shahar, 2001), and—according to US and European intelligence sources—between 15 and 50 cargo freighters around the world (Mintz, 2002).

Based on a United Nations report, the war on terrorism seems to have had little effect thus far on Osama bin Laden's fortune. "A large portfolio of ostensibly legitimate businesses," Douglas Farah reported in the *Washington Post* on 3 September 2002, "continue to be maintained and managed on behalf of Osama bin Laden and Al Qaeda by a number of as yet unidentified intermediaries and associates across North Africa, the Middle East, Europe and Asia [and the United States]."

Osama bin Laden's legitimate front businesses make it easier for him to achieve his stated goal: to destroy the US economy. As he said in a video released after the 9/11 attacks: "It is very important to concentrate on striking the American economy with every possible means. Hit hard the American economy and its heart and its core" (bin Laden, 2001). The 9/11 attacks were estimated by the end of 2002 to have cost the US economy at least USD 135 billion (Thachuk, 2002).

---

12 Among the company's clients were the FBI, the FAA, the US Air Force, the US Naval Air Systems Command, the Department of Energy, and NATO (see Belluck and Lichtblau, 2002).

13 It is not surprising that bin Laden was welcomed in Sudan, for it was here that state-sponsored jihad over two decades caused the deaths of at least two million people and displaced another four million. The slogan of the ruling party was "Jihad, victory, and martyrdom." With government sanction, jihadis there "have physically attacked non-Muslims, looted their belongings and killed their males … then enslaved tens of thousands of females and children" (Pipes, 2002).

Where the Money Is ... And How it Got There

If you want to move money in large quantities, you need a bank. The bigger the bank, the easier it is to avoid scrutiny, especially when you regularly use the bank to conduct business transactions. Never mind the SWIFT network (Society for Worldwide Interbank Financial Telecommunication)—there are many alternative avenues and financial institutions through which to transfer money without any scrutiny. For example, the growing number of Islamic banking institutions in the West, operating according to the *Shari'a*—a system unfamiliar to most Western bank supervisors—can be used to hide and/or transfer money for illegal purposes.

For instance, Osama bin Laden's financial officer in Sudan until 1996, Mustafa Ahmed al-Hisawi (aka Sheikh Saeed), held an account at the Dubai Islamic Bank. In the months prior to the 9/11 attacks, al-Hisawi deposited USD 148,895 into bank accounts in Dubai that were held by two of the 9/11 hijackers. These accounts were in the Dubai Islamic Bank, as well as in the Hong Kong Shanghai Bank (HSBC Holdings) and Citibank. The money was then wire-transferred to the hijackers' accounts with SunTrust Bank in Florida. This transaction was executed in violation of the Bank Secrecy Act (BSA) and the Suspicious Activity Report (SAR) requirements, which are designed to prevent money laundering.

In 1999, the US government had identified the Dubai Islamic Bank as having laundered money for bin Laden.[14] Even so, it was only after 9/11 that SunTrust reported one of the suspicious transactions to the US Treasury Department's Financial Crimes Enforcement Network (Willman, 2001). Further, on 25 September 2001, Luxembourg's commission for supervising financial institutions cited the Dubai Islamic Bank as having links with Osama bin Laden and terrorism (Civil Action, 2002, 251). Despite all this, as of 3 December 2002, the Dubai Islamic Bank was still absent from the US Specially Designated Nationals and Blocked Persons list.

In another example, in 2002 the Israel Defense Forces discovered Palestinian documents in Ramallah indicating that the Amman-based Arab Bank had been a primary recipient of funds from Saudi Arabia, Syria, and Iran to be awarded to families of Palestinian suicide bombers.[15] The documents also revealed that Saudi charitable organizations had been transferring money through Arab Bank branches in the West Bank to organizations linked to Hamas, also to be given to families of suicide bombers (Levitt, 2002). The Arab Bank was also used by Iran to funnel money to Fatah's al-Aqsa Martyrs Brigades for weapons, bomb-making materials, and other expenses, such as preparations for an attack that killed six Israelis (Israeli Prime Minister's Media Adviser, 2002). In addition, the Arab Bank was identified by the Spanish authorities as having transferred money from an Al Qaeda cell in Spain

---

14 The bank's prior history in money laundering goes back to its USD 80 million investment in the Bank of Credit and Commerce International (BCCI). It was also involved in other illegal financial activities, including a USD 242 million money laundering operation through gold trading with a rogue billionaire from Mali (See Civil Action, 2002, 248–9).

15 PLO documents captured by the IDF, dated 12 April, 6 May, and 5 June 2002. These are only samples of the voluminous Palestinian Authority paper trail documenting the PA's many methods and sources of funding terrorism that were captured by the IDF. For more information, see the archive at the IDF website, <www.idf.il>

to members involved in the 9/11 attacks, and as having wired money to Al Qaeda members in Yemen and Pakistan (Civil Action 2002, 352).

Oppression, Corruption, and Terrorism

The precursors of state sponsorship for terror organizations are corruption, domestic terrorism, and the absence of democracy. Although there are claims that poverty pushes people into the arms of terrorists, the 9/11 hijackers all belonged to the middle and upper middle classes. As President George W. Bush said, "Poverty does not make poor people into terrorists and murderers. Yet poverty, weak institutions and corruption can make weak states vulnerable to terrorist networks and drug cartels within their borders" (Bush, 2002).

The West has long been guilty of supporting the most repressive Third World régimes, despite evidence of their corruption and often abysmal human rights records. Of the 169 countries on the World Bank's list of recipients of development loans, 135 are afflicted with various degrees of systemic corruption, according to my analysis. The disbursement of close to USD 400 billion in loans to these countries between June 1946 and June 2002 has done little to diminish this corruption.[16] If anything, the money has only served to strengthen the corrupt systems and further entrench those in power.

Much of the money given to Third World countries seldom reaches its intended recipients; instead, it often finds its way into secret offshore bank accounts. Former Zairian President Mobuto Sese Seko, for example—who advised Zairian civil servants, "If you want to steal, steal a little in a nice way" (Sandbrook, 1986, 95)—looted the national treasury of USD 4 to 10 billion and fled to the French Riviera, leaving his nation bereft. Only USD 4 million in Swiss bank accounts was frozen. In another example, Pakistani Prime Minister Benazir Bhutto's husband was sent to prison for abusing his status to increase the family's wealth through government contracts; no money was recovered. Similarly, Philippine President Ferdinand Marcos and his wife Imelda made off with USD 5 billion from the Philippine people—only USD 2 billion was recovered. In over 32 years in office, the family and cronies of former Indonesian President Suharto helped themselves to USD 80 billion. No money was recovered, and the three Indonesian governments that succeeded him never seriously tried to retrieve it (Masland and Bartholet, 2000). To curtail the growing industry of terrorism, it is mandatory to combat corruption and lawlessness, even though fighting these phenomena requires the cooperation of the very entities that most benefit from them.

---

16   The number of countries afflicted with various degrees of systemic corruption has been identified by the author, using a more encompassing definition than that of the World Bank. The total sum of loans was calculated based on each country's respective loan over this period.

What Is to Be Done?

By now, the evidence that drugs are a major financial lifeline for terrorist groups is overwhelming. However, neither the American government nor its allies consider it a priority to aggressively target this source of funding.

A relatively simple way to eradicate these drugs already exists in the form of mycoherbicides. According to David Sands, a scientist who spent years researching these naturally occurring plant-pathogenic fungi as a means of targeting either coca bushes or poppy plants, "mycoherbicides do not need to be genetically engineered. They can be taken directly from nature … if the pathogen is effective in controlling the target[ed] weed … a battery of six tests to verify the safety of the mycoherbicide from the point of toxicity and probable environmental impact … would cost USD 40,000 for each fungal strain." However, instead of developing this method of eradication in America, the Department of Agriculture handed over USD 10 million to the Department of State, which in turn asked the United Nations Office of Drug Control and Crime Prevention to develop mycoherbicides that could be used on coca, but not on the poppy plant. But if the UN's track record on making this world a better place is any indication, we should not hold our breath for the development of this relatively simple means of ridding the world of the scourge of illegal drugs, which would cut off a major financial lifeline to terrorist groups.

Using mycoherbicides while subsidizing the Afghan economy until other crops and industries can replace the illegal heroin trade that leaves most Afghans poor seems a better way for America to succeed in the war on terrorism and in spreading democracy and the market economy (Ehrenfeld, 2005). Without heroin and cocaine, the major lifeline of the most dangerous terrorist organizations will be cut off. Without these vast amounts of money, their ability to fund their activities and subvert the economies and political systems of new and old democracies alike could be limited.

The US faces a monumental challenge in its efforts to stop international corruption, international money laundering, and international terrorism. To make matters worse, despite the provisions of the Patriot Act, and despite international conventions, few countries seem to be willing to cooperate fully with the US or with each other in this struggle. Even those that do cooperate do so mainly because of their own security concerns, and often claim that the US is not providing sufficient evidence to require action, or that cooperation might conflict with their own laws, especially their bank secrecy laws, and might discourage people from depositing money in their banks, thus hurting their economies. The international condemnation of the United States' use of the SWIFT system to monitor suspicious transactions illustrates that attitude.

US and international efforts to combat terrorist financing require high-functioning, transparent economies, with appropriate legal frameworks set up to counter money laundering that regulate both the formal and informal financial and trade sectors. They demand law-enforcement abilities and real-time intelligence and documentary evidence, which require well-trained financial intelligence experts, regulators, criminal investigators, prosecutors, customs agents, and honest bank officers, as well as vigilant and enterprising bank employees.

Moreover, governments must establish policies and programs to train and sustain the necessary human capital. Already, there is a critical shortage of expertise and trained and experienced staff for organizations such as the Canadian Financial Intelligence Units or the US Foreign Terrorist Asset Tracking Center (FTATC and FinCEN), as well as a dearth of analysts in the intelligence community. It is unclear how the US, Canadian, and European governments will plan for the future. In short, the West still lacks the proper legal mechanisms to stop terror financing, and their financial intelligence professionals are ill-prepared to serve as front-line defenders against terror-financing cash flows.

According to an October 2005 report from the Government Accountability Office, the US has not been successful at stopping terror financing because it lacks a comprehensive policy and guidelines to do so. In May 2006, another GAO report noted: "Despite the formation of an interagency coordination entity—the Terrorist Financing Working Group—U.S. efforts to coordinate the delivery of training and technical assistance lack an integrated strategic plan" (GAO, 2006).

Presenting the *National Security Strategy of the United States of America* in September 2002, President George W. Bush said: "The United States will continue to work with our allies to disrupt the financing of terrorism. We will identify and block the sources of funding for terrorism, freeze the assets of terrorists and those that support them, deny terrorists access to the international financial system, protect legitimate charities from being abused by terrorists, and prevent the movement of terrorists' assets through alternative financial networks."

As illustrated by President Bush, the war on terrorism needs to be waged on all possible fronts. The most urgent task is to stop the flow of terrorist funding—especially that which is state-sponsored—and the funds derived from the drug trade. The funding of this evil is enormous in scope, broad in diversity, ingenious in method, and aggressive in approach. The West should change its approach and treat terror financing as a criminal act, and develop the legal instruments to combat it.

References

9/11 Commission (2004), *The 9/11 Commission Report: Final Report of the National Commission on Terrorist Attacks Upon the United States* (New York: W.W. Norton & Company).

Ashcroft, John (2002), prepared remarks to the DEA/Drug Enforcement Rollout, Washington, DC (19 March).

Beckett, Paul (2002), "Sept. 11 Attacks Cost $303,672; Plot Papers Lacking, FBI Says," *Wall Street Journal* (15 May).

Belluck, Pam, with Lichtblau, Eric (2002), "Federal Agents Raid a Software Company Outside Boston, Seeking Links to al Qaeda," *The New York Times* (7 December).

Bin Laden, Osama (2001), videotape broadcast on *Al Jazeera* TV, Doha, Qatar (27 December); translated in "Bin Laden Calls Sept. 11 Attacks 'Blessed Terror,'" CNN.com (27 December).

Bodansky, Yossef (1999), *Bin Laden: The Man Who Declared War on America* (Rocklin, CA: Forum).

Bosworth-Davis, Rowan, and Saltmarsh, Graham (1994), *Money Laundering* (London: Chapman and Hall).

Bush, George W. (2001), remarks upon signing Drug-Free Communities Act Reauthorization Bill, Omni Shoreham Hotel, Washington, DC (14 December).

Bush, George W. (2002), *The National Security Strategy of the United States of America.* (Washington, DC: The White House).

Carr, Rebecca (2002), "Authorities Say Terrorists Planned Drugs-for-Guns Plots," Cox News Service (7 November).

CBSNews.com (2002), "Drug Money for Hezbollah?" (1 September).

Central Intelligence Agency (2006), *CIA World Factbook 2006* (Washington, DC: Central Intelligence Agency); at <https://www.cia.gov/cia/publications/factbook/index.html>

Civil Action (2002), The United States District Court for the District of Columbia, Case Number 1:02CV01616(JR), Third Amended Complaint (September 2002).

Debussman, Bernd (2006), "War on Drugs: Elusive Victory, Disputed Statistics," Reuters (7 March).

Ehrenfeld, Rachel (1992), *Evil Money* (New York: HarperBusiness).

Ehrenfeld, Rachel (2005), "Afghanistan and Heroin," *New York Sun* (3 January).

Ehrenfeld, Rachel (2006), "A 'Political Party' Unveiled," *The Washington Times* (11 August).

Farach, Antonio (1983), testimony in "The Cuban Government's Involvement in Facilitating International Drug Traffic," joint hearing before the Senate Committee on the Judiciary, Subcommittee on Security and Terrorism and the Senate Foreign Relations Committee and the Drug Enforcement Caucus, Subcommittee on Western Hemisphere Affairs, 98th Cong., 1st sess. (30 April), serial J-98-36 (Washington, DC: US Government Printing Office).

Government Accountability Office (GAO) (2006), "International Financial Crime: Treasury's Responsibilities Relating to Selected Provisions of the USA PATRIOT Act," Report to the Chairman, Committee on the Judiciary, House of Representatives (April), Report GAO-06-483; at <http://www.gao.gov/new.items/d06483.pdf>

Hosenball, Mark (2002), "High-Tech Terror Ties?" *Newsweek* web exclusive (6 December); at <www.msnbc.com/news/844098.asp>

Hutchinson, Asa (2002), "Narco-Terror: The International Connection Between Drugs and Terror," speech presented at the Heritage Foundation, Washington, DC (2 April).

Intelligence and Terrorism Information Center (2006), "Crime and terrorism: During the current confrontation in Lebanon, Hezbollah again used the drug trade to collect intelligence in Israel" (10 August); at < http://www.terrorism-info.org.il/malam_multimedia/English/eng_n/html/hezbollah_100806e.htm>

International Monetary Fund (2006a), "Asian Development Outlook: Afghanistan"; at <http://www.adb.org/documents/books/ado/2006/documents/afg.pdf>

International Monetary Fund (2006b), "IMF Executive Board Concludes 2005 Article IV Consultation with the Islamic Republic of Afghanistan" (Washington,

DC: International Monetary Fund); at <http://www.imf.org/external/np/sec/pn/2006/pn0627.htm>

International Monetary Fund (2006c), *World Economic Outlook: Globalization and Inflation* (Washington, DC: International Monetary Fund); at <http://www.imf.org/Pubs/FT/weo/2006/01/index.htm>

International Monetary Fund, Monetary and Exchange Affairs Department (2000), "Offshore Financial Centers," IMF Background Paper (23 June); at <www.imf.org/external/np/mae/oshore/2000/eng/back.htm#II>

International Monetary Fund, Monetary and Financial Systems Department (2006), "Offshore Financial Centers: The Assessment Program—A Progress Report" (8 February); at < http://www.imf.org/external/np/pp/eng/2006/020806.pdf>

IRIN (2006), "Afghanistan: Opium Harvest to Increase by 60 Percent—UN Report," Reuters AlertNet (4 September); at <http://www.alertnet.org/thenews/newsdesk/IRIN/d037e072e25983e66f5ef527b1fff7f3.htm>

Israeli Prime Minister's Media Adviser (2002), "Senior Fatah Militant in Lebanon Directed and Financed Serious Terror Attacks in Territories and Israel" (26 May); at <www.imra.org.il/story.php3?id=12156>

Israeli, Raphael, ed. (1983), *PLO in Lebanon: Selected Documents* (London: Weidenfeld and Nicholson).

Johnson, Kirk (2006), "Officials Seeking Source of Deadly Heroin Mixture," *The New York Times* (14 June).

Karmon, Ely (2003), *'Fight on All Fronts': Hizballah, the War on Terror, and the War in Iraq*, Policy Focus #46 (Washington, DC: Washington Institute for Near East Policy).

Kurtz-Phelan, Daniel (2005), "A Big Drug Party: Cheap Cocaine on the Way, Thanks to a New Colombian Law," *Slate* (2 August); at <http://www.slate.com/id/2123343/%20-%2035k>

Levitt, Matthew (2002), "The Political Economy of Middle East Terrorism," *Middle East Review of International Affairs (MERIA)* 6: 4.

Library of Congress, Federal Research Division (2002), "A Global Overview of Narcotics-Funded Terrorist and Other Extremist Groups" (May; draft).

Masland, Tom, and Bartholet, Jeffery (2000), "Tracking Abacha's Billions," *Newsweek* (13 March).

McCraw, Steven (2003), Testimony before the Senate Judiciary Committee, hearing on "International Drug Trafficking and Terrorism" (20 May); at <http://www.fbi.gov/congress/congress03/mccraw052003.htm>

McKeeby, D. (2006), "Rumsfeld Reflects on Five Years of Progress in Afghanistan," News from Washington, USINFO (11 July); at <http://usinfo.state.gov/xarchives/display.html?p=washfile-english&y=2006&m=July&x=20060711171130idybeekcm0.7739221>

Mintz, John (2002), "Fifteen Freighters Believed to be Linked to al Qaeda," *The Washington Post* (30 December).

Molyneux, Joseph (2002), "The Worldwide Terror Network: Operations and Financing" (unpublished paper).

National Drug Intelligence Center (NDIC) (2006), "National Drug Threat Assessment 2006; The Impact of Drugs on Society"; at <http://www.justice.gov/ndic/pubs11/18862/impact.htm#Top.>

Pipes, Daniel (2002), "What Is *Jihad?*" *New York Post* (31 December).

Pope, S. (1987), "Diversion: An Unrecognized Element of Intelligence?" *Defense Analysis* 3: 2.

Public Information Notice (2006), No. 06/27 (8 March); at <http://www.imf.org/external/np/sec/pn/2006/pn0627.htm>

Robles, Frances (2003), "Poppy Crops Down: U.S. Expects Weaker Heroin," *Miami Herald* (10 May).

Sandbrook, R. (1986), *The Politics of Africa's Economic Stagnation* (Cambridge: Cambridge University Press).

Shahar, Yael (2001), "Tracing bin Laden's Money: Easier Said Than Done," International Policy Institute for Counter-Terrorism (21 September); at <www.ict.org.il/articles/articledet.cfm?articleid=387>

South Asia Intelligence Review (2002), "Weekly Assessments and Briefings" 1: 22 (16 December); at <http://www.satp.org/satporgtp/sair/Archives/1_22.htm>

Sovetskaya Voyenna Entsiklopedia (1979), vol. 7 (Moscow: Voyenizdat).

Suvorov, Victor (1983), "Spetsnaz: The Soviet Union's Special Forces," *International Defense Review* (September).

Thachuk, Kimberley (2002), "Terrorism's Financial Lifeline: Can It Be Severed?" *Strategic Forum* 191.

The White House (2005), "Fact Sheet: Progress on the 9/11 Commission Recommendations"; at
<http://www.whitehouse.gov/news/releases/2005/12/20051205-5.html>

USAID (2006), "Asia and the Near East: Afghanistan"; at <http://www.usaid.gov/locations/asia_near_east/afghanistan/>

US Department of State (2003), *Patterns of Global Terrorism 2002* (Washington, DC: US Department of State); at <www.state.gov/secretary/rm/2003/20067.htm>

US Department of the Treasury (2002), "Contributions by the Department of the Treasury to the Financial War on Terrorism: Fact Sheet" (September); at <www.ustreas.gov/press/releases/reports/2002910184556291211.pdf>

US Department of the Treasury (2003), "U.S. Treasury Department Announces New Executive Office for Terrorist Financing and Financial Crimes" (3 March); at <www.ustreas.gov/press/releases/js77.htm>

US Department of the Treasury, Customs Service (2001), "Green Quest: Finding the Missing Piece of the Terrorist Puzzle"; at <www.customs.ustreas.gov/xp/cgov/enforcement/investigative_priorities/greenquest.xml>

US Departments of the Treasury and Justice (2002), *National Money Laundering Strategy* (Washington, DC: Department of the Treasury).

US Drug Enforcement Administration (DEA) (2001), "Afghanistan Country Brief: Drug Situation Report, September 2001"; at <www.usdoj.gov/dea/pubs/intel/intel0901.html>

US Drug Enforcement Administration (DEA) (2002), "More Than 100 Arrested in Nationwide Methamphetamine Investigation" (10 January); at <www.usdoj.gov/dea/major/me3.html>

Willman, John (2001), "Trail of Terrorist Dollars That Spans the World," *Financial Times* (29 November).

World Islamic Front (1998), "Jihad Against Jews and Crusaders," *al-Quds al-Arabi,* (February 23), translation available at <www.fas.org/irp/world/para/docs/980223-fatwa.htm>

Chapter 3

Substantiating the Nexus between Diaspora Groups and the Financing of Terrorism

Michel Hess

Terrorism and Diaspora Populations

Financial transactions for terrorist purposes support the logistical preparation and implementation of a specific terrorist attack. They can also provide the material means for general terrorist activities, including propaganda, recruitment, infrastructure, and maintenance. Terrorism financing therefore has either an immediate pragmatic or fundamental programmatic significance in the implementation of overall terrorist objectives (see Ehrenfeld, 2005; Pieth, 2003). In this context, there are at least four distinct reasons why law enforcement, security, and intelligence services have focused recent attention on diaspora groups. These reasons can be classified as tactical–operational or strategic–political (see Gunaratna, 2000; Pérouse de Montclos, 2005; UNODC, 2005; and 9/11 Commission, 2004, Ch. 5).

First, at the tactical–operational level, law enforcement-based intelligence anticipates that a disturbance or disruption of financial transactions between diaspora fund-raisers and terrorist operatives has a direct preventive effect on specific terrorist incidents and undermines terrorist preparations. This assumption presumes a clear identification of specific financial transactions, a certain level of funding, a clear identification of the potential terrorist end-use, and finally, a proof of evidence. In contrast, the second tactical–operational dimension concerns the more diffuse link between diaspora groups and the general financing of terrorist networks, not of specific attacks that may be carried out by the same networks. A substantiation of this connection requires a clear identification of terrorist networks and groups, their official and unofficial sources of material support, and the broader socio-economic contexts in which they operate.

At the strategic–political level, the third reason that the role of diaspora groups has received increased attention is due to the unprecedented degree to which terrorist networks have taken advantage of trans-national opportunities in a globalized world. These opportunities include, but are not limited to, sophisticated financial services, payments systems, and funding instruments. In this view, terrorist networks and groups are not too different from corporations operating in global competitive markets; ostensibly, they take advantage of local value-added and human resource expertise for specific operational needs and purposes, but ultimately possess a global vision. Finally, the fourth reason for the focus on diasporas at the strategic–political level is rooted in the concern that diaspora-based terrorism financing benefits from disparities in levels of income and purchasing power, whereby communities in relatively high-income countries would be in a position to cover a disproportionate share of the total costs of specific and general terrorist expenditures. This concern is bolstered by the local and national political and ideological marginalization of individuals that belong to the pertinent diaspora communities. Not infrequently, this level of individual social isolation contrasts sharply with the perceived collective empowerment gained as a result of playing a proactive sponsorship role in support of an allegedly "higher cause" with which individual diaspora members can identify.

The first two scenarios describe the broad operational parameters within which law enforcement, intelligence, and security agencies tackle the linkages between national diaspora communities and terrorism financing. The focus on diaspora groups is straightforward and instrumental—namely, to apprehend suspects accused of supporting terrorism in kind, through services, or through monetary payments. The second two scenarios raise fundamental governance issues. While they are of some limited strategic interest to intelligence services, these scenarios can be more effectively addressed by institutions that take a long-term view, supporting good governance—for example, the World Bank—and standards for transparent financial practices—for example, Financial Action Task Force (see <www.fatf-gafi.org>), Wolfsberg Group (see Pieth and Aiolfi, 2004), or the Egmont Group of Financial Intelligence Units (see <www.egmontgroup.org>).

This chapter makes a four-pronged claim regarding the nexus between diaspora groups and the financing of terrorism:

- This nexus is of critical importance, since a number of terrorist networks and groups are supported by well-organized diasporas in Western Europe and North America that are instrumental in raising funds and spreading propaganda.
- Understanding the specific connections is crucial, since terrorists purportedly rely on funding sources that are close to their basic ethnic or cultural roots. Terrorists with a fundamentalist religious agenda and motivation would typically be supported by funds donated for religious purposes.[1] The diaspora fund-raising efforts depend on culturally specific practices.
- While terrorist networks or groups may have legally constituted political or other front organizations (for example, political parties, firms, non-governmental organizations, religious sects), these branches generally transfer some of the donations to their armed factions.
- Informal methods of transferring funds between crisis regions and diaspora groups emerge and intensify in times of open conflict or war (see Maimbo, 2003). While most of these remittances have a humanitarian purpose, the same channels are also misused for transferring funds donated by diaspora groups to terrorist networks in the countries of origin. In any circumstance, terrorist networks and groups only rely on transfer methods that they know and trust.

---

1   This motivational nexus is replicated in other types of terrorism financing not necessarily related to diaspora groups. State-sponsored terrorism, by definition, uses public funds. Likewise, terrorist activities sponsored by private groups (corporate or other) are supported by private and business sources.

Caveats

This four-pronged claim argues that a focus on diaspora groups is warranted as far as the financing of terrorism is concerned. However, it also argues that, while maintaining this focus on diaspora groups, both intelligence and security agencies and governance institutions need to keep in mind certain deterministic pitfalls— namely, the fact that money is not the root cause of the terrorist scourge. While effective measures against the financing of terrorist acts and activities are important, they are not sufficient to eliminate the root causes of the problem: unsolved ethnic, political, religious, ideological, or socio-economic conflicts and disparities.

Similarly, it is always important to clarify and differentiate between two sets of issues—humanitarian assistance versus the financing of specific terrorist acts— and two sets of practices—money laundering and terrorism financing. Diaspora- supported non-governmental and humanitarian organizations fulfill an extremely important role in conflict zones where regular state services have been interrupted and can no longer provide for basic necessities. In these difficult circumstances, humanitarian funding may well indirectly and inadvertently support general terrorist groups due to the nature of the conflict environment. It may, for example, improve the livelihoods of families of suicide-bombers. Private, non-governmental, and even official intergovernmental humanitarian assistance in complex emergencies or post- conflict rehabilitation environments is no different in this regard. Nonetheless, it is important to keep in mind the principal objective of humanitarian aid, which is to alleviate human suffering.

At the same time, we have to acknowledge that under the given circumstances the potential "collateral damage" with regard to indirect support of terrorist violence must be controlled and managed, with clear standards of ethics and rules of engagement. Should, for instance, humanitarian organizations cease their activities in Chechnya only because it is exceedingly difficult to differentiate between victims and perpetrators? The answer to this question is clearly "No"—the primary task of humanitarian aid is not to resolve issues of structural violence. This dilemma has, for instance, recently become the subject of policy discussions after Hamas' victory in the Palestinian parliamentary elections: is the European Union's and the United States' decision to stop providing financial support for the Palestinian Authority meaningful? What does this mean for the 140,000 government employees (who are primarily young men)? What are the potential repercussions for radicalization? For these reasons, it is critical to refer back to the distinction raised earlier: indirect financing of general terrorist group activities is not the same as the targeted financing of a specific terrorist act.

Regarding the second distinction, it is important to keep in mind that terrorists may not necessarily have the need to launder money. If funds that are ultimately intended to be used for terrorist purposes are gained from the outset in legal markets (diaspora-based or otherwise), potential sponsors of terrorism do not have to work with obscure financial investors in offshore markets in order to launder the proceeds. In cases of so-called reversed money laundering for terrorist purposes, legal funds are kept as long as possible in legal financial flows in order to avoid detection by financial intelligence.[2] These funds reach their terrorist end destination shortly before they are needed. Conversely, illegal funds can remain in the shadow economy, and terrorist networks can form alliances to manage and divert funds for operational purposes using illegal or non-institutionalized methods of transfer, thus escaping any oversight mechanisms. This practice is particularly widespread when it comes to the operational use of funding from profitable narcotics businesses, as shown by the Madrid train bombings in 2003.

The Origins: Forms of Diaspora-based Financing

The main sources of funding for globally operating terrorist networks and groups include state sponsorship; private and corporate sponsorship (for example, Al Qaeda assets and related financial networks); funds obtained through criminal activities (extortion, drugs, organized crime); and general fund-raising in diaspora and other sympathetic communities. This chapter will focus primarily on the last form of financing, and will not elaborate on the other forms of possible financial support, however important these may be. In the subsequent section, the chapter also examines money transfer systems, as these are particularly relevant to a basic understanding of diaspora-based funding.

Fund-raising activities are a common practice in all diaspora communities. In the absence of public support from state budgets, diaspora communities resort to fund-raising in order to maintain social, cultural, and political community-based activities. Some of these fund-raising projects are specifically targeted toward humanitarian projects in the groups' countries of origin. Fund-raising activities designed to directly or indirectly support terrorist organizations take many different forms: they can be membership dues of associations, parties, and clubs; they can be voluntary donations; they can also be the creation of foundations under public law specifically working for terrorist fund-raising. For all these forms of gathering funds to support terrorism, an understanding of the functioning of diaspora groups is key.

There is hardly any terrorist network or group that does not enjoy at least the moral support of a sympathetic diaspora in Europe or North America. Religious fundamentalist and nationalist or separatist groups in particular have traditionally relied on "extraterritorial" support. The "new" trans-national, networked style of the global jihadist movement is in this respect not that different from "old-style" terrorist movements. Let us remember, for instance, that back in the 1970s and 1980s, the Armenian Secret Army for the Liberation of Armenia (ASALA), operating primarily out of the Lebanese Armenian community, was very much dependent on diaspora

---

2   In his remarks at a luncheon with the Congressional Legislative Staff Association in 2002, Swiss Attorney General Valentin Roschacher said: "But let me remind you—we are not only talking about money laundering in the classic sense of the word, which means illegal money out of illegal actions is transformed into legal money. What we are also facing in the fight against the financing of terrorism is reversed money laundering, which is legal money out of legal actions which is then used via legal channels to fund illegal acts. Here we face the challenge to determine illegal sources or to prove illegal intentions" (Roschacher, 2002). Full text available online at <www.swissemb.org>

support. The main difference from "old-style" diaspora-supported terrorism is the extent to which contemporary radical Islamist movements benefit from trans-national opportunities. As such, the diaspora dimension is only one segment of a more complex picture. Not infrequently, diaspora groups are well networked, and fundraising activities open up an opportunity to deliver a tangible contribution to the conflict in the countries of origin. What are the specific forms of diaspora-based fund-raising?

For Islamist groups, the first form that comes to mind is of course the *zakat*, or tax. It is the third of the five pillars of Sunni Islam, and one of the ten branches of religion in Shi'a Islam. *Zakat* is a mandatory duty which the Qur'an states must be performed when certain prerequisites are fulfilled, though it is also possible to donate additional amounts as an act of voluntary charity in order to receive additional divine reward.[3] For example, the Internet provides online calculators for the two types of *zakat* that exist: one is a per head payment to the *zakat* collector equivalent to the cost of around 2.25 kilograms of the primary food of the region, which is paid during the month of Ramadan by the head of a household; the second is a wealth and property tax on business, savings, income, crops, livestock, gold, minerals, and hidden treasures. For practical purposes, a flat rate of 2.5 percent is generally applied on valuables and savings beyond the minimum of life subsistence, currently rated in North America and Europe at USD 1300 per year. The *zakat* benefits eight types of people in need, or in difficult life circumstances.[4]

It is estimated that several billion dollars are collected worldwide annually through *zakat*. Islamic financial institutions typically donate several million dollars each. However, there is disagreement as to the percentage figure of these funds that is dedicated to terrorist activities, and even a general estimate would not be very useful. Fund-raisers occur at regular intervals in religious centers. On some of these occasions, believers are specifically requested to donate money for the families of suicide bombers. Significant shares of these funds are, as a rule, transferred in small amounts of cash by couriers across national borders, thus escaping any effective financial oversight by authorities. The rest remains within the diaspora communities, and could (at least in theory) also be used for extremist activities there. Based on the purposes of *zakat*, however, it is only reasonable to assume that significant funds are transferred to regions suffering from complex humanitarian emergencies. Since terrorist networks and groups often emanate from these same regions, *zakat* most likely also supports these networks and groups. Whether or not individual donors are consciously or unconsciously aware that some of their taxes end up being used for a larger terrorist purpose cannot be judged conclusively.

---

3   "And what you give in usury, so that it may increase through (other) people's wealth it does not increase with Allah, but what you give in *zakat*, seeking Allah's Pleasure, then it is those who shall gain reward manifold ..." (30:39).

4   People who have neither material possessions nor means of livelihood; people with insufficient means to meet basic needs; workers associated with the collection and distribution of *zakat*; converts to Islam; people who want to escape slavery and bondage; someone who is in debt; people who strive for the cause of Allah; people who are stranded on a journey.

The second form of diaspora-based financing is membership dues of political or quasi-religious parties. Political factions can support armed factions financially. Examples of this type of diaspora-based support abound in Europe, where the Basque ETA, the Irish IRA, and many other terrorist groups with a Marxist, nationalist, or separatist agenda have pursued dual-track strategies to achieve their objectives. Religious factions, however, have not enjoyed nearly as much of this kind of support from possible corresponding political factions. The reason is primarily rooted in the non-territorial dimension of religiously motivated terrorism.

It may be worthwhile to expand briefly on the most prominent historical case of this second form of diaspora-based financing: the substantial funding of terrorist activities of the Provisional IRA by Irish-American Catholic communities, which retained a strong sense of exile and diaspora.[5] As leading Ulster Unionist Jeffrey Donaldson remarked in the 1970s, without funding coming from the diaspora community in the northeast United States, the IRA would not have had nearly the same potential for violence (see Adams, 1986; Horgan and Taylor, 2002).

Though the IRA received financial support from Europe and Libya,[6] its complex and sophisticated fund-raising activities and mechanisms focused on the northeastern United States, where over 70 percent of the roughly 34 million Americans reporting Irish ancestry reside. Before its de-designation as a political terrorist branch of the IRA, Sinn Fein benefited from funding emanating from Noraid, the Irish-American Northern Aid Committee, which traditionally supported the families of republican paramilitary prisoners in Ireland. Sinn Fein, in turn, acted as a political branch supporting the military faction at the time. Even though Noraid openly expressed support for the IRA, it was always emphatic as to the humanitarian end destination of its donations. Expenditures of the Provisional IRA focused on weapons (though some were imported directly from the United States), munitions, training, salaries, payments to supporters (safe houses), and welfare payments. Expenditures of Sinn Fein focused on covering maintenance costs of offices and meeting premises, election and campaign costs, and salaries.

The key to understanding the magnitude and sustainability of the support that the Irish diaspora provided for the Provisional IRA is to recognize the extent to which already existing institutions and organizations within diaspora communities, such as the *Clann na Gael* (the US branch of the Irish Republican Brotherhood) facilitated fund-raising from the very beginning of the funding process. The second key element is to recall the respectable political standing of Irish nationalists and militants in the US diaspora community. Michael Flannery of the North Tipperary

---

5   For example, a declassified FBI Director Memorandum, dated 20 November 1973, stated: "... financial contributions in the past have been rather substantial and the Irish Northern Aid Committee (INAC) has collected the bulk of this money and has forwarded same to its representative in Northern Ireland. As investigations have disclosed, some of the money collected in the US is finding its way into the hand of the militant Provisional Irish Republican Army (IRA). *These financial contributions currently are being forwarded from the headquarters of INAC, Bronx, NY, either by bank drafts or by personal courier ...*" (accessible online at <http://www.paperlessarchives.com/ira.htm>; emphasis added).

6   The total budget range of the Provisional IRA was estimated between £6.5 million and £15 million; this had diminished to £5.3 million by the mid-1990s.

Brigade, for instance, tapped very skillfully into currents of Irish Catholic radicalism in the US for instrumental purposes. Both of these elements reemerged in the recent controversy around the banning of Sinn Fein fund-raising efforts by Gerry Adams associated with St Patrick's Day celebrations in the US. Security sources within the United States claim that Sinn Fein fundraising efforts have netted between £15 million and £20 million since the ban on such activities was lifted by President Clinton in March 1995 ("U.S. Calls Halt to Sinn Fein Fundraising in IRA Backlash, *Times of London*, 14 March 2005). Both the magnitude and success of the fund-raising efforts by this political branch have no equivalents in jihadist movements, as the latter lack the support of formally constituted political factions, and usually have no nationalist ambitions or territorial claims.

Donations and non-governmental fund-raising are the third and fourth forms of diaspora-based support with a potential terrorist end-use. Some of these donations may be obtained voluntarily, while others are generated through extortion or blackmail. For instance, the now defunct Kurdish PKK and current Kongra-Gel has in the past used both voluntary and forceful means of fund-raising. The key consideration with regard to non-governmental and humanitarian fund-raising efforts in the diaspora is the degree to which funds are obtained with explicit statements that they will be exclusively applied toward a specific terrorist end-use. While many forms of terrorism rely on non-governmental support, it is particularly Islamic fundamentalist terrorism that benefits from funds received from humanitarian agencies. Governments have as a result increasingly recognized the need for financial oversight of institutions that do not fall typically within the standard range of institutions that deal professionally with transfers of funds (and would therefore be excluded by money laundering legislation), such as private foundations, diamond dealerships, and private investment firms. These loopholes have been closed in many countries. In Saudi Arabia, for instance, all non-governmental organizations are subject to regulation by the Ministry of Interior, and therefore the Kingdom. In Russia, a new law regulating non-governmental organizations clearly gives the government greater discretion in outlawing private institutions under public law. Major private grant-giving foundations apply the regulations as if they were financial intermediaries themselves, clearly a sign that their reputation is perceived to be at stake.

Given the considerable civil liberties concerns, a viable working alternative to excessive oversight responsibilities of government agencies has been quality-labeling for foundations and humanitarian agencies—similar to ethical quality-labeling on consumer products, such as "dolphin-free tuna"—by a recognized certification agency that maintains financial compliance and accounting regulations and standards. Though this form of certification or labeling may not be very effective when it comes to the purposeful abuse of non-governmental institutions for financing terror, it is nonetheless useful for potential donors interested in contributing to a charitable organization. Finally, though organized criminal activities, state sponsorship, and private corporations may have a link to diaspora-based terrorism funding, this link is indirect at best, as the diaspora is not the primary vehicle through which funds are raised and through which terrorism is supported in these models.

Financial Transfer Systems Linked to Diaspora Fund-raising

The fight against the financing of terrorism addresses two dimensions: the origins of funds, and the transfer of funds. Effective transfers are key for operational terrorist purposes. Without targeted transfers, funds are useless. Though significant funds may be raised in diaspora communities, these funds only achieve their ultimate objective if they reach the intended destination, at the right time, for the specific purpose they are meant to support. Transfer systems deserve more detailed attention than they have received so far in the context of diaspora groups. Their importance is obvious: transfers bridge the spatial and temporal gap between the place where funds are collected and the place where funds are to be spent for terrorist goals.

There are at least three forms of financial transfers relevant to diaspora-based fund-raising. First, large sums of money can be transferred from legal sources. Second, large sums can also be transferred from illegal sources. Third, smaller sums of money can be transferred from both legal and illegal sources.

The transfer of funds from legal sources essentially concerns the full range of formally regulated banking services, and practices in Islamic banking in particular, as only institutional banks can execute these forms of transfers. Institutionalized Islamic banking is primarily based on three forms of financial partnerships, which may or may not involve members of the diaspora community: wealth management based on partnership *(mudaraba)*; a joint enterprise *(musharaka)*; a corporate enterprise form in which the bank buys and sells goods with profits *(murabaha)*. These financial partnerships have nothing in common with informal practices such as *hawala*, which is described in greater detail below.

It is important to understand the regulations of Islamic banking, as these regulations are tantamount to the business practices of what can be considered otherwise to be essentially investment associations or financial placement institutes. While the customer benefits and profits are roughly the same as in regular commercial banking, the customer has no insight into the financial institutions' concrete business operations or business strategies. This practice contrasts with the relative transparency of investment funds, which in general provide an overview of their range of holdings. Western banks also offer investment funds that adhere to Islamic laws (not holding shares in companies related to pornography, alcohol, and pork);[7] the acquisition of shares by Muslims is permitted, because dividends are not considered the same as regular interest, which is prohibited under Islam. Whether or not large amounts of money earmarked for terrorists are transferred from legal sources in either Islamic or Western financial institutions is irrelevant. What is relevant is the presence of effective financial oversight. This oversight is

---

7   See, for example, Al Rajhi Global Equity Fund of UBS Asset Management; Al-Alhi Equities of Deutsche Bank; Al-Dar World Equities and Al-Khair Global Equities, both of Pictet & Cie; Arab Investor Crescent Fund of Schroder Investment Management International; and Miraj Global Equity of the Royal Bank of Canada. These investment funds provided by Western banks have recently gained in importance, especially within European banking institutions, due to the large-scale shift of funds from the United States and the Middle East to Europe after the political uncertainties surrounding the Iraq war and the intensified oversight of Middle Eastern funds in American banks.

circumvented, for instance, in cases where organizations with direct or indirect links to terrorism create their own financial institutions through which they can execute the payments. This is, for example, the case with regard to the Liberation Tigers of Tamil Eelam (LTTE), who control the Eelam Bank in Sri Lanka. The available legal mechanisms do not offer an effective solution to the issue of financial intermediaries that are affiliated or associated with terrorist groups. While a terrorist network can be simply outlawed or blacklisted, a bank cannot, because only a segment of its overall activities may or may not be related to terrorist activities.

Second, the transfer of funds from illegal sources in general results from a desire to avoid excessive exposure to financial oversight mechanisms. For this reason, illegal funds intended for terrorist use are preferably kept in the shadow economy, and will as a rule not enter the channels of public banking services. Funds of illegal origin are transferred illegally for illegal purposes. As simple as this equation may seem, the question is, how are these funds being transferred around the globe? There are two well-known transfer mechanisms that have been used over the past years, particularly in Europe: travel agencies, and gold and diamond dealerships.

Specialized travel agencies cultivate a natural affinity with certain ethnic diaspora groups, as these groups serve as the main customer base for their legal businesses. At the same time, these agencies are also quite naturally involved in large-scale currency exchange and money transfer activities involving courier services and family or clan relationships. In countries where significant refugee populations established themselves after the outbreak of a war in their home country, travel agencies stepped in to fill the vacuum left by the collapse of the banking system. This was, for example, most prominently the case with regard to Kosovo, Serbia-Montenegro, and Bosnia in the 1990s. There are substantial grounds to suspect that legitimate travel agencies both knowingly and unknowingly transferred funds from diaspora sponsors to terrorist and extremist groups.

Complementing the substitute banking services provided by travel agencies, gold and diamond dealerships have offered a second ideal transfer mechanism. Both gold and diamonds maximize the value of transfers while they minimize the risk of detection due to their small size and volume. As a result, one could assume that precious stones such as sapphire or lapis lazuli will further gain in importance in terrorism financing in general, not just when it comes to the transfer of funds. Commerce in precious stones and metals used to be a quasi-monopoly held by central banks and governments. The continuous erosion of this quasi-monopoly will only render the gold and diamond trade more attractive, as trade heterogeneity can more easily circumvent government oversight and regulations. However, effectively coordinated, integrated border management strategies; intelligence and information exchange; computerized profiling of cash couriers; and enhanced implementation of more refined customs systems for both declaration and disclosure represent several methods that states have used quite successfully to take up the slack of domestic regulatory regimes that are increasingly insufficient to deal with diverse global trade flows.

Third, the transfer of smaller sums emanating from both legal and illegal sources relies as a rule on the well-known *hawala* system.[8] Though this rather archaic legal money transfer system is widespread, primarily in the Middle East and in Asia, it has also become more commonly used in non-Islamic diaspora communities and countries. Again, it is important to mention from the outset that *hawala* as such is a completely legitimate and relatively low-cost service that gives small businesses or private individuals the chance to transfer funds in non-banking environments. Since relatively few people from diaspora groups have access to banks, credit cards, and electronic payment systems to begin with, *hawala* continues to play a necessary role for this important market segment. The keys for a successful *hawala* are trust and trans-national clan-based structures with diversified business activities. For instance, funds can be given to a small shop, with the order to have these funds paid out at another point of contact to the person presenting the correct password. *Hawala* payment orders are communicated through standard means such as e-mail, phone, or fax. The *hawala* payment system, however, can only function if the person disbursing the funds knows that the reimbursement is guaranteed at another unrelated time or place, through either a physical transfer of funds or a cancellation of outstanding debts.

While using *hawala* is financially cost-effective, offering *hawala* is also attractive due to the sizeable market of potential customers who do not have access to regular banking services. In many of the destination countries for diaspora-raised funds, formal banking and credit services are only open to a few, if available at all. However, unlike Western Union, *hawala* providers do not keep any systematic written or electronic records documenting the transfer of funds. For this reason, the arrangement facilitates illegal transactions, as transfers can be tracked only with great difficulty. The most prominent and financially powerful terrorist networks use *hawala*. The World Bank estimates that roughly over USD 300 billion have been transferred around the world in the past two decades using *hawala* networks. In addition, the World Bank estimates that remittances by migrant workers amounted to USD 110 billion in 2004. The Persian Gulf/Indian Subcontinent sector was the second-largest recipient of these remittances, after the US–Mexico corridor; about USD 16 billion in remittances were made in 2004 through the Persian Gulf/Indian Subcontinent corridor (World Bank, 2003).[9] There is a significant overlap between *hawala* and migrant worker remittances. While law enforcement agencies have stepped up measures to prohibit, penalize, formalize, and register *hawala* transfers, these regulatory efforts have been largely unsuccessful.

When it comes to diaspora-based transfers of funds, especially from European countries to countries of origin, the role of the US-based transfer firm Western Union cannot be overstated. Somewhat similar to *hawala*, though more institutionalized and

---

8   Roughly translated from Hindi, *hawala* means trust. In Pakistan, Afghanistan, Central Asia, and parts of the Middle East, the *hawala* equivalent can be *hundi*. *Hundi* refers to a kind of money order or exchange check which allows for the transfer of funds. See El-Qorchi, 2002; El-Qorchi, et al., 2003; and Nawaz, et al., 2002.

9   Two of the most important *hawala* recipient countries have been Pakistan and Iran. See the older study by Jost and Sandhu, 2000; and Central Bank of the UAE, 2005.

regulated, Western Union provides fast, relatively informal cash transfer services to 225,000 agent locations in over 195 countries and territories. Depending on country-specific legislation, mandatory identity checks are required by Western Union agents for transfers exceeding a certain amount, though the recipient can remain anonymous by presenting a fake identity. Increasingly, though, the firm has enforced more stringent identity checks, and works closely with financial intelligence services and money laundering reporting offices in many countries.[10]

Finally, cash couriers are the third most significant channel through which diaspora funds for terrorist purposes cross borders from donors to recipients. Law enforcement agencies have stepped up their efforts in this area as well, especially in border and customs controls. Indicative in this respect is the recent best practices report (available at <www.menafatf.org>) issued by the Middle East and North Africa Financial Action Task Force (or FATF), which provides general profiling of likely cash couriers, disclosure systems (declaration and disclosure), international directives, and possible implementation mechanisms under both the declaration and the disclosure system.[11] The report reveals that cash couriers today deserve the utmost attention in any credible strategy designed to combat money laundering and terrorism financing.

Conclusions

The magnitude of fund-raising efforts and monetary transactions in support of terrorist organizations through institutionalized and non-institutionalized means suggests a close nexus between diaspora-based community support and armed or unarmed political activism in zones of conflict. This chapter argues that the term *nexus*—though admittedly rhetorically and politically appealing—is indeed justified when it comes to the business relationship between sympathetic diaspora groups and trans-national extremist and terrorist networks. The analysis here does not fully explore the use of diaspora funding for extremist and terrorist activities in countries where funds are being raised, and focuses instead on trans-national financial flows to zones of conflict or insurgency. For the purposes of this chapter, a differentiation between the financing of insurgencies and the financing of terrorism does not seem to suggest itself. This analysis does not deal with the business relationship between organized crime and terrorism, as diaspora groups are clearly not the main focus for raising and transferring funds for terrorist ends in this model. Finally, for the same reason, the chapter does not deal with state, private, or corporate sponsorship of terrorism.

---

10   Based on this cooperation, we know from newspaper reports that Western Union services were used regularly for terrorism financing purposes, such as 9/11 preparations. See, for instance, *Der Spiegel*, 9 September 2002.

11   Briefly, under the declaration system for natural persons and financial institutions, implementation mechanisms include cash limits, registration details, compliance with customs obligations, customs inspection methods, sanctions, and penalties. Under the disclosure system, these mechanisms include the responsibilities of both travelers and customs officials without any predefined limit on cash and bearer-negotiable instruments.

What is commonly known, however, about the linkage of terrorism to organized crime nonetheless confirms the conclusions of this analysis in two ways. The 2003 Madrid train bombing, for instance, validates the anecdotal connection between the use of profits from organized crime (specifically, narcotics trafficking) and the financing of a major terrorist attack.[12] More importantly, the Madrid bombing demonstrated the motivation and potential or real operational capabilities of radicalized organized criminals who became terrorists. Furthermore, the terrorist threat potential of radicalized second-generation members of diaspora populations clearly confirmed the argument that an intelligence focus on diaspora groups is justified.[13] The Madrid incident also revealed no significant financial transfers or transactions that could have been tracked by financial intelligence. A superficial conclusion seems therefore to support the notion that the counter-terrorism utility of FATF and other standards is not to prevent specific attacks—however desirable and ambitious this goal may be—but rather to identify anonymous conscious and unconscious donors and supporters of more diffuse terrorist activities.

A focus not only on the origin, but also on the transfer methods of funding, however necessary, will not be sufficient. Going beyond the origin and the transfer methods, there are three interconnected reasons why the diaspora-terrorism funding nexus deserves special attention from a security and counter-terrorism perspective. First, if we are able to address the radicalization of second-generation immigrants as potential fund-raisers, if not as terrorist operatives, then we can go a long way in managing the security deficits associated with the terrorist threat. Second, if we are able to see behind the relationship between diaspora communities and zones of conflict, then we can also begin to effectively disrupt the flow of money and to perhaps prevent specific attacks, or, at a minimum, to disturb the money flow and general terrorist preparations. Finally, if we are able to understand the extent to which terrorist groups exploit quality financial services and disparities in purchasing power in a globalized, trans-national economy, then we will also be able to identify more precisely the law enforcement loopholes that would yet have to be closed through either more stringent national legislation or closer multilateral cooperative frameworks.

Armed or unarmed political activism can easily take on terrorist and extremist dimensions. Crisis-prone regions, which disproportionately harbor terrorist activities, depend for both legitimate humanitarian and illegitimate material support on the development of informal money transfer systems. Financial support for terrorist activities can emanate from both legal and illegal diaspora sources. Depending on the purpose and destination, these funds may have to be laundered in order to

---

12   As National Court Judge Juan del Olmo observed after the Madrid bombing investigation, it was "not possible to determine … the existence of transnational transfers or financial transactions that might have contributed to the funding of the attacks." Jamal Ahmidan, for instance, earned more than 1.6 million Euros in cash from drug trafficking, but only spent about 41–54,000 Euros for the Madrid bombing. See Goodman, 2004.

13   As the saying goes, "Most immigrants are not terrorists, but most terrorists are immigrants."

enter legal financial flows, in which case money-laundering techniques are used for terrorist ends. If the funds remain in the shadow economy, instrumental alliances between various diaspora groups will continue to allow funds to be managed illegally, deploying illegal or non-institutionalized methods of transfer in order to feed terrorist operations.

While many terrorist networks and groups enjoy material, spiritual, or political support from sympathetic and well-organized diasporas in Western Europe and North America, they overwhelmingly rely for financial support on sources that are close to their own ethnic or cultural roots. We cannot exclude the "collateral damage" of informally transferred funds for humanitarian purposes being misused for terrorist sponsorship. Again, as money is not the root cause of terrorism, a focus on the origins of terrorism in structural violence is an important long-term preventive instrument. As a first priority, it is critical to replace the excessive responsibilities for the oversight of diaspora-based fund-raising that have been taken on by government agencies with certification of diaspora non-profit organizations that can confirm to donors that their contributions will not be used to support terror. As a second priority, a focus of financial intelligence and oversight on institutions that do not fall under the classic notion of financial intermediaries has become an urgent necessity. Finally, a focus of financial intelligence on informal transfers of small sums of illegal money, an emphasis in border management on profiling and identifying cash couriers, and a more systematic and professional integration of financial intelligence in all criminal investigations is paramount. As we have seen, specific terrorist attacks are relatively cheap; therefore, multilateral and national legislative measures to combat terrorism financing will not be able to stop specific attacks. Anti-terrorism financing legislation has a long-term impact on general terrorist activities. This is a key decision-making consideration when it comes to civil liberties trade-offs.

A range of carefully elaborated national and multilateral measures have been implemented or are in the process of being implemented, with varying degrees of tangible commitment. The FATF developed 40 recommendations on money laundering, and nine special recommendations related to the financing of terrorism, including in particular the freezing of assets, an evaluation of alternative and electronic forms of transfer, and an evaluation of the role of non-profit organizations and foundations. In addition to the United Nations Resolutions 1267 and 1333, the European Union's terrorism list, intensified cooperation between operational security services (Europol, Eurojust), and the World Customs Organization's resolution on intensified control of air and naval commerce, Interpol has engaged in the collection and evaluation of terrorism-related financial information.

At the national level, measures that have been taken include intensified regulation of the fund-raising and propaganda activities of immigrant groups, intensified undercover or preventive investigations of non-governmental organizations, new legislation to close legal gaps, and intensified financial analysis in criminal investigations. The targeted financial and other security investigations against specific immigrant and diaspora communities have sparked a significant civil liberties debate in many European and North American countries. The controversy relates to the trade-offs between privacy, human rights, and individual and public security and safety. If the funding that is required for the launching of a specific and concrete terrorist act is indeed rather modest compared to the potential damage (to say nothing of the simple maintenance of terrorist organizations, leaders, and operatives), are the measures that can be deployed to combat the financing of terrorism, but that compromise civil liberties, really worth it?[14]

This chapter argues that a measured approach to this question has to address the extent to which a society is politically willing to pay the price for prevention. For example, how much are we willing to pay for information-based insurance premiums? A strategic and operational focus on the origins and transfer methods of diaspora-based funding delivers powerful data and information on terrorist leadership, networks, groups, and operational activists. Above all, the data can reveal anonymous supporters of and donors to terrorist causes, and could therefore indirectly serve to save the life of yet another innocent bystander.

References

9/11 Commission (2004), *The 9/11 Commission Report: Final Report of the National Commission on Terrorist Attacks Upon the United States* (New York: W.W. Norton & Company).

Adams, James (1986), *Financing of Terror: The PLO, IRA, Red Brigades, and M-19 and Their Money Supply* (New York: Simon & Schuster).

Bell, Stewart (2004), *Cold Terror: How Canada Nurtures and Exports Terrorism Around the World* (New York: Wiley).

Central Bank of the UAE (2005), "Proceedings of the Third International Conference on Hawala 2005" (Abu Dhabi: Central Bank of the UAE); at <www.cbuae.gov.ae>

Ehrenfeld, Rachel (2005), *Funding Evil* (Los Angeles: Bonus Books).

El-Qorchi, Mohammed (2002), "Hawala: How Does this Informal Funds Transfer System Work, and Should it Be Regulated?" *Finance & Development* (December).

El-Qorchi, Mohammed, et al. (2003), *Informal Funds Transfer Systems: An Analysis of the Informal Hawala System* (Washington, DC: International Monetary Fund).

Goodman, Al (2004), CNN Madrid Bureau Chief, "Tunisian Led Madrid Group" (posted 1 April); at <www.edition.cnn.com/2004>

Gunaratna, Rohan (2000), "Transnational Terrorism: Support Networks and Trends," *Faultlines* 7; at <www.satp.org>

Horgan, John, and Taylor, Max (2002), "Playing the Green Card—Financing the Provisional IRA," in *Terrorism and Political Violence* 11:2 (London: Frank Cass).

Jost, Patrick, and Sandhu, Harjit Singh (2000), *The Hawala Alternative Remittance System and its Role in Money Laundering* (Lyon: Interpol).

---

14 Suicide bombings without any major devices, such as airplanes or other vehicles, are particularly cost-effective. The cost of the 9/11 attack is estimated between USD 250,000 and 1 million. This figure includes flight training, business-class airline tickets, and general maintenance costs of all operatives.

Maimbo, Samuel Munzele (2003), *The Money Exchange Dealers of Kabul: A Study of the Hawala System in Afghanistan* (Washington, DC: World Bank).

Nawaz, Shahid, et al. (2002), "Informal and Formal Money Transfer Networks: Financial Service or Financial Crime?" in *Journal of Money Laundering Control* 5:4.

Pérouse de Montclos, Marc-Antoine (2005), "The Dark Side of Diaspora: Networking Organized Crime and Terrorism," in *African Terrorism Bulletin*, Monograph no. 112 (Cape Town: Institute for Security Studies).

Pieth, Mark, ed. (2003), *Financing Terrorism* (Boston: Kluwer Academic Publishers).

Pieth, Mark, and Aiolfi, Gemma (2004), "The Private Sector Becomes Active: The Wolfsberg Process," (Basel: University of Basel Paper); at <www.wolfsberg-principles.com.>

Roschacher, Valentin (2002), Swiss Attorney General, "Fight Against Terrorism and its Financing: The Role of Switzerland and International Cooperation," remarks delivered to the Congressional Legislative Staff Association, Washington, DC (27 February).

United Nations Office of Drugs and Crime (UNODC) (2005), "Proceedings of the Conference on Combating Terrorism Financing," (Vienna: United Nations Office of Drugs and Crime); at <www.unodc.org>

World Bank (2003), *Informal Funds Transfer Systems: An Analysis of the Hawala System* (Washington, DC: World Bank), full-text document no. 25803; at <www.worldbank.org>

Chapter 4

An Analysis of the Role of the Iranian Diaspora in the Financial Support System of the Mujahedin-e Khalq

Mark Edmond Clark

Following the outset of Operation Iraqi Freedom in 2003, the *Mujahedin-e Khalq*, or People's Mujahedin (MEK)—designated by most Western governments as a terrorist organization, and sworn to destroy the Islamic government in Iran—was crippled by a dramatic shift in its financial resource profile.[1] Since 1982, the MEK had received substantial financial support from the nemesis of the Iranian people, Saddam Hussein. Along with money, Saddam Hussein's regime established bases of support for the MEK in Iraq and supplied the organization with large hauls of weapons and materiel, as well as training (US Department of State, 1994, 9). Saddam Hussein also supported the MEK's planning for its terror campaigns against Iran, and allowed the organization to maintain the goal of bringing about regime change in Iran and installing an MEK-controlled government in Tehran (US Department of State, 1994, 12). Yet, although the MEK has lost its main benefactor, and with him the ability to conduct operations against Iranian government interests worldwide as in the past, it still maintains an ability to conduct significant activities.

Long before 2003, the MEK had the ability to maintain and develop a financial support system independent of Saddam Hussein's assistance. The primary foundation of that financial support system was the Iranian diaspora throughout North America, Europe, and Australia. As considerable secrecy surrounds the MEK's financial activities, it is difficult to calculate the degree to which it has drawn funds from its diaspora resources. Nevertheless, through an examination of the MEK's financial support system using available sources as well as conversations with former MEK members at the Nejat Society in Tehran, a picture emerges of how those fund-raising activities are conducted.[2] That examination sheds light on the MEK's potential

---

1   The *Mujahedin-e Khalq*, or People's Mujahedin, is the shortened version of its Persian name, *Sazeman-e Mujahedin-e Khalq-e Iran*, or Organization of People's Holy Warriors of Iran (US Department of State, 1994, 3; Office of the Coordinator of Counterterrorism, 2004).

2   Conversations on 24–25 January 2006 with former members of the MEK at the Nejat Society. My interviews with former members were arranged by the Nejat Society under the provision that their identities be kept confidential. Founded in 2002 by former MEK members and their families, the Nejat Society is the first non-governmental organization created that has worked to get members of the MEK "released." The Nejat Society has arranged to have families of MEK members visit their relatives in Iraq. The organization remains in close contact with the UN and the International Committee of the Red Cross. The Nejat Society is

ability to use the Iranian diaspora in Western countries for financial support, allows a better understanding of the size and scope of activities the MEK might be able to conduct with such support, and paints a picture of what that may mean to Western countries in the present and the near future.

The MEK: an Overview

The MEK was formed in 1965 as a nationalistic group committed to creating a radical socialist state in Iran. Its ideology was developed from a combination of Marxist and militant Islamic theories (Mackey, 1998, 303). On the Marxist side, it espouses theories of class struggle and historical determinism and neo-Marxist concepts of armed struggle, guerilla warfare, and revolutionary heroism (*ibid*). On the Islamic side, it embraces both the Islamic concept of *tawhid*, a divinely inspired classless society in which all men are equal and all women are entitled to basic social and political rights, and militant concepts of martyrdom (*ibid*). Since 1997, the MEK has held a place on the list of groups designated by the US Secretary of State as Foreign Terrorist Organizations. The EU added the MEK to its list of terrorist groups in 2000.

At the time of its organization in 1965, the MEK filled its ranks with recruits from among Iran's poor and middle classes, with the goal of turning them into soldiers (Mackey, 1998, 303). The MEK provided training administered by the Palestine Liberation Organization in Syria, Lebanon, and Jordan. In 1971, the MEK, inspired by the revolutions in Cuba and Vietnam, began to deploy its members against the Shah of Iran. Over the years leading to the Islamic Revolution of 1979, they struck at the Shah's installations. They also focused attacks on US businesses and citizens throughout Iran, with the goal of resolving the "fundamental contradictions between the people and the CIA imposed regime" (*ibid*). They attacked facilities run by Pepsi-Cola, General Motors, Shell Oil Company, Pan Am, and the Iran–American Society (US Department of State, 1994, 5). They killed a number of US military officers and corporate employees, mostly from Rockwell International (*ibid*). Retribution from SAVAK, the Shah's secret police force, for these acts against the regime and its allies' interests in Iran included imprisonment, torture, and execution (*ibid*, 7).

The MEK temporarily split in 1975 due to a conflict over issues of faith. One faction published a manifesto saying the organization was discarding Islam in favor of Marxist terrorism (Abdo and Lyons, 2003, 212). A new faction declared Islam a "mass opiate" and a utopian ideology, in contrast to Marxist–Leninism, which was the ideal scientific philosophy of the underclass and the true road for mankind (*ibid*). Despite the rift, the MEK regrouped and got involved in the revolutionary fervor that swept Iran in 1978 (*ibid*).

After the Ayatollah Khomeini returned to Iran, the MEK expressed even greater militancy (US Department of State, 1994, 7). Following the seizure of the US embassy in Tehran, the MEK participated physically at the site by assisting in

---

registered with the Iranian Ministry of the Interior. See the Nejat Society website at <www.nejatngo.com>

defending it from attack (*ibid*). The MEK also offered strong political support for the hostage-taking action. Yet, at the same time, the MEK was not very supportive of the new Islamic constitution (Mackey, 1998, 303–4). When, using his powers under the new constitution, the Ayatollah Khomeini barred the MEK leader Masoud Rajavi from standing as a candidate in the 1981 election for President on the basis that he was "un-Islamic," the MEK went into active opposition against the government (US Department of State, 1994, 7). Through the first months of 1981, the MEK— whose supporters at that time allegedly numbered several hundred thousands— initiated a campaign of terror and revenge in which countless acts of violence were committed against the Iranian people. During the summer and fall of 1981, more than a thousand government officials, including religious leaders, judges, and police officials, fell victim to the MEK (Mackey, 1998, 306). The MEK staged a failed attempt to assassinate Ayatollah Ali Khamenei in 1981 with a bomb planted in a tape recorder, and successfully murdered several of his aides (*ibid*). A bomb blast in the headquarters of the Islamic Republican Party killed 74 of its leaders (*ibid*, 304). The President and Prime Minister that had been elected in 1981, along with the Chief Justice, were killed in a bomb attack. When security measures around the remaining key officials were strengthened, the MEK struck at lower-level members of the civil service and the Revolutionary Guards (*ibid*). Countless ordinary citizens who the MEK declared to be government supporters were shot (*ibid*, 306). In response, thousands of MEK members were executed in the early 1980s; more than 2,000 died in 1988 alone (Sciolino, 2000, 238).

With its record of resistance against the Shah's regime and against the West, particularly its role in the 444-day hostage drama at the US embassy, the MEK provided a rallying point for nationalists who opposed the new Islamic government (US Department of State, 1994, 7). While other opposition groups demonstrated, the MEK took action (Mackey, 1998, 306). Many of the main parties in opposition to the new Islamic government—such as the Kurdish Democratic Party of Iran (KDPI), the National Democratic Front, the Hoviyat Group, the Union of Iranian Communists, and the Worker's Party—united with the MEK and the first President of the new Iranian government, Abolhassan Bani Sadr, to form the National Council of Resistance (NCR) (US Department of State, 1994, 8). After the KDPI withdrew from the NCR over the dominant role played by MEK leaders with their autocratic style, suppressing dissent and dismissing other views, a mass exodus of members occurred. Most of the groups that remained were under MEK control (*ibid*, 9). Bani Sadr left the NCR after the MEK formally sided with Iraq against Iran in 1983 (on 22 September 1980, 50,000 troops of the Iraqi Army had invaded Iran) (US Department of State, 1994, 9; Mackey, 1998, 304). The move toward Saddam Hussein was allegedly an attempt by the MEK to maneuver against the government, with the goal of acquiring arms, training facilities, and financial resources.[3]

---

3   Saddam Hussein established bases of support for the organization in locations such as Baghdad, Ashraf, and Fallujah. His provision of large supplies of weapons and materiel for the organization—such as ammunition, small arms, armored personnel carriers, tanks, artillery, rocket launchers, and training, as well as Iraqi intelligence and special operations

In 1986, Masoud Rajavi and 1000 MEK members relocated to Baghdad, where they were welcomed with great ceremony by Saddam Hussein. By 1987, Rajavi had established the National Liberation Army (NLA). The NLA was provided with training facilities, staging grounds for attacks at its primary base in Ashraf, headquarters facilities in Baghdad, and training bases in locations such as Fallujah (Rubin, 2000). The NLA conducted attacks against the border towns of Mehran, Karand, and Islamabad-e Gharb, hitting industrial and civilian targets (US Department of State, Office of the Coordinator of Counterterrorism, 2004). The NLA also fought (reportedly poorly) alongside the Iraqi Army. It willingly participated in a June 1988 incursion into Iran during which Iraqi forces used chemical weapons (*ibid*). Once the war ended, the NLA was useful to Saddam Hussein against the Kurds and Shia in Iraq. According to Jalal Talabani of the Patriotic Union of Kurdistan, nearly 5000 NLA troops joined Iraqi forces in the battle for Kirkuk during his brutal repression of the Kurdish rebellion (*ibid*). In Iran, the MEK—supported by the Hussein regime—launched regular raids on civilian targets such as automobiles, highways, government buildings, businesses, and private homes with mortars, mines, booby-traps, bombs, and fire, using Iraqi military tactics and equipment (*ibid*).

While it struck out against Iranian civilians and attacked Iranian government sites worldwide, including a raid on Iran's UN Mission in New York, the MEK's political wing's propaganda effort continued as well (US Department of State, 1994, 13). Under the rubric of the MEK-dominated NCR, which is considered the MEK's political wing, the group has sent numerous unsolicited books, brochures, and other publications and communications to Western leaders as well as the UN Secretary-General, often filled with false data (*ibid*, 14). It has sought political support and financial backing from Western public figures. Masoud Rajavi, head of the MEK's political and military wings and chairman of the NCR, and his wife, Maryam (the future leader of the NCR) have provided many press interviews. Yet, back in Iran, neither the MEK nor the NCR were able to garner much support from the Iranian people. Foreign policy analysts and other specialists on Iran assert that both organizations are discredited among the Iranian populace due to their leaders' decision to flee to Iraq and align with Saddam Hussein, as well as to the internal environment of fear in which members operate, where dissent is suppressed and tolerance of differing views is eschewed (*ibid*).[4] Masoud Rajavi, ruling by fiat, has allegedly fostered his own cult of personality. The MEK now claims to have abandoned its revolutionary ideology in favor of liberal democracy (Salhani, 2006). However, its leadership cannot present any track record to substantiate a capability or intention to be democratic (*ibid*).[5]

---

support—served to bolster MEK terror campaigns against Iran (US Department of State, 1994, 9).

4   As is stated in the Council on Foreign Relations report on Iran entitled, *Iran: Time for a New Approach*, the MEK's "collaboration with Saddam Hussein throughout the Iran-Iraq War means that the group retains little if any validity as an alternate political movement among Iranians" (Council on Foreign Relations, 2004, 83).

5   Michael Rubin, a Bush Administration consultant and an Iran expert at the American Enterprise Institute, wrote an article entitled "Monsters of the Left—The Mujahedin al-Khalq," in which he argued that in public the MEK "say the right things about freedom and democracy,

Although the MEK's military wing's campaign of terror appeared to be declining by the end of the 1990s, it actually remained deadly. In 1999, the MEK targeted key military officers in Iran, and assassinated the deputy chief of the Armed Forces General Staff (US Department of State, Office of the Coordinator of Counterterrorism, 2004). In 2000, the MEK attempted to assassinate the commander of the Nasr Headquarters—Tehran's interagency board responsible for coordinating policies on Iraq (*ibid*). The pace of attacks increased during the MEK's "Operation Great Bahman" in February 2000, when it launched dozens of attacks against Iran, including one on the complex in Tehran that houses the offices of the supreme leader and the President (*ibid*). In 2000 and 2001, the MEK was regularly involved in mortar attacks and hit-and-run raids on Iranian military and law enforcement units and government buildings near the Iran-Iraq border. In 2003, US forces in Iraq encountered the MEK. Some measures were taken against the organization; for example, United States Central Command bombed its base camps (*ibid*). However, after that action, US forces provided garrisons for approximately 3,800 MEK members at Camp Ashraf in Iraq near the Iranian border (Jehl and Gordon, 2003). Although confined to their new garrisons, the organization's fighters have maintained their heavy and small weapons, are protected from Iraqi retribution, and continue to conduct training exercises (*ibid*). Some MEK leaders operate from Auvers-Sur-Oise, France, and other sites outside Paris (Sciolino, 2003; US Department of State, Office of the Coordinator of Counterterrorism, 2004). The MEK claims an unknown number of sympathizers inside Iran, the US, and Europe (Slavin, 2005; US Department of State, Office of the Coordinator of Counterterrorism, 2004).

The MEK's Use of Aliases and Other Deceptive Practices

The MEK's outreach and lobbying efforts are critical to its existence. Using aliases to take on the guise of other, unrelated groups, the organization has sought to exploit fears in Western capitals about Iran's government. By doing so, the MEK hopes that it can also attract support for itself as an alternative to the government in Tehran (US Department of State, 1994, 14). However, under those aliases, the MEK often disseminates false and misleading information about Iran. It was the MEK that presented satellite imagery that allegedly showed Iranian nuclear facilities; the group also reported on alleged "secret" Iranian weapons laboratories (Jehl, 2004).[6] Yet it was also an MEK website that presented photos from the 1979 US embassy takeover in Tehran, incorrectly claiming that one included a young Mahmoud Ahmadinejad, the current President of Iran, handling a hostage (Slavin, 2005). In the United States, the MEK has found support from the Bush Administration. President George W. Bush alluded to the organization in a 16 March 2005 news conference, when he

but in reality is dedicated to the opposite. Maryam Rajavi, and her husband Masoud, are adept at public relations and adroit at reinvention, but the organization over which they preside eschews democracy and embraces terrorism, autocracy, and Marxism" (Rubin, 2006).

6   The MEK is generally viewed as being helpful to US intelligence authorities that are seeking to gauge the extent of Iran's nuclear program (Slavin, 2005).

stated Iran's nuclear program had been revealed by a "dissident" group ("Bush on Iran, Baseball, DNA and Judges," *The New York Times*, 17 March 2005).

Since the MEK does not engage in military activities in North America, Europe, or Australia, Western governments typically close their eyes to its activities. Ignoring MEK activities is made easier by the fact that these activities are often concealed by the use of aliases. The MEK actually became an organization of many names as early as 1981, when other key opposition elements initially united with the MEK to form the NCR, referred to in more recent times as the National Council of Resistance of Iran (NCRI) (US Department of State, Office of the Coordinator of Counterterrorism, 2004; Salhani, 2006). In spite of the departure of numerous organizations from the NCRI's ranks that occurred after 1983, when the MEK formally sided with Saddam's Iraq against Iran, the MEK-controlled NCRI still claims that it includes multiple member groups under its umbrella (US Department of State, 1994, 18). Most are in fact shell organizations, established by the MEK to make the NCRI appear more representative (*ibid*).[7] The NCRI has formed associated groups with innocuous names, such as the "Association of Iranian Scholars and Professionals" and the "Association of Iranian Women" (US Department of State, 1994, 18). To promote itself, the MEK has also taken on the names of unaffiliated professional associations. In California, the MEK once applied for a demonstration permit using the name of "The Society of Iranian Professionals." California state officials alerted the actual organization with that name, which later issued a statement explaining it had no direct or indirect connections to the MEK (*ibid*).

Deception and the MEK's Acquisition of Financial Support

Reportedly, the MEK does not pursue financial gain as an end in itself (US Department of State, Office of the Coordinator of Counterterrorism, 2004). However, through the further use of aliases, funds acquired are directed to media campaigns and used to build political influence, undertake special projects to retain members, recruit new members, and attract sympathizers.[8] In the United States and Europe, laws exist to prohibit the MEK from soliciting or receiving such support. For example, in the US, it is unlawful for a person to knowingly provide "material support or resources" to a designated Foreign Terrorist Organization (FTO) such as the MEK (US Department of State, 2004). The term "material support or resources" is defined in 18 U.S.C., Section 2339A(b) as:

> currency or monetary instruments or financial securities, financial services, lodging, training, expert advice or assistance, safe houses, false documentation or identification,

---

7   Other organizations in the NCRI that supported the MEK included: the Muslim Student Association, the Towhidi Society of Guilds, the Movement of Muslim Teachers, the Union of Instructors in Universities and Institutions of Higher Learning, and the Society for the Defense of Democracy and Independence in Iran (US Department of State, 1994, 18).

8   The Muslim Iranian Students' Society is one group recognized specifically by the US government as an MEK front organization used to garner financial support (Office of the Coordinator of Counterterrorism, 2004).

communications equipment, facilities, weapons, lethal substances, explosives, personnel, transportation, and other physical assets, except medicine or religious materials (US Department of State, 2004).

Any US financial institution that becomes aware that it has possession of or control over funds in which a designated FTO or its agent has an interest must retain possession of or control over the funds and report the funds to the Office of Foreign Assets Control of the US Department of the Treasury (US Department of State, 2004). A substantial portion of the MEK's funding is derived from individual contributors, many of whom are unaware of the true intent of the organization (author's conversations at the Nejat Society). However, most contributors do know that they are in contact with the MEK, and are cognizant of what the MEK is. Some who have been solicited by the MEK are unaware of laws prohibiting the provision of material support (*ibid*).

Using a financial support system based within Iranian diaspora communities in Western countries, the MEK has used various approaches to secure funds from the public. They include raising funds from families of MEK members; "international financing operations," which focus on street solicitation; what the organization refers to as "psychological methods"; and activities known as "special financing operations" (*ibid*).

Financial Support From MEK Members' Families

One key source of financial support for the MEK is the family members of its younger members. Many of the younger members of the MEK—as well as some of the long-time fighters—did not join the MEK by choice (author's conversations at the Nejat Society). At colleges and universities in the United States, Canada, and throughout Europe, young men and women from the Iranian diaspora are drawn to the organization through seemingly innocuous cultural events, social gatherings, conventions, and rock concerts; the name of the MEK is usually not initially mentioned (*ibid*). Typically, even after one joined the MEK in a Western country, the organization would not present itself as controlling in any way, nor would it attempt to threaten members' freedom of movement or action. That experience would be quite different from the interaction they would have with the MEK after they had come into contact with the formal organization in Iraq. Eventually, selected members that had been introduced to the organization in North America or Europe would be sent to Iraq for training. In Iraq, they would join others from Western countries, as well as other members from Iran who were lured to Iraq under the pretense that they were seeking job opportunities with a company based in the West (*ibid*). Prospective employees would usually first be brought to Turkey for job interviews, where they would then be told that their formal interview would take place at the company's main office in Iraq, where the final decision would also be made on their employment. Upon their arrival, they would be informed that the company they were in contact with was in fact the MEK, their passports would be confiscated, and their indoctrination into the MEK would begin (*ibid*).[9]

New members of the MEK would be directed to participate in financial support activities (author's conversations at the Nejat Society). They would be asked to contact their families and inform them that they were safe and in Iraq. However, they would also be ordered to solicit money from their families for the organization to pay for their expenses; families would occasionally be told that their children were sick, and that money was required for their care. Families were given a confidential bank account number and asked to deposit money in the account for their children (*ibid*). However, MEK managers who controlled the accounts would use the deposits solely for the organization's activities. Families that traveled to Iraq and were allowed to see their children were asked to deposit money in MEK accounts and then attend meetings on how to best transport money. Families would bring things such as books, seeds, and cooking utensils for their relatives to use, but the MEK would again keep everything. Families would give gold, silver, and diamonds to the MEK for the support of their children, but the organization would appropriate these as well (*ibid*). The MEK's goal with the families was to put them in a situation in which they had to keep giving money. In return for their "donations," families often received compact discs and t-shirts with Rajavi's picture on them (*ibid*).

International Activities

Recognizing that most Western countries would not allow it to solicit funding publicly under its name, the MEK had its members engage in street solicitation as representatives of front organizations (author's conversations at the Nejat Society). One MEK operation in California that was attempting to raise money under the guise of charitable fund-raising activity was uncovered by the US government (US Department of State, Bureau for Narcotics and Law Enforcement Affairs, 2002). Solicitors at Los Angeles International Airport (LAX) asked travelers and others

---

9   Elizabeth Rubin, in an article in *The New York Times Magazine*, described the conditions for MEK members in Iraq and the experiences of MEK recruits, particularly a recent recruit from Germany named Mohammed, now confined in a Kurdish Iraqi prison: "A Mujahedeen recruiter spotted him and a friend sleeping on the streets, so hungry they couldn't think anymore. The recruiter gave them a bed and food for the night, and the next day showed them videos of the Mujahedeen struggle. He enticed them to join with an offer to earn money in Iraq while simultaneously fighting the cruel Iranian regime. What's more, he said, you can marry Mujahedeen girls and start your own family. The Mujahedeen seemed like salvation. Mohammad was told to inform his family that he was going to work in Germany and given an Iraqi passport. The first month at Ashraf, he said, wasn't so bad. Then came the indoctrination in the reception department and the weird self-criticism sessions. He quickly realized there would be no wives, no pay, no communication with his parents, no friendships, no freedom. The place was a nightmare, and he wanted out. But there was no leaving. When he refused to pledge the oath to struggle forever, he was subjected to relentless psychological pressure. One night, he couldn't take it anymore. He swallowed 80 diazepam pills. His friend, he said, slit his wrists. The friend died, but to Mohammad's chagrin, he woke up in a solitary room" (Rubin, 2003).

to donate money to the Committee for Human Rights (CHR), an entity which the solicitors are alleged to have known was a front organization for the MEK. Based on the results of a federal investigation, it is believed that the funds were collected for the purpose of financing the activities of the MEK (*ibid*).

Seven individuals, including those who are believed to have knowingly donated and raised money for the MEK, were charged in a 59-count indictment with providing and conspiring to provide material support or resources to a Foreign Terrorist Organization in violation of Title 18 U.S.C. Section 2339B(a)(1). Under this indictment, it was alleged that one defendant coordinated the fund-raising activities for the MEK, while several other defendants solicited donations for the CHR—a front organization for the MEK—at LAX, knowing and intending that those donated funds would go to the MEK. Yet another group of defendants was charged with donating money to the MEK. One defendant transferred money via wire from a CHR bank account to bank accounts in Turkey for the benefit of the MEK. Several defendants participated in conference calls during which fund-raising for the MEK was discussed. During one such conference call with an MEK leader, several defendants learned that the MEK had been designated as a Foreign Terrorist Organization and were nonetheless instructed (and continued) to raise funds for the MEK (*ibid*).

In Virginia, groups called the "Iranian–American Community of Northern Virginia" and the "Union Against Fundamentalism," both MEK front organizations, sought a Congressional permit for a 19 November 2004 demonstration in support of the MEK and NCRI in front of the Capitol building in Washington, DC (author's conversations at the Nejat Society). Congress granted a permit, not knowing that they were actually providing material support to the MEK as defined in 18 U.S.C., Section 2339A(b). Funds for the demonstration were transferred in USD 9,000 increments to the US bank account of a Houston, Texas member of the MEK's US network (*ibid*). The bank may not have been aware that it had possession of funds belonging to a Foreign Terrorist Organization or its agent. Yet, if it had been, it would have been required under the law mentioned above to retain possession or control of the funds and report them to the Office of Foreign Assets Control of the US Department of the Treasury. Pointing further to the possible illegality of the operation, a Washington, DC residence of a veteran MEK member was selected by the MEK as a "safe house" for the planning of the demonstration. All instructions from the MEK's leaders, based in Paris, were sent to this residence (*ibid*). By maintaining contact with the MEK in Paris and providing the MEK with a safe house, the MEK member provided material support and resources for the MEK as defined under the law. Local and state law enforcement officials failed to investigate and respond to the use of this residence as a safe house.

In Great Britain, the organization "Iran Aid" was closed by the government for being an MEK front (author's conversations at the Nejat Society). In Germany, a non-governmental organization was used by the MEK to support asylum seekers and refugees. Another front organization allegedly supported children whose parents had been killed in Iran. The front organization would go as far as placing pictures of children falsely identified as those who would receive support in an album for prospective supporters to review. To collect funds, front organizations typically used sealed and stamped boxes placed in city centers; at first, the boxes only attracted coins. However, the MEK determined that it should be announced that public donations would be matched, and that contributions of DM 20 to 30 were customary. The intake soon increased to DM 600 to 700 a day. Nearly 30 to 40 people in each city were used in this operation. In 1988, the Nürnberg MEK front organization was uncovered by police, and the tactic was exposed (*ibid*). Initially, these false fronts, given their mission, received support from the Green Party in Germany, which was unaware of their true purpose. However, once these organizations got in trouble with the police, they lost the support of the Green Party (*ibid*).

Psychological Methods

One approach used by the MEK to secure larger sums of money from supporters was through the use of what were referred to as "psychological methods." Such activities allegedly entailed the solicitation of funds from the rich and famous at their homes, under the guise of raising money for Iranian people in need (author's conversations at the Nejat Society). Personnel from the higher levels of the MEK were specially trained to do this work. Members selected to do these solicitations were chosen based on the particular situation; members of the highest rank in the MEK were included in the selection process. The soliciting members were to work privately with these benefactors. Planning for these contacts took into account what would be most attractive to the potential donor in question, and the operations were allegedly quite successful (*ibid*). It has also been alleged that there were wealthy and prominent individuals contacted by MEK solicitors who were well aware of the MEK's purpose, and openly discussed the organization during meetings (*ibid*). The identities of these benefactors were kept completely confidential within the MEK.

Special Finance Operations

These operations were normally controlled by the financial deputy of the MEK (author's conversations at the Nejat Society). One approach included the establishment of special MEK-run companies. These seemingly average companies would engage in typical commercial activities; however, profits from these businesses would be made available for the sole and exclusive use of the MEK (*ibid*; US Department of State, 1994, 20). Other types of front companies were created to receive investments from supporters as well as unsuspecting private investors (author's conversations at the Nejat Society). In the early 1990s, an Italian reporter claimed that the MEK's financial support was derived from international businesses, noting: "The opposition has established a flourishing network of international companies trading in carpets, gold, and automobiles" (*ibid*; US Department of State, 1994, 20).

Under another approach, MEK members would work in diverse occupations—as taxi and limousine drivers, waiters, and other restaurant workers—and send the money they earned to the organization (author's conversations at the Nejat Society). Allegedly, a used car dealership in Northern Virginia had also served to fund the MEK (according to members of the Nejat Society, the dealership was located in Chantilly, VA). Until 1985, all money from the special finance operations was sent to a confidential bank account in Switzerland (US Department of State, 1994, 20). In the initial years of the MEK, bank robberies were committed in Iran, and it has been suggested by former members that some overseas bank robberies have been committed since to fund MEK operations (author's conversations at the Nejat Society).

Globally, control over MEK financial support activities is managed through encoded communication by telephone and computer, and members are trained to encode messages (*ibid*). An electronic mail system at one time existed over a private computer network. In Iraq in particular, laptops with satellite modems and special dishes as well as code-encrypted pocket computers have been used. It was understood within the MEK that the Iranian government had no ability to intercept such communications along the border with Iraq (*ibid*).

Conclusion

Western countries have been quite tolerant of MEK activity, particularly its practices involving recruitment, organizing, and especially soliciting financial support by skirting laws against providing material support to terrorist organizations. Some Western political figures, impressed by its activities against the Iranian government, have pledged their support for the organization. By promising to avoid "military activities," the MEK has established a *modus vivendi* with Western governments that has opened the door for the organization to maintain offices and conduct activities separate from its MEK title. However, Western governments have no need to recognize the MEK's avoidance of military activities as an act of goodwill; even more, they should not excuse anything else the MEK might do within the borders of Western states based on the MEK's decision not to engage in violent activities in those countries. Additionally, by pointing to its avoidance of such activities in Western countries, the MEK itself calls attention to the fact that it *could* potentially engage in a type of harmful activity in Western countries. This capability makes the organization, de facto, a potential threat to those societies.

Yet, on the question of whether or not the MEK is doing harm in Western countries, it is equally important for Western governments to consider MEK efforts to co-opt members of the Iranian diaspora in their respective countries for participation in its activities, particularly in its financial support system. The MEK pulls diaspora members backward; rather than allowing them to focus on being good citizens and making a positive and successful place for themselves and their families in their respective new countries of residence, it asks them to focus on making a place for the MEK in Iran. Although they tend not to react aggressively to such activities, as they are protected by basic rights such as the freedoms of speech and association, Western governments likely would prefer less external interference in the lives of immigrant groups. Some protection of the diaspora community from such efforts appears necessary. Given the MEK's current standing as a designated FTO, such interference, along with its nearly superfluous use of deception and secrecy, provides further support for a decision by Western governments to continue to list the MEK as a terrorist organization whose activities must be more closely monitored.

References

Abdo, G., and Lyons, J. (2003), *Answering Only to God* (New York: Henry Holt).

Council on Foreign Relations (2004), *Iran: Time for a New Approach*, Independent Task Force Report (New York: Council on Foreign Relations).

Jehl, D. (2004), "Group Says Iran Has Secret Nuclear Arms Program," *The New York Times* (17 November).

Jehl, D. and Gordon, M. (2003), "Aftereffects: Policy; American Forces and Terror Group Reach Ceasefire," *The New York Times* (29 April).

Mackey, S. (1998), *The Iranians: Persia, Islam, and the Soul of a Nation* (New York: Plume).

Rubin, E. (2003), "The Cult of Rajavi," *The New York Times Magazine* (13 July); at <http://www.nytimes.com/2003/07/13/magazine/13MUJAHADEEN.html>

Rubin, J. (2000), State Department Spokesman, "Excerpt from the Daily Press Briefing" (Washington, DC: U.S. Department of State, 24 March); at <http://www.state.gov/www/regions/nea/000324-rubin-excerpt.html>

Rubin, M. (2006), "Monsters of the Left—The Mujahedin al-Khalq," *FrontPageMagazine.com* (13 January); at <http://www.meforum.org/article/888>

Salhani, C. (2006), "Exclusive Interview: Maryam Rajavi," United Press International—International Intelligence (26 June); at <http://www.upi.com/InternationalIntelligence/view.php?StoryID=20060626-025421-9269r>

Sciolino, E. (2000), *Persian Mirrors: The Elusive Face of Iran* (New York: Touchstone).

Sciolino, E. (2003), "Iranian Opposition Movement's Many Faces," *The New York Times* (30 June).

Slavin, B. (2005), "Iran's Terrorists Helped Disclose Nuke Program," *USA Today.com* (14 April); at <http://www.usatoday.com/news/world/2005-04-14-mek>

US Department of State (1994), "Report on the People's Mujahedin of Iran" (Washington, DC: US Department of State); at <http://www.iran-interlink.org/files/child%20pages/USstatedept.htm>

US Department of State, Bureau for Narcotics and Law Enforcement Affairs (March 2002), "International Narcotics Control Strategy Report" (Washington, DC: US Department of State); at <http://www.state.gov/g/inl/rls/nrcrpt/2001/rpt/8487pf.htm>

US Department of State (2004), "US Identifies 39 Groups as Foreign Terrorist Organizations" (19 October); at <http://usinfo.state.gov>

US Department of State, Office of the Coordinator of Counterterrorism (2004), *Patterns of Global Terrorism–2003*, Appendix B: Background Information on Designated Foreign Terrorist Organizations "Mujahedin-e Khalq Organization (MEK or MKO)" (Washington, DC: US Department of State, 29 April); at <http://www.state.gov/s/ct/rls/pgtrpt/2003/31711pf.htm>

PART 2
Issues and Analyses

Chapter 5

Arms and Terrorism: Tracing the Links

William D. Hartung and Frida Berrigan

Introduction: Arming Terrorists

How do terrorist organizations build their weapons stockpiles? During the Cold War, insurgents, terrorist groups, and other non-state actors depended primarily upon governments for arms and training. By contrast, in the current period it is possible for these organizations to become virtually self-financing, or to find their own sources of armaments without any significant help from governments. The process of non-state groups getting their weaponry from "state sponsors" is not nearly as prevalent as it was during the Cold War. Understanding this shift—both with respect to the small arms and light weapons that are currently the weapons of choice for terrorists and other non-state groups, and regarding their pursuit of nuclear weapons—is a key to curbing their access to weapons and undermining their ability to inflict violence.

This chapter will explore the techniques used by terrorists, insurgents, and militias to acquire weaponry, in hopes of shedding new light on this phenomenon. We will also explore the vulnerabilities in the international regimes that are currently in place to control the spread of these instruments of war.

Small Arms and Light Weapons: the Immediate Threat

The literature on small arms and light weapons routinely refers to the potential and actual dangers of these armaments being acquired by terrorist organizations. That being said, there are relatively few concrete examples available that trace the flow of small arms and light weapons to specific terrorist organizations.

The most cogent (but brief and skeletal) analysis of the links between small arms and terrorism comes from a fact sheet produced for the International Action Network on Small Arms (IANSA), which uses the State Department's 2003 *Patterns of Global Terrorism* report as a departure point:

> Small arms and light weapons are the weapons of choice for many terrorists. Of the 175 terrorist attacks documented in the U.S. State Department's 2003 report, *Patterns of Global Terrorism*, approximately half were committed with small arms and light weapons. These incidents ranged from targeted assassinations to indiscriminate attacks on crowded public places.
>
> An example of the latter occurred in Bogotá in November 2003 when members of the Revolutionary Armed Forces of Colombia lobbed fragmentation grenades into two crowded bars, killing one person and wounding 72.

The 2005 State Department report, now titled *Country Reports on Terrorism*, also includes a list of terrorist acts. One avenue of study could be to trace the weapons used in each act to ascertain where the weapons used came from and how the actors acquired them.

This chapter will attempt to advance the state of knowledge on the small arms issue by looking at the following issues:

- Definitions of small arms and light weapons, and of "terrorism" or "terrorist groups"
- An overview of stockpiles and new production of key small arms and light weapons
- An analysis of some of the mechanisms used to finance and distribute small arms and light weapons
- A sampling of measures that have been proposed to make it more difficult for non-state actors to acquire small arms and light weapons.

This will be followed by a profile of how collusion between state and non-state actors risks putting nuclear weapons or bomb-making materials in the hands of terrorist groups.

Terrorism and Small Arms/Light Weapons: Definitions

Before launching into a detailed analysis of the links between arms and terrorism, it is useful to explore contrasting definitions of two of the major terms of reference, *terrorism* and *small arms/light weapons*.

What is Terrorism?

Any analysis relating to the phenomenon of terrorism needs to at least *discuss* the competing definitions of who qualifies as a terrorist or of what groups should be considered terrorist organizations. Terrorism is a tactic, not an ideology. Terrorist attacks are generally—but not exclusively—aimed at civilian populations, and are designed to instill fear and provoke reactions from the targeted group or nation. Except in the case of the "lone gunman" or disturbed individual, terror attacks are usually designed to achieve political ends, however unrealistic or outrageous these ends may be. Unlike one working definition of pornography—you know it when you see it—the question of who is a terrorist requires a more detailed and nuanced definition. As the saying goes, one person's terrorist might be another person's freedom fighter, even though the individuals/organizations may employ similar tactics.

The United Nations General Assembly has defined terrorism quite broadly, as "criminal acts intended or calculated to provoke a state of terror in the general public, a group of persons, or particular person for political purposes." The definition further notes that these acts are "in any circumstance unjustifiable, whatever the considerations of a political, philosophical, ideological, racial, ethnic, or other nature that may be invoked to justify them" (UN General Assembly Resolution 54/110, 9 December 1999).

Despite this apparent resolution of the issue, the definition of terrorism remains a contentious issue at the United Nations. Countries such as Egypt, Syria, Saudi Arabia, and Sudan have sought to distinguish between terrorism and "legitimate resistance to occupation," a term they would apply, for example, to Palestinian attacks on Israeli citizens or soldiers. In addition, many UN delegates come from developing nations where armed violence was part and parcel of the struggle for independence, and are therefore disinclined to accept too broad a definition of terrorism.

Even different agencies within the US government use different definitions of terrorism. For example, the Pentagon defines it as "the unlawful use of—or threatened use of—force or violence against individuals or property to coerce or intimidate governments or societies, often to achieve political, religious, or ideological objectives" (cited at <www.pbs.orgwgbh/pages/frontline/teach/alqaeda/ glossary.html>). By contrast, the CIA defines terrorism as "premeditated, politically motivated violence perpetrated against noncombatant targets by sub-national groups or clandestine agents, usually intended to influence an audience" ("Terrorism FAQs," at <www.cia.gov/terrorism/faqs.html>). Note that the CIA definition does not speak explicitly of "violence against property," efforts to "coerce or intimidate governments," or the "threatened use of" violence as opposed to actual violent acts. The Pentagon version casts such a wide net that it could in theory be used to punish speech ("threatened use of force") or even aggressive demonstrators (for example, anarchists kicking in the window of a Starbucks at a demonstration against globalization).

Given these conflicting definitions, this chapter will address the supply of small arms and light weapons to non-state actors, a category that includes terrorists, insurgent groups, and paramilitary forces. This choice is reinforced by the fact that most non-state actors, terrorists or not, use similar channels of finance and distribution to acquire small arms and light weapons.

Small Arms and Light Weapons Defined

Most writing on small arms and light weapons uses as its point of departure the definition developed by the UN General Assembly's 1997 *Report of the Panel of Governmental Experts on Small Arms* (see, for example, *Small Arms Survey 2002*, 2002, 10). The most comprehensive assessment of the global trade, global stockpiles, and global impacts of small arms and light weapons is the *Small Arms Survey*. The survey defines small arms and light weapons as follows:

- Small Arms: revolvers and self-loading pistols, rifles, and carbines, assault rifles, sub-machine guns, and light machine guns
- Light Weapons: heavy machine guns; hand-held, under-barrel, and mounted grenade launchers; portable anti-tank and anti-aircraft guns; recoilless rifles; portable launchers of anti-tank and anti-aircraft missile systems; and mortars of less than 100mm caliber (*Small Arms Survey 2002*, 2002, 10).

The main problem with this definition from the point of view of studying the link between small arms and terrorism is that it excludes explosives, an increasingly popular tool of terrorist groups and insurgents, whether used by suicide bombers or in improvised explosive devices (IEDs).

The original report of the UN Panel of Experts recognized the importance of explosives as a weapon of war and terror, and included them in their definitions of small arms or light weapons. By contrast, the *Small Arms Survey* and other non-governmental organizations researching this issue originally excluded explosives from their main fields of research and activism (United Nations General Assembly, 1997, 8). The UN's rationale for putting explosives in the small arms category was because its panel of experts saw the link between explosives and violence by terrorist groups and other non-state actors:

> [V]iolence perpetrated through improvised explosive devices has recently exacerbated conflicts and caused severe destruction and death. Even a small quantity of such explosive devices has been used to devastating effect by terrorists and insurgents in various parts of the world (United Nations General Assembly, 1997, 9).

The group of UN experts also noted that, "Ammunition and explosives form an integral part of the small arms and light weapons used in conflicts" (United Nations General Assembly, 1997, 9). Non-governmental organizations have recently focused on ammunition as a critical part of the attempt to curb small arms and light weapons, but the market and methods through which non-state groups acquire explosives has yet to be the topic of substantial research.

This chapter will touch on the issue of explosives, but absent the kind of tracking of stockpiles and markets for explosives that has been done for the more narrowly defined category of small arms and light weapons, this discussion will be brief and anecdotal. This approach is not entirely satisfactory, both because explosives wreak so much damage on human beings and because they have become weapons of choice for many terrorist organizations.

A brief anecdote makes the need for more work on explosives clear. In an article in the April 2006 issue of the *Atlantic Monthly*, Matthew Teague talks with Kevin Fulton, an IRA explosives man who was also an agent for the British government. As part of the fascinating story, Teague describes a 1993 trip that Fulton made to the United States to acquire infrared flash technology for IRA bombs. An MI5 officer went ahead of him to make the arrangements. Fulton then arrived with thousands of dollars provided by British intelligence, met with American handlers, and bought the hardware to make infrared photo-sensor bombs. The new, more deadly bomb worked so well that other terrorist groups made efforts to acquire the technology. Infrared flash technology—taken from the United States, provided to the IRA by British intelligence as a way of keeping their informant indispensable, and shared through terrorist networks the world over—is now in the hands of Iraqi insurgents, where it is proving terribly effective against US troops (Teague, 2006).

Small Arms, Terrorism, and UN Efforts to Curb the Trade

The word *terrorism* is mentioned four times in the 2001 Program of Action developed by the United Nations "Conference on the Illicit Trade in Small Arms and Light Weapons in All Its Aspects." The small arms/terrorism link is mentioned twice in the preamble to the Program of Action (emphasis added):

> I. 5 *Recognizing* that the illicit trade in small arms and light weapons in all its aspects sustains conflicts, exacerbates violence, contributes to the displacement of civilians, undermines respect for international humanitarian law, impedes the provision of humanitarian assistance to victims of armed conflict *and fuels crime and terrorism,*

> I. 7. *Concerned also about the close link between terrorism,* organized crime, trafficking in drugs and precious minerals and the illicit trade in small arms and light weapons, and stressing the urgency of international efforts and cooperation aimed at combating this trade simultaneously from both a supply and demand perspective ...

The connection is also mentioned in the section on combating the illicit trade in small arms: "38. To encourage States to consider ratifying or acceding to international legal instruments *against terrorism and* transnational organized crime."

In addition, the connection between small arms and terrorism is mentioned in the section on implementing the Program of Action: "15. Upon request, States and appropriate international or regional organizations in a position to do so should provide assistance to combat the illicit trade in small arms and light weapons linked to drug trafficking, transnational organized crime *and terrorism*." In short, a review of statements in the UN Program of Action reveals that the links between the small arms trade and acts of terrorism are referred to often but not elaborated upon. Statements at the two major UN conferences on small arms and light weapons have been similarly vague.

Current Stockpiles of Small Arms and Light Weapons

According to a rough estimate by the *Small Arms Survey*, there are 639 million small arms in the world. This estimate covers firearms only, not light weapons like mortars or rocket-propelled grenades. Compared to the roughly eight million new small arms produced each year, the market in second-hand weapons is dominant, due to the sheer size of the stockpiles.

The bulk of the world's small arms stockpile—378 million, or nearly 60 percent— is in civilian hands (*Small Arms Survey 2002*, 2002, 63, 75, 79). Many of these are handguns, which one would think would not be the weapons of choice of terrorists or insurgents, even if stealing or buying them from individuals were an efficient way to acquire an arsenal. However, there have been a number of documented cases of terrorists or insurgents purchasing weapons from US-based gun dealers, taking advantage of the relatively lax gun control laws that prevail in the United States.

Since the late 1980s the Colombian government has repeatedly called for the United States government to take steps to restrict the ability of Colombian drug cartels to purchase pistols and firearms in the US According to the head of the US Bureau of Alcohol, Tobacco, and Firearms (BATF), 87 percent of a sampling of 292 firearms seized from Colombian drug traffickers during 1988 and 1989 were of US origin (Isikoff, 1989a). During that same time period, *The Washington Post* reported that:

> [l]aw enforcement officials report growing evidence that agents of the cartels operating in the United States have made major new efforts to purchase large caches of semi-automatic weapons—including AR-15 and Uzi assault guns—since the August 18 [1989] assassination of Colombian presidential candidate Luis Carlos Galan (Isikoff, 1989a).

As Jack Killorin, then a spokesperson for the BATF, put it, "what we have is a constant flow of guns out of the country using the same trail that drugs are coming into the country ... the cocaine traffickers are not going back empty handed" (Isikoff, 1989b).

The flow of weapons from the US to Mexican drug syndicates appears to be even larger than in the Colombian case. A 1994 article in the *Cleveland Plain Dealer* reported that in 1992 and 1993, Mexican authorities identified over 8,700 guns from the United States, noting that "officials on both sides of the border say the real numbers are far higher" (Gogek, 1994). Among other crimes, guns that originated in the US were used in the March 1994 killing of Mexican presidential candidate Luis Donaldo Colosio; the September 1994 murder of Jose Francisco Ruiz Massieu, the secretary general of Mexico's Institutional Revolutionary Party (PRI); a Roman Catholic cardinal in 1993; and in the slaughter of 19 men, women, and children in Ensenada, Mexico ("Unwanted Export," 2001; Thomas and Anderson, 1996).

Apparently, not much has improved since the Mexican and Colombian governments raised these issues from the late 1980s through the mid-1990s. For example, a January 2005 report by the Government Accountability Office (GAO) found that, between February and June 2004, 35 of 47 individuals on US government terrorist watch lists who attempted to purchase guns had been cleared to buy them by the FBI. In fact, as the GAO noted, "According to the Department of Justice, under federal and state law, neither suspected or actual membership in a terrorist organization would prohibit a person from possessing or receiving a firearm" (GAO, 2005, 1). Since February 2003, the FBI has been required to give extra scrutiny to requests to purchase a gun from individuals on a terrorist watch list, but they are only denied the right to buy the firearm if "prohibiting information" is found—for example, if they are in the country illegally—not merely because they are a "suspected or actual" member of a terrorist organization.

In addition to guns in civilian hands, an additional 241 million firearms—about 38 percent of the world's stockpile of small arms—are controlled by traditional military forces (that is, uniformed military forces answerable to states, not private militias or other military or paramilitary organizations) (*Small Arms Survey 2002*, 2002, 63, 75, 79). Some of these weapons also end up in the hands of terrorists or insurgents, either through capture, theft, or corruption—primarily sales to the groups by members of regular military forces. For example, it is suspected that weapons accumulated by Al Qaeda members involved in the May 1993 bombing of three residential compounds in Saudi Arabia were sold to them by members of the Saudi Arabian National Guard (Finn, 2003). On a larger scale, it is believed that much of the weaponry used by Chechen rebels at the height of their war with the Soviet military in the mid-1990s was *bought* from those very same Soviet personnel, in a sort of "weapons for food" program. As one Soviet soldier asserted: "The Chechens bought all of their weapons from us; otherwise, we wouldn't have had money to eat" (Klare, 1995, n. 20; see also Renner, 1997, 36, 46–7).

It is believed that there are 70 to 100 million copies of just one type of automatic weapon—the Russian-designed AK-47 assault rifle (and its variants)—worldwide. The AK is a popular weapon with insurgents, terrorists, and armed forces alike (*Small Arms Survey 2002*, 2002, 63, 66). For example, when the United States went about building a new Iraqi military in the wake of the overthrow of Saddam Hussein, it was decided to arm them with AK-47s, to which many Iraqis were already accustomed— and which were less likely to jam in the windy, dusty climate of Iraq (Landay, 2005). The failure to procure the US-built M-16 rifle drew some criticism from Congress, particularly from Senator Lindsey Graham (R-SC), who has an M-16 factory in his state.

More importantly for the purposes of this chapter, because AK-47s are durable, portable, easy to maintain, and easy to use, they are an ideal system for terrorist organizations that may have to move people and weapons across borders on a regular basis. Most AK-47s used by terrorist groups are purchased from middlemen who draw upon existing stockpiles, not new production.

After the estimates for civilian and government stockpiles are taken into account, there are still an estimated 20 million small arms and light weapons remaining in global stockpiles. The bulk of the remaining weapons are controlled by police forces, while the remaining percentage—about 0.2 percent, or roughly 320,000 weapons—are not in official hands. An unknown percentage of these 320,000 find their way into the hands of non-state actors. While small relative to global stockpiles, the stocks held by non-state actors are still substantial. In Africa, many insurgent groups are able to do considerable damage with small arms stocks in the 2,000 to 15,000 range (*Small Arms Survey 2002*, 2002, 81). Rebel factions in the Republic of Congo (Brazzaville) have an estimated 41,000 small arms. In Colombia, there are three major non-state actors vying for small arms to increase their capacity to inflict violence on civilians and military personnel: the rebel groups FARC and Ejercito de Liberacion Nacional (ELN), and the right-wing paramilitary United Defense Forces of Colombia (AUC). The FARC appears to have well in excess of 10,000 small arms, and the 11,000-member AUC may rival the FARC in its small arms stockpiles (*ibid*, 82–3).

Finally, a number of analysts have suggested that, for certain key weapons like man-portable air defense systems (MANPADS), looting of government stockpiles is the primary method of distribution to non-state groups. After an unsuccessful 2002 attempt to shoot down a charter plane filled with Israeli passengers as it was taking off from the airport in Mombasa, Kenya, there has been a renewed focus on the dangers of MANPADS (Nelson, 2002; Marino, 2004).

Dissemination of Small Arms: Financing and Logistics

How do non-state groups get their hands on small arms and light weapons? Two examples were mentioned in the previous section: theft or purchase from government forces, and taking advantage of lax local gun laws. But another major source of small arms and light weapons destined for terrorist and insurgent groups comes from illegal, clandestine sales, commonly referred to as the black market. This market operates on a global scale, taking advantage of state-of-the-art communication, transportation, banking, and brokering services.

For example, covert US supplies of billions of dollars worth of weapons and training provided to Afghan rebels during the 1980s were often redirected to Islamic fundamentalist groups. An Algerian official described the creation of a "floating army" of fundamentalist fighters who received arms and training in Afghanistan in the 1980s, and have since mounted terrorist attacks against US-backed governments in Algeria, Egypt, Israel, and Saudi Arabia (Hoagland, 1993). There is reason to believe that fighters who went on to join Osama bin Laden's Al Qaeda network tapped into the Afghan arms pipeline, perhaps through Pakistan's Inter-Services Intelligence agency (ISI), which was also instrumental in the founding of the Taliban. US arms destined for the Afghan *mujahedin* for use in the war against the Soviet occupation in the 1980s were skimmed off in considerable numbers by Pakistan's ISI, and then redistributed to their allies in the region, including rebel groups fighting for the independence of Kashmir ("India: Arms and Abuses," 1994, 5–11).

Although no comprehensive figures are available, it is widely believed that the bulk of the small arms and explosives being used by the anti-US insurgency in Iraq came from internal sources. Analysts for the *Small Arms Survey* have written that, "[a]s the forces of Saddam Hussein collapsed in April 2003, there was little left of his armies but one of the largest small arms inventories in the world. With a large proportion of these weapons already gone and the rest unguarded, the collapse precipitated what was almost certainly one of the largest and fastest transfers of small arms ever" (*Small Arms Survey 2004*, 2004, 44). There is evidence to suggest that members of Iraq's armed forces spread the country's weapons stockpiles to locations throughout the country prior to the US intervention on the assumption that they would end up fighting a guerilla war after US forces toppled the regime itself. To give a sense of the scale involved, the *Small Arms Survey* has estimated that as many as 4.2 million firearms were in the hands of Iraqi military and reserve forces prior to the March 2003 US invasion, and that "many of these largely military weapons were abandoned, pilfered, looted, and sold to the Iraqi public after Saddam Hussein's defeat and disappearance" (*ibid*, 46).

As journalist George Packer noted, "[b]etween August 2002 and January 2003, Iraqi commanders had removed weapons and equipment from bases and hidden them in farms and houses all over the countryside" (Packer, 2005, 299). In addition, there was considerable looting of warehouses that contained these materials. One of the most deadly weapons of the war—the improvised explosive device, or IED—is described by Packer as "a home-made bomb composed of an artillery shell or other military munitions (available at unguarded factories and ammo dumps throughout Iraq)" (*ibid*, 299). Last but not least, several hundred thousand members of the Iraqi

Army—which was disbanded by Paul Bremer, the head of the Coalition Provisional Authority in Iraq, in May 2003—took their weapons with them when they left military service.

Beyond cases where non-state actors have small arms literally handed to them, as in Iraq and Afghanistan, there remains the question of how these weapons are purchased and transported from place to place and conflict to conflict. Financing and logistics are closely intertwined in the illegal trade in small arms and light weapons, since in many cases the deals involve barter arrangements in which guns are traded for timber, diamonds, or other natural resources. The same transport companies are often involved on both ends of the deal, and the transactions are coordinated by arms brokers who procure weapons and oversee the provision of transport and financing.

One of the best-documented examples of how small arms and light weapons are procured by a non-state paramilitary force emerged from an investigation by the United Nations sanctions committee of violations of the arms embargo against UNITA (National Union for the Total Independence of Angola) forces in Angola. The committee had the advantage of interviews and documentation provided by defectors who had been involved in UNITA's arms procurement efforts, resulting in detailed information on the methods used to transport and finance weapons shipments to the group. The report emphasized the importance of brokers, and noted that "a small number of brokers accounted for the bulk of UNITA's weapons imports." It further emphasized the "one-stop shopping" element of brokering services: "As a general rule, the broker who supplied the arms was also responsible for arranging transport and delivery, any necessary training on the use of the system, maintenance and sometimes even spare parts" (United Nations Security Council, 2000, 7).

During 1993–94, for example, UNITA's main arms brokers were the De Decker brothers, one of whom—Joe De Decker—was in the diamond business in South Africa. This proved to be a key advantage, since UNITA paid for its arms imports with rough diamonds that had been mined in the areas of Angola that were under its control. The second brother, Ronnie De Decker, known as "Watson," was in charge of procuring weapons from Eastern Europe. Among the items he acquired on behalf of UNITA were "mortar bombs, anti-tank weapons, anti-aircraft weapons, grenades and ammunition of various kinds, and a variety of small arms and light weapons." At one point Watson even brought foreign trainers to Angola to teach UNITA personnel how to use the SAM-16 surface-to-air missile. Meanwhile, Joe De Decker used his experience in the diamond industry to assess the value of the packets of diamonds UNITA was offering in exchange for a specific arms package. The UN report notes that the diamonds were "generally packaged in parcels worth between USD 4 million and 5 million." It also indicates that on occasion Watson would take the packets to the diamond market in Antwerp, Belgium, and see what he was offered for them. If the price was lower than the original assessment, UNITA would have to provide additional diamonds to close the deal (United Nations Security Council, 2000, 8).

There were also points at which UNITA actually involved heads of state as middlemen in its arm procurement network. From roughly 1994 through 1997, Zairian dictator Mobutu Sese Seko agreed to let Jonas Savimbi and UNITA use his country as a trans-shipment point for weapons destined for UNITA-controlled areas of Angola. Zaire provided end-user certificates, a required form of documentation in all international arms transfers. The certificates indicated that the weapons were being transferred to Zaire; only later, after being stored in warehouses near Kinshasa and other Zairian cities, were the arms forwarded on to Angola. Procurement of weapons in this arrangement (again from Eastern Europe) was handled by Imad Kabir, an arms broker described as "part of Mobutu's entourage" who had been introduced to Savimbi by Mobutu. In exchange for the end-user certificates and warehousing services, Savimbi paid Mobutu directly in diamonds and cash (United Nations Security Council, 2000, 8).

Another UN panel of experts, this time focused on violations of the arms embargo against Liberia, shed further light on the methods used to transport illicit weaponry. Liberia had long provided a lax registration process for both aircraft and ships that allowed middlemen and third countries to transport weaponry and other illicit items under Liberian "flags of convenience." This permissive system "enabled arms trafficking networks to camouflage their operations through fake registrations, document fraud and … the setting up of a mystery airline with the full knowledge of Liberian authorities in order to avoid detection" (United Nations Security Council, 2001, 33).

As noted above, one of the most important needs of arms brokers and their governmental or non-governmental clients seeking illicit weaponry are real or forged end-user certificates. These allow weapons shipments to clear customs in any country on their transport route, after which they are either delivered to the country listed on the certificate and then transferred to a third country, or sent directly to a third country not listed on the certificate. Once again, the best-documented cases come from West Africa. For example, a popular mechanism for getting "small arms, missiles, helicopters, and cargo aircraft" to Liberia from Eastern Europe was by using forged end-user certificates indicating that the weapons were destined for the armed forces of Guinea (United Nations Security Council, 2001, 36). In late November 2000, the Ugandan government impounded 1,250 sub-machine guns allegedly destined for Guinea when authorities decided, based on the cargo plane's flight plan, that the shipment was heading to Liberia (*ibid*, 39).

This seemingly straightforward deal involved a long chain of front companies and illicit transport operators. Among the companies involved in the attempted shipment of the 1,250 sub-machine guns to Liberia were Centafrican Airlines, registered in Bangui, Central African Republic and operating out of the United Arab Emirates; Pecos, an arms dealing company based in Conakry, Guinea; Vichi, "a private agent for the Moldovan Ministry of Defense"; and MoldTransavia, a company that was chartered to fly the aircraft used in the arms shipments. The UN panel of experts that investigated the incident also learned that the aircraft used in the transfer was owned by the arms dealer Victor Bout, and leased from his company Transavia Travel Agency of the United Arab Emirates. San Air, another UAE-registered company, supplied insurance for the deal. The majority of the companies involved were ultimately owned either by Victor Bout, his brother Sergei, or current or former associates of Victor Bout (*ibid*, 39–42). Bout is one of the most active players in the illicit arms trade, involved in deals with UNITA in Angola, the Charles Taylor regime in Liberia, and the rebels in Sierra Leone. In addition, according to intelligence documents uncovered by the International Consortium of Investigative Journalists (ICIJ), Bout was also involved in supplying USD 50 million in weaponry to the Taliban during the period that they were hosting and supplying Al Qaeda (International Consortium of Investigative Journalists, 2002, 147).

Non-state groups like Al Qaeda generally have multiple sources of funding, from diaspora funding resulting from the creation or infiltration of charities in diaspora communities, to skimming profits from ownership of legitimate businesses, such as a series of honey shops controlled by Osama bin Laden and Al Qaeda throughout the Middle East. However, as Al Qaeda's annual budget has been reduced from USD 35 million per year to USD 5–10 million per year, according to a US Treasury Department expert, it has sought more innovative forms of financing. As Don Van Natta of *The Washington Post* reported in September 2003, "Terrorists have embraced more daring and unorthodox methods to raise and move cash—credit card fraud, cigarette smuggling, transferring cash into gems, gold, and diamonds, and counterfeiting everything from 20-euro notes to baby formula" (Van Natta, 2003). Of these various financing methods, one of the most important and best documented is the illicit acquisition and sale of natural resources such as timber, diamonds, gold, copper, and coltan (an element important for the production of cell phones and laptop computers).

Democratic Republic of the Congo

One of the most lucrative conflicts for internal warlords and foreign armies has been the multi-sided war in the Democratic Republic of the Congo (DRC), in significant part because of the diversity of natural resources in the country available for plunder by regular and paramilitary forces. These forces are often armed primarily or entirely with small arms and light weapons, which they use to seize territory, forcefully recruit personnel, and commit extreme human rights abuses in the course of looting local resources and selling them on the international market. The profits from this illicit trade can then be used to buy more weapons and support more fighters in a vicious cycle of guns, resources, and money that can sustain non-state parties in a civil war or terrorist groups seeking to engage in attacks on civilians. Unlike during the Cold War, this "business of war" can be sustained with or without state sponsors. According to an analysis by the NGO Global Witness, the following DRC resources have been sold off for guns or profit: coltan, tin, copper, cobalt, diamonds, gold, oil and gas, timber, coal, lead, iron ore, and manganese.

The Rwandan and Ugandan armies have backed rebel groups in the Eastern Congo in exchange for control over coltan and tin exports supervised by hastily incorporated companies like Rwanda Metals. Most of these firms benefit either government officials of the invading countries or individuals with close ties to the governments of Rwanda and Uganda. A report by Global Witness describes how the process works:

> the only role assigned to Congolese people is extraction and handing over to Rwandese (or sometimes Ugandan) brokers. ... The exploitation and taxation is organized centrally from an administrative entity known as the Congo Desk, located in a cell of Rwanda's Ministry of Defence. Throughout the war, Rwanda has been benefiting directly from

coltan exploitation in eastern DRC, and it has been suggested that between late 1999 and late 2000 the Rwandan army alone reaped revenues of at least US $20 million a month (Global Witness, 2004, 21).

Rwanda and Uganda use similar channels to seize cassiterite (tin) from Eastern Congo and sell it to companies from Belgium, Germany, Canada, Malaysia, Tanzania, the Netherlands, Russia, and India (Global Witness, 2004, 22). These foreign companies are the ultimate financiers of war and repression in the DRC, but they are rarely held accountable, nor are they likely to ask too many questions about where their Rwandan or Ugandan suppliers acquired these resources.

Katanga province, in the southern DRC along the Zambian and Angolan borders, is a rich source of copper and cobalt. Throughout the country's multi-sided civil war, the government in Kinshasa has controlled this region, so none of the revenues from these resources have made their way to rebel groups. However, the DRC's government has given preferential concessions to Zimbabwean individuals and companies in exchange for that nation's military support during the civil war. Over one-third of the revenues from one of the richest copper/cobalt mines in Katanga go to Zimbabwe through a Zimbabwean-controlled company called Kababancola Mining Company (KMC). It has been alleged that part of the profits of this venture are used to buy weapons for the armed forces of Zimbabwe and the DRC (Global Witness, 2004, 26). If the regime in Kinshasa reaps the benefits of the DRC's cobalt and copper reserves, significant quantities of diamonds from the DRC are in areas controlled by Rwandan or Ugandan forces and the rebel groups they support.

In Liberia, timber sales have been used to fuel one or both sides of a conflict. Other examples include Cambodia, Burma, and Indonesia. But the Liberian case has been studied in more detail due to the work of UN expert groups, the imposition of sanctions, and the series of reports done by NGOs like Global Witness.

Like the trade in timber, Liberia's diamond trade had regional and even global implications during the years of Charles Taylor's rule. Not only did Liberia sell its own diamonds in exchange for cash and armaments; it also served as a trans-shipment point for diamonds it marketed for groups like the Revolutionary United Front (RUF) of Sierra Leone, a brutal paramilitary group responsible for killing and maiming thousands of citizens of that nation. In exchange for access to diamonds, Taylor provided the RUF with refuge and training areas inside the Liberian border with Sierra Leone (Klare, 2001, 199–200).

While Taylor's role in Sierra Leone is fairly well known, his regime also harbored members of Al Qaeda and helped them acquire diamonds as a better way to conceal their assets in the run-up to the 9/11 attacks and beyond. *The Washington Post* has reported that Western intelligence officials have indicated that, "Even Osama bin Laden's Al Qaeda network was linked to Taylor, allegedly laundering millions of dollars by buying diamonds from Sierra Leonean rebels under Taylor's protection" (Farah, 2002). In a more recent piece, Douglas Farah cites eyewitness reports by the United Nations Special Court on Sierra Leone, as well as banking and telephone records, in suggesting that, "While he was president, Taylor sold diamonds to Al Qaeda, Hezbollah, and Russian organized crime" (Farah, 2005).

Ahmed Khalfan Gailani, a Tanzanian citizen under arrest for his role in the 1998 bombings of the US embassies in Kenya and Tanzania, was involved in setting up the Al Qaeda–Liberia–Sierra Leone diamond connection, which some government investigators assert was part of a "\$20 million operation to corner the market on African gemstones" (Khan, 2004). Other estimates of Al Qaeda's investments in Sierra Leonean diamonds go as high as USD 100 million or more (for more analysis of Al Qaeda's role in the diamond trade, see Global Witness, 2003).

Small Arms and Terrorism: Policy Options

While some of the specific examples cited above have changed due to peace agreements in Angola and Sierra Leone and the arrest of exiled Liberian dictator Charles Taylor, the same channels used to arm the regimes and the non-state actors involved in such conflicts remain open. In addition, despite numerous efforts at stemming the conflict, the resources of the Congo continue to be looted by both governments and non-state groups.

A November 2005 Amnesty International report discusses a possible shipment of "hundreds of thousands of small arms and light weapons from Bosnia and Herzegovina's war-time stockpiles together with tens of millions of rounds of ammunition," sent to Iraq "clandestinely and without public oversight" with the approval and support of the US Department of Defense from 2004 to 2005. None of the private brokers involved in the sale have supplied documentation proving that these massive shipments ever made it to Iraq, or whether, as some Western European officials believe, some of the weapons may have been "siphoned off" to non-state groups in Iraq or other end-users (Amnesty International, 2006, 14).

As this example indicates, along with those from West Africa, dealing with the sheer size and complexity of the problem of small arms and light weapons is a daunting task. A few solutions have been proposed, none of which has been put forward as *the* answer, but rather as part of an array of measures designed to at least make it more difficult for terrorists, warlords, insurgents, and other non-state actors to acquire small arms and light weapons.

Reducing Global Stockpiles

As long as there are hundreds of thousands or millions of small arms and light weapons stockpiled and ready to be accessed by brokers or seized or bought by terrorists, slowing down the flow of these weapons will be difficult, if not impossible. The United Nations has done some work on disarming combatants in the wake of conflicts, under the rubric of Demobilization, Disarmament, and Reconstruction (DDR). States like Mali, El Salvador, South Africa, Mozambique, and Albania have put considerable energy into gun destruction and buyback programs. But so far, these efforts have only scratched the surface of what needs to be done to significantly reduce global stockpiles. More concerted, far better funded efforts are needed.

Cracking Down on Brokers, Shippers, and Arms Dealers

Amnesty International has identified an emerging problem in the area of arms brokering and shipping: the use of private companies by countries that control 90 percent of the world's arms transfers. Absent improved legal and regulatory frameworks, Amnesty argues that this situation contributes to the "diversion and easy availability of such arms by those perpetrating serious violations of human rights ... including those believed to engage in terrorism" (Amnesty International, 2006, 3).

Some of the recommendations put forward by Amnesty include the following:

• All countries should include brokering, transport, and dealing in weaponry in their national laws, including coverage of these activities when engaged in by their own citizens
• Screening of brokers, shippers, and dealers every two years to determine whether they have violated laws relating to arms exporting, trafficking, or money laundering, at which point their licenses should be revoked
• Annual reports naming all brokers, shippers, and other transporters of arms, including an indication of what type of documentation they are using to legitimate their activities.

The importance of individual countries having their own strong laws was underscored on 7 June 2006 when Gus Kouwenhoven, a major player in the illicit timber trade, was tried in the Netherlands and sentenced to eight years in prison for breaking a UN arms embargo on Liberia. Global Witness, the NGO most involved in researching the trade in conflict diamonds, applauded the verdict as "precedent-setting" and indicated that it should serve as a model for other countries (Global Witness, 2006). It is incredible to think that some of these simple measures do not already exist, but it also suggests that their implementation should make it considerably harder for arms to be diverted to terrorists, militias, and other non-state groups.

Marking and Tracing Small Arms and Ammunition

Marking and tracing are potentially powerful tools for holding countries of origin accountable for their explicit support of illicit arms transfers to non-state groups. At a minimum, such countries can and should be called to account for their lax regulation of their own arms stockpiles, and/or their transfer of small arms to middlemen or untrustworthy governments without adequate screening.

Curbing Arms Export Financing

As noted above, an important source of funding for non-state actors is the illicit trade in natural resources, including gemstones, precious metals, oil, and timber. Measures need to be taken that will allow international authorities to track nations and groups engaged in these "arms for resources" swaps, including governments and groups in the areas of origin, and states and organizations that serve as middlemen in these transactions.

One of the most promising and fully developed efforts to deal with the use of resources to fund violence perpetrated by non-state groups is the Kimberley process, which requires the certification that diamonds sold on the international market are not "conflict diamonds." The process, supported by groups like Global Witness and Physicians for Human Rights, aims to produce a distinct system of marking rough diamonds so that their place of origin can be traced, and countries and non-state actors that are regular sources of conflict diamonds can be boycotted or otherwise regulated. Governments and the diamond industry are participants in the process, which seeks to create an effective global system for regulating and ultimately ending the sale of diamonds emanating from conflict zones. Some NGOs have been highly critical of the implementation of the Kimberley process, while agreeing that it has achieved a number of important steps, like banning exports of diamonds from the war-torn Democratic Republic of the Congo and sending a review mission to the Central African Republic to investigate that nation's possible role in selling conflict diamonds. As Global Witness spokesperson Susie Sanders noted in late 2005, "The Kimberley process has taken real steps to stop the trade in conflict diamonds, but the problem has not been solved. Governments must audit all sectors of the diamond trade and take credible action against members of the diamond industry that are known to trade in conflict diamonds" (Global Witness, 2005).

A less comprehensive process is being developed to monitor timber cutting in key nations to make sure it is not being done illegally. This effort has two benefits, one environmental and one security-related. Curbing illegal logging preserves forests that might otherwise be destroyed, and it makes it harder to use illicit transfers of timber to fund conflict. The process, known as "Independent Forest Monitoring," involves work by NGOs in cooperation with government agencies and, at times, timber companies. NGOs like Global Witness generally take the lead in ensuring that government-approved forest plots are not overlogged, via site visits or using tools such as Global Positioning System monitors. In Honduras, for example, the International Forest Monitor (IFM) uncovered illegal logging near the municipality of Salama, where the government and illegal loggers used a cooperative to hide the fact that they were taking logs from unauthorized areas (Comisionado Nacional de Herechos Humanos and Global Witness, 2006). The findings were reported to the central government of Honduras for enforcement action. Global Witness has also undertaken IFM missions in Cambodia and Cameroon. Other IFM missions have been carried out by other organizations in Indonesia, the Philippines, Ecuador, and Canada (IFM fact sheet, downloaded 12 June 2006 from <www.globalwitness. org>). With international support, including the financing of an IFM trust fund, these kinds of activities could be expanded to a much wider range of countries.

Conclusions

Efforts to curb the distribution of small arms and light weapons to non-state groups face daunting challenges. First and foremost, the millions of military-style firearms,

(MANPADS), light mortars, grenades, and other small arms and light weapons in existing stockpiles make it virtually impossible to keep these weapons out of the hands of militias, insurgents, terrorists, and other non-state actors. The absence of uniform regulations on arms brokering, dealing, and shipping constitute another set of obstacles to curbing the trade. Finding ways to cut off funding that comes from techniques like "resource for weapons" swaps is also a considerable task.

Despite these challenges, working on all of these fronts—stockpile reduction, coordinated international regulation of brokers, shippers, and arms dealers, and tracking and monitoring systems that may eventually be used to cut off financing and transfers of illicit small arms and light weapons at the source—should make it considerably harder and more expensive to get hold of small arms and light weapons. It will not stop the flow entirely, but even slowing the flow of these weapons can have important long-term consequences. To the extent that restricting the proliferation of small arms and light weapons increases the time needed for non-state actors to get these tools of war, it may increase the time and space available to negotiate peaceful resolutions of disputes and develop alternative solutions to the problems that fuel the spread of small arms in the first place.

Proliferation of Weapons of Mass Destruction: the A.Q. Khan Network

While the transfer of small arms and light weapons to terrorist organizations and other non-state actors is an ongoing concern, their pursuit of weapons of mass destruction—and nuclear weapons in particular—has proved futile to date. However, this is no reason to be complacent about the possibility. Even if the probabilities of terrorists getting control of a nuclear weapon are low, the consequences of their acquiring these weapons could be catastrophic, costing tens or hundreds of thousands of lives and rendering large parts of major cities or other targeted areas uninhabitable for years to come. One model for how a nuclear black market might operate is the extensive nuclear smuggling network established by the Pakistani nuclear scientist A.Q. Khan.

Anatomy of the Khan Network

Born in Bhopal before the partition of India and Pakistan, Abdul Qadeer Khan migrated to Pakistan in 1952 along with millions of other Muslims. After completing studies in Karachi, Khan moved to Europe, receiving an engineering degree in Holland and a doctorate in metallurgy in Belgium.

In 1975, A.Q. Khan began work as a consultant for the Dutch team at URENCO (a for-profit nuclear consortium of the Netherlands, the United Kingdom, and Germany), where teams were designing centrifuges to enrich uranium. As India began to develop nuclear weapons, Khan felt he had something to contribute to Pakistan's nuclear aspirations. According to Dutch prosecutors, when Khan returned to Pakistan in 1976 (ostensibly on holiday with his wife), he brought the blueprints for the Dutch and German centrifuge designs, as well as lists of specifications and materials suppliers. From these designs, Khan expected he would be able to replicate the hollow metal tubes that enrich natural uranium into bomb fuel. A set of thousands of centrifuges, called a cascade, spins millions of times per second to concentrate U-235 to levels sufficient to build a nuclear weapon.

With these plans, and a blank check from the Pakistani government of Zulfikar Ali Bhutto, Khan built a vast centrifuge facility at Kahuta, near Islamabad. By the early 1980s, the facility was able to enrich significant quantities of uranium. Khan claims that by 1984 he had completed work on a nuclear bomb. He later boasted about this feat in the context of his country's lack of development, saying: "A country which could not make sewing needles [or] good bicycles … was embarking on one of the latest and most difficult technologies" (Edidin, 2004). But he did not do it alone. The so-called Father of the Pakistani Bomb took advantage of weak export controls and loopholes in national and international regulations that focused on plants and complete systems rather than components. Using this approach, Khan was able to purchase much of what was needed for the Pakistani bomb on the open market.

By the late 1970s, the US State Department was regularly expressing its concerns to European officials about specific component sales to Pakistan. In addition, the Central Intelligence Agency was monitoring Khan's dealings. Their subsequent analyses reveal that Pakistan obtained one or more of almost every component needed to build a centrifuge enrichment plant (Weissman and Krosney, 1981).

Sellers from all over the world flocked to Pakistan to offer price lists for high-technology goods applicable to Pakistan's nuclear program, according to *The New York Times*. "They literally begged us to buy their equipment. … My long stay in Europe and intimate knowledge of various countries and their manufacturing firms was an asset," Khan bragged (Broad, Sanger and Bonner, 2004).

Reversing the Network

Once Pakistan had the bomb and the capacity to enrich uranium, Khan "reversed the network" he had developed to bring nuclear components and materials into Pakistan, using the same illicit channels to disseminate nuclear know-how and plans throughout the world—to those willing to pay. International Atomic Energy Agency (IAEA) director Mohamed ElBaradei described the elaborate model Khan perfected for disseminating nuclear materials: "Nuclear components designed for one country would be manufactured in another, shipped through a third country (which often appeared to be a legitimate user) assembled in a fourth and designated for eventual turnkey use in a fifth" (ElBaradei, 2004). The network included suppliers from Switzerland, the United Kingdom, the United Arab Emirates, Turkey, South Africa, Malaysia and elsewhere. It was responsible for the transfer of nuclear weapons-related technology, centrifuge parts, and blueprints to Iran, North Korea, Libya, and elsewhere (Lin, 2004).

According to Christopher Clary from the Center for Contemporary Conflict, Iran was Pakistan's first major customer, and Libya was its most recent. Writing in *Disarmament Diplomacy*, Clary asserts that Pakistan's role in nuclear proliferation grew steadily more complex, noting that "sharing with Iran was fairly limited, Pakistani–North Korean cooperation was more significant, while Libya was in the midst of acquiring the most extensive 'package' when it made the strategic decision to forego weapons in 2003" (Clary, 2004).

Clary cites reports by Mohamed ElBaradei to the IAEA Board of Governors that found that Iran received centrifuge plans through a foreign intermediary around 1987. The report goes on to note that between 1985 and 1997 "about 2,000 components and some sub-assemblies had been obtained from abroad through foreign intermediaries or directly by Iranian entities, but no help was received from abroad in the assembly of centrifuges or in training, nor were any completed centrifuges imported" (International Atomic Energy Agency, 2003).

Nuclear sharing with North Korea is thought to have begun in 1997, and in his confession Khan admitted to "supplying old and discarded centrifuge and enrichment machines together with sets of drawings, sketches, technical data and depleted Hexaflouride (UF6) gas to North Korea" ("Re-imposition of Sanctions Feared," 2004).

By the time Khan began supplying materials to Libya, Khan Research Laboratories was reportedly able to offer a "turnkey" nuclear package ready for immediate implementation. Robert Joseph, US Under-Secretary of State for Arms Control and International Security, asserted that "A.Q. Khan and company" was "the principal supplier for the entire program. Khan provided the design, the technology, the expertise, and the equipment, primarily for the centrifuges. He also provided the warhead design" (Motta, 2006).

While Khan maintains that he "transferred nuclear technology so that other Muslim countries could enhance their security," money was also a factor. One account in *The New York Times* pointed out that Khan spent millions buying homes and properties, including a tourist hotel in Africa that he named after his wife, Henny (Broad and Sanger, 2004). Bush Administration officials estimate that the Khan network netted USD 100 million from its sales to Libya alone (*ibid*).

The World Responds

In early 2004, the world learned what the intelligence community had long known: A.Q. Khan oversaw a vast nuclear supermarket, what Dr ElBaradei called the "WalMart of private sector proliferation" (Landler, 2004). Dismissed from his post amid an "investigation into alleged acts of nuclear proliferation by a few individuals," Khan and as many as six nuclear scientists were detained and questioned by the Pakistani military's Inter-Services Intelligence agency in the first days of February 2004. Pakistani President Pervez Musharraf vowed to punish "with an iron hand" anyone who leaked nuclear weapons secrets to foreign governments. But, by 5 February 2004, Khan was pardoned, dubbed a national hero, and Musharraf announced he would block any international probe into Pakistan's nuclear program. In response, a US State Department spokesman said only that the issue of whether or not to punish Khan was "a matter for Pakistan to decide" (Hersh, 2004).

For the past two and a half years, Khan has lived under comfortable house arrest. The IAEA does not have direct access to Khan, is only able to submit written questions for the scientist to answer, and even the text of his 12-page confession has not been made public. The Bush Administration has not publicly challenged

Pakistan's refusal to allow US intelligence officials access to Khan, and continues to provide Islamabad with millions in military aid. In 2006, the United States provided USD 698 million in military and economic assistance to Pakistan as part of a five-year, USD 3 billion aid package (Cronin, et al., 2005).

While a White House spokesman said that the administration valued Musharraf's assurances that, "Pakistan was not involved in any of the proliferation activity," the Congressional Research Service concluded that, "A.Q. Khan must have had significant logistical support from elements in the Pakistani military and the civilian nuclear establishment" (*ibid*). Writing in *The New Yorker* in March 2004, veteran investigative journalist Seymour Hersh quoted an unidentified Bush Administration intelligence officer as saying:

> One thing we do know is that this was not a rogue operation. Suppose Edward Teller had suddenly decided to spread nuclear technology and equipment around the world. Do you really think he could do that without the government knowing? How do you get missiles from North Korea to Pakistan? Do you think A.Q. shipped all the centrifuges by Federal Express? The military has to be involved, at high levels (Hersh, 2004).

The Bush Administration took advantage of the Khan disclosure to call for measures aimed at strengthening domestic and international non-proliferation efforts. At the National Defense University in Washington, President George W. Bush called for a wide set of reforms; including:

- Expanding the Proliferation Security Initiative (PSI), a program designed to intercept ships suspected of carrying nuclear materials, nuclear components, or materials that could be used to deliver these weapons (the PSI was also concerned with stopping shipments of chemical and biological weapons, which lie beyond the scope of this chapter)
- Strengthening the legal framework governing proliferation, expanding efforts to secure nuclear material in the former Soviet Union and other states
- Denying enrichment and reprocessing technology to any states that do not already possess them
- Requiring countries to implement the IAEA's Advanced Safeguards Additional Protocol as a necessary condition for supplying equipment and materials for civilian nuclear programs. The protocol calls for more intrusive inspections of nuclear programs to ensure that they are not being used to develop nuclear weapons
- Reforming the IAEA to improve its capabilities to enforce states' obligations under the nuclear non-proliferation treaty (NPT).

Missing from this list of useful counter-proliferation tools is an acknowledgement that the United States knew enough about Khan's network to stop it long before 2004. "We had every opportunity to put a stop to the A.Q. Khan network fifteen years ago. Some of those involved today in the smuggling are the children of those we knew about in the eighties. It's the second generation now," a US intelligence officer told Hersh (Hersh, 2004).

Defense Secretary Donald Rumsfeld has asserted that, "the network has been dismantled" (Suryanarayana, 2004). In an appearance on "CNN Late Edition with Wolf Blitzer" on 3 October 2004, Secretary of State Condoleezza Rice went further, saying that the "important thing is that the A.Q. Khan network is out of business, and people are being brought to justice." While some players are being punished (albeit very gently), evidence points to facets of Khan's network still being intact. Leonard Weiss, a consultant with the Center for Global Security Research at Lawrence Livermore Laboratory, testified before the House Subcommittee on International Terrorism and Proliferation in May 2006 that, "at least some parts of the network are definitely still functioning" (Weiss, 2006). As evidence of this, Weiss noted that the Khan Research Laboratories "is the size of a small city, and there are large numbers of scientists and engineers working there who ... can carry out the work that Khan has been heading for all these years. And they have reason to be motivated" (*ibid*).

Weiss also outlined a 2004 plan by "a South African electronics salesman and former Israeli army major named Asher Karni" to illegally ship oscilloscopes and spark gap triggers to Pakistan from the US via South Africa. As Weiss described it, the final destination of this hardware was a:

> company described by U.S. officials as a front for Pakistan's nuclear weapon program. ... When federal investigators asked for State Department permission to go to Pakistan to interrogate the head of the company, a man named Humayun Khan, permission was denied. ... Asher Karni was ultimately convicted and is serving a three-year prison sentence, but Humayun Khan, who was indicted, is scot-free in Pakistan at this time.

Finally, Weiss asserted that, "an educated guess based on the unclassified literature is that a good part of the network is still intact, and that additions to it are being actively sought" (Weiss, 2006).

Hersh posits that Pakistan gained US support for Khan's slap on the wrist by granting US Special Forces permission to search for Osama bin Laden in northwestern Pakistan. This access had long been sought by US Army commanders eager to carry out sweeps in the remote mountainous regions, but Musharraf had refused. In addition to granting access, a former senior intelligence official said: "Musharraf told us, 'We've got the guy inside. The people who provide the fresh fruit and vegetables and herd the goats'" for Osama bin Laden and Al Qaeda members. The official continued, "it's a quid pro quo: we're going to get our troops inside Pakistan in return for not forcing Musharraf to deal with Khan" (Hersh, 2004).

Aside from not having succeeded, this deal-making overlooks the fact that deterring nuclear proliferation should be a central US policy objective on a par with defeating radical Islamist terrorism. But, instead of pursuing both objectives simultaneously, the United States failed to act to thwart a pernicious form of proliferation, all the while strengthening fundamentalist groups. "If a nuclear weapon destroys the U.S. Capitol in the coming years," writes *The New York Times* columnist Nicholas Kristof, "it will probably be based in part on Pakistani technology. The biggest challenge to civilization in recent years is not from Osama or Saddam Hussein but Abdul Qadeer Khan" (Kristof, 2004).

Osama bin Laden remains at large, Al Qaeda continues to menace the West, and nuclear proliferation remains a vexing concern for policy makers throughout the world. Absent additional information from Khan himself, it will be difficult for global intelligence agencies to determine whether his network has been "rolled up," or whether elements continue to operate without Khan's leadership. To the extent that private actors are involved, there is always a danger that terrorist organizations can acquire nuclear components for cash. Unfortunately, the Bush Administration appears to have placed priority on the war on terrorism—narrowly conceived—at the expense of a systematic approach to non-proliferation.

References

Amnesty International (2006), "Dead on Time: Arms Transportation, Brokering and the Threat to Human Rights" (London: Amnesty International) (10 May).

Broad, W. and Sanger, D. (2004), "Pakistani's Nuclear Earnings: $100 Million," *The New York Times* (16 March).

Broad, W., Sanger, D. and Bonner, R. (2004), "How Pakistani's Network Offered the Whole Kit," *International Herald Tribune* (13 February).

Clary, C. (2004), "Dr. Khan's Nuclear WalMart," *Disarmament Diplomacy* (March/April).

Comisionado Nacional de Herechos Humanos [Honduras] and Global Witness (2006), "New Independent Forest Monitoring Reports Illegal Activities in Honduran Forests" (29 March).

Cronin, R., et al. (2005), "Pakistan's Nuclear Proliferation Activities and the Recommendations of the 9/11 Commission: U.S. Policy Constraints and Options" (Washington, DC: Congressional Research Service) (24 May).

Edidin, P. (2004), "Pakistan's Hero: Dr. Khan Got What He Wanted, and He Explains How," *The New York Times* (15 February).

ElBaradei, M. (2004), "Nuclear Non-Proliferation: Global Security In A Rapidly Changing World," presentation at the Carnegie International Non-Proliferation Conference (21 June).

Farah, D. (2002), "Liberian Leader Again Finds Means to Hang On; Taylor Exploits Timber to Keep Power," *The Washington Post* (4 June).

Farah, D. (2005), "Standing By as a Brutal Warlord Plots His Return," *The Washington Post* (2 October).

Finn, P. (2003), "Al Qaeda Arms Traced to Saudi National Guard; 3 Attackers Identified in Riyadh Bombing," *The Washington Post* (19 May).

Global Witness (2003), "For a Few Dollars More: How Al Qaeda Moved Into the Diamond Trade" (April).

Global Witness (2004), "Same Old Story: Background Study on Natural Resources in the Democratic Republic of the Congo" (June).

Global Witness (2005), "Making It Work: Why the Kimberley Process Must Do More to Stop Conflict Diamonds" (15 November).

Global Witness (2006), "Arms Dealer and Timber Trader Gus Kouwenhoven Found Guilty of Breaking UN Arms Embargo" (7 June).

Gogek, J. (1994), "U.S. Guns Fuel Political Killings in Mexico," *Cleveland Plain Dealer*, (18 October).

Government Accountability Office (GAO) (2005), *Gun Control and Terrorism: FBI Could Better Manage Firearm-Related Background Checks Involving Terrorist Watch List Records*, Report GAO-05-127 (Washington, DC: Government Accountability Office).

Hersh, S. (2004), "The Deal: Why is Washington Going Easy On Pakistan's Nuclear Black Marketers?" *The New Yorker* (8 March).

Hoagland, J. (1993), "No More Frankensteins," *The Washington Post* (13 July).

"India: Arms and Abuses in Indian Punjab and Kashmir," *Human Rights Watch Arms Project* 6: 10 (1994) (Washington, DC: Human Rights Watch).

International Atomic Energy Agency (2003), "Implementation of the NPT Safeguards Agreement in the Islamic Republic of Iran," report by the Director General to the Board of Governors (10 November).

International Consortium of Investigative Journalists (2002), *Making a Killing: The Business of War* (Washington, DC: Public Integrity Books).

Isikoff, M. (1989a), "Cartels Turn to U.S. for Weapons; Colombians Said to Rely on 'Easy Availability' for War of Terror," *The Washington Post* (2 November).

Isikoff, M. (1989b), "Colombia Urges U.S. to Curb Flow of Semi-Automatic Guns; Drug Cartels Said to Be Hoarding Weapons," *The Washington Post* (8 September).

Khan, K. (2004), "Pakistan Holds Top Al Qaeda Suspect; Key Figure in 1998 Embassy Bombings Arrested After 10-Hour Shootout," *The Washington Post* (30 July).

Klare, M. (1995), "Stemming the Trade in Small Arms and Light Weapons," *Issues in Science and Technology* (Fall).

Klare, M. (2001), *Resource Wars: The New Landscape of Global Conflict* (New York: Metropolitan Books).

Kristof, N. (2004), "Twisting Dr. Nuke's Arm," *The New York Times* (25 September).

Landay, J. (2005), "Chinese Firm Picked by U.S. to Arm Iraq Tied to Smuggling," *Pittsburgh Post-Gazette* (25 April).

Landler, M. (2004), "Trafficking in Nuclear Arms Called Widespread," *International Herald Tribune* (24 January).

Lin, S. (2004), "The A.Q. Khan Revelations and Subsequent Changes to Pakistani Export Controls," Center for Nonproliferation Studies, Monterey Institute of International Studies (October).

Marino, J. (2004), "House Bill Would Push Airline Missile Defense," *Los Angeles Times* (31 March).

Motta, M. (2006), "Reporters Get First-Hand Look at Libyan WMD," *VOA News* (14 March).

Nelson, C. (2002), "Israelis Targeted in Kenya Attacks; Bombers Kill 12 at Resort Hotel Just After Missiles Are Fired at Jetliner," *Austin American-Statesman* (29 November).

Packer, G. (2005), *The Assassin's Gate: America in Iraq* (New York: Farrar, Straus and Giroux).

"Re-imposition of Sanctions Feared: U.S. Aid May Be Jeopardized," *Dawn* (Karachi) (5 February 2004).

Renner, M. (October 1997), "Small Arms, Big Impact: The Next Challenge of Disarmament," Special Report (Washington, DC: Worldwatch Institute).

Rio, V. (2006), *Targeting Ammunition: A Primer* (Geneva: Small Arms Survey).

Small Arms Survey 2002: Counting the Human Cost (2002) (Oxford: Oxford University Press).

Small Arms Survey 2004: Rights at Risk (2004) (New York: Oxford University Press).

Suryanarayana, P.S. (2004), "No assurance that A.Q. Khan network is dismantled," *The Hindu* [India] (6 June).

Teague, M. (2006), "Double Blind," *The Atlantic Monthly* (April).

Thomas, P. and Anderson, W. (1996), "Mexico Asks U.S. to Track Guns Being Imported by Drug Cartels," *The Washington Post* (5 November).

United Nations General Assembly (1997), "General and Complete Disarmament: Small Arms—Note by the Secretary General," Document A/52/298 (27 August) (New York: United Nations).

United Nations Security Council (2000), "Report of the Panel of Experts on Violations of Security Council Sanctions Against UNITA" (New York: United Nations) (28 February).

United Nations Security Council (2001), "Report of the Panel of Experts pursuant to Security Council Resolution 1343 (2001), paragraph 19, concerning Liberia" (New York: United Nations) (26 October).

"Unwanted Export; Flow of Illegal U.S. Guns to Mexico," *San Diego Union-Tribune* (19 July 2001).

Van Natta, D. (2003), "Terrorists Blaze New Money Trail," *The Washington Post* (28 September).

Weiss, L. (2006), "Testimony on the A.Q. Khan Network," given to the House Committee on International Relations, Subcommittee on International Terrorism and Nonproliferation (25 May).

Weissman, S. and Krosney, H. (1981), *The Islamic Bomb* (New York: Times Books, Quadrangle/The New York Times Book Co.).

Chapter 6

The United States, Small Arms and Terrorism

Rachel Stohl

Introduction

Small arms are ideal tools for terrorists. They are lethal, portable, concealable, and— most importantly—readily available. In newspaper and video images, terrorists often brandish small arms and light weapons (SALW), and they make use of them as well; fully half of the terrorist incidents reported in the US State Department's 2003 *Patterns of Global Terrorism* report were perpetrated with small arms and light weapons (Schroeder, 2005). Although carefully orchestrated, large-scale efforts, such as the attacks of 9/11, come to mind when most people think about terrorism, the use of small arms makes even the simplest terrorist plot incredibly effective. As Terry Gander puts it:

> In terror situations, the use of firearms can be every bit as effective as a bomb. The mere sight of a determined guerrilla appearing armed in a crowded environment is enough to cause all manner of panic and dismay in any crowd. If the weapon involved is something as menacing in appearance as an assault rifle or sub-machine-gun, the effect of its appearance alone can be every bit as extreme as the weapon firing; even the sight of a pistol can have a numbing effect on group behavior … (Gander, 1990, 20–21).

This chapter will examine the issue of small arms and terrorism in the United States, explaining how US domestic firearms laws are exploited in ways that allow terrorists to acquire weapons. The chapter will also describe the evolution of US policy responses to the terrorist threat of small arms, focusing on man-portable air defense systems (MANPADS) policies, export controls, and official policy statements linking small arms and terrorism.

Terrorist Acquisition of Weapons: Exploiting US Policy Loopholes

Terrorists obtain weapons using many of same means that other criminals use, including theft of weapons from both individuals and poorly guarded stockpiles, as well as craft production. However, terrorists are also quite familiar with existing loopholes in arms laws and export regulations that allow them to use legal channels to acquire weapons. Indeed, terrorists have singled out the United States as a place where weapons for nefarious purposes can be easily and legally acquired.

The United States has some of the most comprehensive arms export regulations in the world, and has a complex web of federal and state laws governing the purchase and ownership of guns. However, critical loopholes remain in US gun laws that terrorists can exploit in order to obtain US weapons. US Special Forces discovered a manual in Afghanistan that urges members of Al Qaeda living in the United States to obtain weapons from US gun shows and gun shops, given the ease of purchase. The manual directs members to "respect the laws of the country," and to use legal channels for purchasing and operating weapons, as many exist (Diaz, 2002, 5).

Terrorists have taken this call to action seriously. In 2003, the Congressional Research Service (CRS) reported that "foreign terrorists could exploit and appear to have exploited, in limited cases, the general availability of firearms in the United States to carry out terrorist attacks in the United States or abroad [and acquired these weapons] through either legal or illegal channels" (Congressional Research Service, 2003). The study revealed that background checks for gun purchases do not include checks of "international terrorist lookout records." Even more shocking, a 2005 Government Accountability Office (GAO) report found that, "under federal and state law, neither suspected nor actual membership in a terrorist organization is a stand-alone factor that would prohibit a person from receiving or possessing a firearm" (Government Accountability Office, 2005, 1). The GAO report also revealed that between 3 February and 20 June 2004, "44 firearm-related background checks handled by the FBI and applicable state agencies resulted in valid matches with terrorist watch list records." Although clearly these were purchases of concern, "of this total, 35 transactions were allowed to proceed because the background checks found no prohibiting information, such as felony convictions, illegal immigrant status, or other disqualifying factors" (GAO, 2005, 3).

The CRS report also noted that background checks are not required at all for transactions conducted "with a private person (within state lines)," nor are they required when purchasing weapons at gun shows (CRS, 2003, 2). Thus, purchasing weapons from individuals is one way for terrorists to bypass federally mandated checks. "Military-type" weapons are readily available at gun shows, and the laxity of regulations on firearm purchases at gun shows means that terrorists could easily acquire arms, including semiautomatic assault weapons and .50-caliber sniper rifles. Furthermore, because only multiple purchases of handguns must be reported under federal requirements, numerous long-gun purchases can be made without triggering any government oversight (CRS, 2003, 2).

The Brady Center to Prevent Gun Violence exposed the weaknesses of US gun laws and their susceptibility to exploitation by terrorists in a 2001 report (Brady Center, 2001). The Brady Center report documented the legal purchase of assault rifles and high-capacity ammunition magazines by terrorists, the availability of gun kits via mail order, the involvement of corrupt gun dealers in providing weapons to would-be terrorists, and the importance of gun shows as sources of weapons. In particular, the report highlighted several incidents where the FBI and other federal authorities intercepted weapons that had been legally and easily acquired in the United States that were destined for international terrorists.

In 2001, Ali Boumelhem was convicted of attempting to supply the terrorist group Hezbollah with weapons he purchased at gun shows in Michigan. Boumelhem was able to avoid detection because of the lack of federal and state laws requiring private sellers to conduct background checks. Even though Boumelhem was a convicted felon, and thus ineligible to purchase weapons of any kind, he was only caught due to information provided by a police informant. In 2000, Conor Claxton, a soldier in the Irish Republican Army, was convicted of supplying guns to the IRA. Claxton purchased the weapons through a legitimate gun dealer in the US, who he simply bribed to not file the appropriate paperwork. Claxton was apprehended when British authorities intercepted the weapons and were able to trace them back to Claxton's dealer (Brady Center, 2001, 6–7). Undoubtedly, these are not the only attempts that have been made by terrorists to acquire weapons in the United States for malevolent purposes, and reflect just a few of the attempts that have actually been discovered.

Although US officials and legislators are aware of the weaknesses of US firearms legislation, little has been done to remedy the situation. Bipartisan efforts to close gun show loopholes that allow terrorists to purchase weapons without detection have met with strong resistance from some Bush Administration officials and from members of Congress pressured by the enormously powerful US gun lobby, namely the National Rifle Association. As a result, these control efforts have been largely unsuccessful, and US gun laws remain vulnerable to exploitation and abuse.

US Policy Responses to Small Arms and Terrorism

Although US domestic firearms laws and regulations have worrisome gaps that have allowed terrorists to purchase weapons in the United States, US rhetoric and official policy statements have called attention to the linkages between small arms and terrorism for years. While in many cases the push to address small arms policy-making has gained in urgency since the events of 11 September 2001, US small arms policy has actually addressed the threat of terrorist acquisition of these weapons repeatedly over the past several decades.

The United States also works to prevent the diversion of small arms through practical means. The Office of Weapons Removal and Abatement (WRA) in the Political-Military Affairs Bureau of the State Department, whose mission is "to contain the weapons and their aftereffects that are most responsible for fueling regional conflicts, unrest and terrorist activity worldwide," conducts a small arms and light weapons destruction program. Since 2001, this program—whose annual budget has never exceeded USD 9 million—has helped destroy over 900,000 illicit or surplus small arms and light weapons and over 80 million rounds of ammunition in 25 countries, as well as more than 18,600 (MANPADS), or shoulder-fired missiles, in 18 countries since 2003 (US Department of State, 2006b). In conjunction with WRA's programs, the Department of Defense's Defense Threat Reduction Agency (DTRA) provides assistance to states interested in securing their national stockpiles of small arms and light weapons, which often "supply international terrorist and insurgent groups" (DTRA, 2006). Through January 2006, DTRA had "conducted MANPADS and SALW Physical Security and Stockpile Management (PSSM) assistance operations in 25 countries in South and Central America, Europe, Africa, and Asia," at a cost of approximately USD 300,000 a year (DTRA, 2006; Myerscough, 2006).

The linkages between small arms and terrorism have been clearly articulated by the United States government in three distinct areas: policies on MANPADS, policies on arms exports, and official policy statements on the illicit trade in small arms. The following sections outline the evolution of these policies; they are not intended to be comprehensive, but rather to provide an overview of US policies.

MANPADS

The United States has been concerned with terrorist acquisition of MANPADS since the 1970s. As early as 1972 the United States contacted the Soviet Union due to US concerns about the acquisition of Soviet MANPADS by terrorist groups (Schroeder, et al., 2006, Ch. 5). In 1976, the United States undertook its first systematic, interagency study of the threat posed by terrorist use of MANPADS. Although the study found a "serious risk" of terrorist acquisition and use of MANPADS, the study had little effect on the actual practices of the United States. Ten years later, the United States was still examining the MANPADS threat, and by 1986 members of Congress began referring to MANPADS as the "terrorists' delight" (Schroeder, et al., 2006, Ch. 5).

However, it would take ten more years—until 1996—for US efforts to counter the terrorist threat from MANPADS to accelerate. The explosion of TWA Flight 800 in 1996 off Long Island—which, despite initial theories, was not due to a MANPADS attack—spurred the United States to pursue more concrete action. President Clinton created a commission chaired by Vice President Al Gore to examine the MANPADS threat to civil aviation. The commission called for immediate action, and three years later the State Department developed "Elements for Export Controls of Man-Portable Air Defense Systems" for the Wassenaar Arrangement—the first international agreement on MANPADS export controls (Schroeder, et al., 2006, Ch. 7). Members of the Wassenaar Arrangement agreed to the "Elements" in 2000; they contain export controls, including eligibility criteria, stockpile security measures, and information sharing requirements pertaining to transfers of MANPADS (Elements for Export Controls, 2000). The "Elements," which were strengthened and made more comprehensive in 2003, have served as a model for other multilateral organizations (see below) and are expanding global norms on MANPADS control (Wassenaar Arrangement, 2003).

More recent events have reinvigorated the US policy response to the MANPADS threat. Between 2002 and 2005, a period encompassing the first three years after the attacks of 9/11 and the 2002 attempted MANPADS attack on an Israeli airliner in Mombasa, Kenya, 14 pieces of legislation related to MANPADS were introduced to the US Congress (Schroeder, et al., 2006, Ch. 8). Two key pieces of legislation introduced in the 109th Congress—the Cooperative Proliferation Detection, Interdiction Assistance, and Conventional Threat Reduction Act of 2006, introduced by Senators Richard Lugar (R-IN) and Barack Obama (D-IL); and the Shoulder-Fired Missile Threat Reduction Act of 2006, introduced by Rep. Ed Royce (R-CA)—would, if passed, allocate considerably more money to the destruction of small arms and light weapons than has been spent in the past, with an emphasis on MANPADS. In addition, Royce's bill would also authorize sanctions against countries that transfer shoulder-fired missiles to known terrorist organizations or governments that support terrorism.

Outside of Congressional action, the US government launched an interagency task force in 2002 to "develop an aggressive plan to assess and counter the MANPADS threat." The task force, using the input of 21 US government agencies, developed a strategy on three fronts—"proliferation control and threat reduction, tactical measures and recovery, and technical counter-measures"—for implementation by various government agencies (Schroeder, et al., 2006, Ch. 8). In 2003 alone, the Transportation Security Administration created a vulnerability map of US airports to determine which airports were particularly susceptible to MANPADS attacks, the House of Representatives held its first closed hearing in many years on MANPADS, and the Department of Homeland Security began evaluating anti-missile systems.

Anti-missile systems represent a huge part of the US approach to the MANPADS threat. According to a May 2006 interview with James Tuttle, the program executive for aircraft protection programs at the US Department of Homeland Security (DHS), the funding for DHS' counter-MANPADS program alone was "$60 million in FY 04, $61 million in FY05, and $109 million in FY06. FY07 funding, still being worked on the Hill, is $4.9 million" (Adams, 2006). Those figures did not include the costs for equipping aircraft or airports with anti-missile systems, which according to a 2005 RAND report would cost an estimated USD 11 billion to install on US commercial airliners. In addition, the systems would cost an additional USD 2.1 billion annually to operate. According to the RAND report, "over 20 years, the cost to develop, procure, and operate these systems would amount to an estimated $40 billion" (RAND, 2005).

The United States has also continued its work to stem the threat internationally within the five regional and international organizations that have recently developed guidelines for export and control of MANPADS (Schroeder, et al., 2006, Ch. 8). In October 2003, the United States expressed support for the Asia Pacific Economic Cooperation (APEC) Initiatives on Counterterrorism, which were crafted "not only to liberalize and facilitate regional trade and investment, but also to protect our peoples and societies against threats to their security." These initiatives commit APEC member states to "adopt strict domestic export controls on MANPADS; secure stockpiles; regulate MANPADS production, transfer, and brokering; ban transfers to non-state end-users; and exchange information in support of these efforts." Leaders also vowed "to continue to strengthen national controls on MANPADS and review progress at next year's Leaders meeting in Chile" (The White House, 2003).

The United States also used its participation and standing in the Group of Eight industrialized nations (G-8) to solidify global action on MANPADS. In 2004, the United States promoted the G-8 Secure and Facilitated International Travel Initiative (SAFTI), which "commits the G-8 to additional steps to counter the threat to civil aviation" posed by MANPADS. The G-8 agreed to "accelerate efforts to destroy excess and/or obsolete MANPADS; strengthen controls on the transfer of MANPADS production technology; and develop a methodology to assess airport vulnerability to the MANPADS threat and effective countermeasures" (G-8, 2004).

In June 2005, the United States pushed the issue of MANPADS defense within the forum of the Organization of American States (OAS), which resulted in the OAS General Assembly passing Resolution 2145, titled "Denying MANPADS to Terrorists." The resolution urged "member states to adopt strict national controls and security measures, ban all transfers of MANPADS and their essential components to non-state actors, destroy surplus MANPADS, and adopt a series of recommended guidelines attached to the resolution" (OAS, 2005).

The United States has also remained committed to working bilaterally with countries to stop terrorist acquisition and use of MANPADS. In April 2006 the United States and Russia issued a joint statement on MANPADS as part of their meeting on the implementation of the US–Russia Arrangement on Cooperation in Enhancing Control of Man-Portable Air Defense Systems, which was signed in February 2005. This arrangement established "a bilateral framework for cooperation in the control of shoulder-fired anti-aircraft missiles" (US Department of State, 2006a).

Export Policies

US export laws emphasize the link between US arms transfers and terrorism in two distinct ways. First, US arms export policy requires consideration of a potential recipient's past or current support of terrorism before approving a particular export. Second, policy makers view export criteria as an essential mechanism with which to prevent terrorist acquisition of small arms and light weapons. Through the US Conventional Arms Transfer Policy, the US International Arms Sales Code of Conduct Act, and through regional agreements—such as the Wassenaar Non-Binding Guidelines on SALW, and the OAS/CICAD Model Regulations on Brokering—the United States has pushed an anti-terrorism agenda as part of its export policies.

In 1995, President Clinton outlined a new US conventional arms transfer (CAT) policy. The CAT policy outlined criteria to which all arms transfers from the US are subject. Included among these criteria that must be taken into consideration are the "human rights, terrorism, and proliferation record of the recipient and the potential for misuse of the export in question" (US Department of State, 1995).

In 1997, the United States signed the Inter-American Convention Against the Illicit Manufacturing of and Trafficking in Firearms. In its fact sheet on the Convention, the United States touted the importance of the agreement, saying, "the Convention will make the citizens of the hemisphere safer by helping to shut down the gray and black arms markets that fuel the violence associated with drug trafficking, terrorism, and international organized crime" (The White House, 1997). The United States has not ratified the OAS Convention, yet it continually proclaims its importance as a tool against terrorism. In a 1998 review of the CAT policy, the US Arms Control and Disarmament Agency stated that regulations at the Departments of State, Commerce, and Treasury would be altered to reflect the 18 April 1998 Summit of the Americas agreement, "in an effort to strengthen common hemispheric security and strengthen protections against new transnational threats facing the region, including the production, distribution, and abuse of narcotics, illegal arms trafficking and terrorism" (US Department of State, 1998).

In November 1999, the US Congress adopted the International Arms Sales Code of Conduct Act, as part of the FY2000 State Department Authorization Act. The code establishes criteria for a party to be eligible to receive a transfer of weapons from the United States, including the provision that the country not support terrorism. In December 2002, the Wassenaar Arrangement adopted non-binding guidelines on small arms and light weapons exports that "list the criteria states should abide by when assessing a possible sale of small arms or light weapons, and detail the situations in which the export of these weapons ought to be refused." In expressing support for these guidelines, the United States referred to the importance of preventing terrorist acquisition and use of small arms. Wassenaar party states also "agreed to review WA guidelines related to MANPADS in order to ensure their ability to prevent terrorist use of these weapons," which led to the expanded "Elements" in 2003 (Wassenaar Arrangement, 2002).

Official Statements on Terrorism and the Trade in Small Arms

In conjunction with the passage of laws and agreements intended to prevent terrorist acquisition of small arms, the United States has also made significant policy statements linking the trade in small arms and terrorism. Even before the United Nations began its concerted efforts to stem the illicit proliferation and misuse of small arms and light weapons, the United States was identifying strategies for global action. As part of a speech to the UN General Assembly in October 1995, President Clinton focused on "the global humanitarian and security threats posed by terrorism, organized crime, and drug trafficking." President Clinton stated that nations, working together under UN auspices, should create a counter-terrorism pact that would work to "urge more states to ratify existing antiterrorism treaties, and work with [the United States] to shut down the gray markets that outfit terrorists and criminals with firearms and false documents" (The White House, 1995).

While several policy statements on small arms have been delivered in the intervening ten years, an elaboration of the specific links between small arms and terrorism has been absent from many of these statements. However, in 2004, terrorism again began to receive mention in US statements on small arms policy. In January 2004, the US Alternate Representative for Special Political Affairs to the United Nations, Ambassador Stuart Holliday, told the UN Security Council that the United States commended the recent expansion of the UN Register of Conventional Arms to include reporting on MANPADS and small arms and light weapons, and called on member states to "provide full and accurate reporting of MANPADS transfers in their annual submissions to the UN Register of Conventional Arms, and encourage the adoption of MANPADS guidelines developed by the G-8 and the Wassenaar Arrangement" (US Mission to the United Nations, 2004).

Reiterating the importance of regional and multilateral cooperation to counter the threat posed by terrorist use of small arms, the United States also spoke in favor of cooperation and coordinated action in various regional forums. In April 2005, US Ambassador Robert G. Loftis highlighted the links between small arms and terrorism at a meeting of the Organization of American States, stating:

> Given the close links between terrorism, organized crime, and drug trafficking, the illicit trade in small arms and light weapons has the potential to affect any country in the world at any time. ... Focused efforts to identify and curb the sources and methods of the illicit trade via robust export controls, law enforcement measures, and efforts to expeditiously destroy excess stocks and safeguard legitimate stocks from theft or illegal transfer are the

best ways to attack the problem (US Department of State, Bureau of Political–Military Affairs, 2006).

Later in 2005, the United States reiterated its commitment to stamping out the spread of small arms and light weapons to terrorist organizations. In his November 2005 address to the 18th Annual Global Trade Controls Conference, Assistant Secretary of State for Political–Military Affairs John Hillen stressed the US commitment to strong arms export controls, stating that he intended to direct all the energies of his office towards preventing the combination of "bad actors and bad materials." In particular, Hillen pointed to WRA's weapons destruction program and the checks conducted by the State Department's "Blue Lantern" end-use monitoring program as defenses against terrorist acquisition of small arms and light weapons (Hillen, 2005).

During the March 2006 hearing of the House International Relations Committee's Subcommittee on International Terrorism and Nonproliferation on "The Terrorist Threat from Shoulder-Fired Missiles," Hillen discussed the United States' strategy to protect the country's aviation from potential terrorist attacks involving unsecured MANPADS which, according to Hillen, "pose the second greatest proliferation threat to the United States, after weapons of mass destruction." Hillen highlighted State Department MANPADS destruction programs, which had already destroyed 18,500 systems, and cited "firm commitments" to destroy 5,000 more of the weapons. Hillen also stressed US efforts in multilateral organizations to combat MANPADS proliferation, such as in the Wassenaar Arrangement, the Organization for Security and Cooperation in Europe (OSCE), the Asia Pacific Economic Cooperation forum (APEC), and the Organization of American States (US Department of State, USINFO, 2006).

Conclusion

The linkages between small arms and terrorism cannot be understated. Small arms proliferation and misuse have multiple effects on societies at large—from hampering sustainable development to limiting access to food, medicine, and educational opportunities. In countries facing insecurity fuelled by small arms, peacekeepers are threatened and business opportunities are diminished by the proliferation of portable, easily acquired weapons. In many cases, the lack of security and the decline of the economy can cause alienation and frustration to fester, particularly among those that are most often affected by such conditions. Terrorists can exploit such conditions to indoctrinate and recruit new members.

A coordinated policy response to small arms proliferation and misuse should do much more than simply prevent terrorist acquisition and use of these weapons. It must be multi-faceted, and should deploy myriad strategies to combat the spread of these weapons, including efforts to reduce the supply of weapons, remove existing weapons from circulation, end the misuse of the weapons, and reduce the demand. The United States has made some important strides in developing and furthering policies on small arms that will indeed make it more difficult for terrorists to acquire such weapons. However, much work remains to be done, and the United States must be increasingly vigilant in its efforts to counter this urgent threat.

References

Adams, Charlotte (2006), "Q&A: James Tuttle Counter-MANPADS Moves Forward," *Avionics* 30: 5.

Brady Center to Prevent Gun Violence (2001), "Guns and Terror," (Washington, DC: Brady Center to Prevent Gun Violence).

Congressional Research Service (2003), "Foreign Terrorists and the Availability of Firearms and Black Powder in the United States," (Washington, DC: Congressional Research Service).

Defense Threat Reduction Agency (DTRA) (August 2006), "Fact Sheet: Small Arms and Light Weapons"; at <http://www.dtra.mil/newsservices/fact_sheets/display.cfm?fs=salw>

Diaz, Tom (November 2002), "Credit Card Armies—Firearms and Training for Terror in the United States" (Violence Policy Center); at <http://www.vpc.org/graphics/creditcardarmies.pdf>

Elements for Export Controls of Man-Portable Air Defense Systems (MANPADS) (2000); at <http://www.wassenaar.org/docs/oth_manpads.pdf>

G-8 (2004), Secure and Facilitated International Travel Initiative (SAFTI); at <http://www.fas.org/asmp/campaigns/MANPADS/safti.pdf>

Gander, Terry (1990), *Guerrilla Warfare Weapons* (New York: Sterling Publishing Company).

Government Accountability Office (GAO) (January 2005), "Gun Control and Terrorism: FBI Could Better Manage Firearm-related Background Checks Involving Terrorist Watch List Records," (Washington, DC: Government Accountability Office); at <http://www.gao.gov/ncw.items/d05127.pdf>

Hillen, John (2005), Assistant Secretary for Political–Military Affairs, "Address to the 18th Annual Global Trade Controls Conference" (November 3); at <http://www.pmdtc.org/docs/Hillen%20Speech.pdf>

Myerscough, Rhea (2006), "Challenging Conventional Threats: FY 06-FY 07 Budgets Show Increase," *The Defense Monitor* (March/April); at <http://www.cdi.org/PDFs/DMMarApr06.pdf>

Organization of American States (OAS) (2005), AG/RES. 2145 (XXXV-O/05), "Denying MANPADS to Terrorists: Control And Security Of Man-Portable Air Defense Systems (MANPADS)," (June 7); at <http://www.fas.org/asmp/campaigns/MANPADS/2005/OASmanpads.pdf>

RAND (2005), "Press Release: RAND Study Says Airliner Anti-Missile Systems too Expensive and Unreliable" (January 25); at <http://www.rand.org/news/press.05/01.25b.html>

Schroeder, Matt (2005), "Issue Brief 3: The Illicit Arms Trade," (Federation of American Scientists, September 2005); at <http://fas.org/asmp/campaigns/smallarms/IssueBrief3ArmsTrafficking.html>

Schroeder, Matt, Smith, Dan and Stohl, Rachel (2006), *The Small Arms Trade* (Oxford: Oneworld Publications).

The White House (1995), "Remarks by the President to the UN General Assembly," (October 22); at <http://www.clintonfoundation.org/legacy/102295-speech-by-president-at-the-united-nations-nyc.htm>

The White House (1997), "Fact Sheet: OAS Convention Against Illicit Firearms Trafficking," (November 14); at <http://www.fas.org/asmp/resources/govern/oasillicit.html>

The White House (2003), "Fact Sheet: New APEC Initiatives on Counter Terrorism," (October 21); at <http://www.whitehouse.gov/news/releases/2003/10/20031021-4.html>

United States Department of State (1995), "Conventional Arms Transfer Policy"; at <http://www.state.gov/t/pm/rsat/c14023.htm>

United States Department of State (1998), "Small Arms Issues: U.S. Policies and Views," (August 11); at <http://www.state.gov/www/global/arms/factsheets/conwpn/small.html>

United States Department of State (2006a), "Media Note: Joint United States–Russian Federation Statement on the USRussia MANPADS Arrangement on Cooperation in Enhancing Control of Man-Portable Air Defense Systems," (April 21); at <http://www.state.gov/r/pa/prs/ps/2006/64968.htm>

United States Department of State (2006b), "Media Note: Stemming the Illicit Trade in Small Arms and Light Weapons," 19 June; at <http://www.state.gov/r/pa/prs/ps/2006/68035.htm>

United States Department of State, Bureau of Political–Military Affairs (2006), "Fact Sheet: U.S. Spent $27 Million To Destroy Small Arms, Light Weapons," (June 9); at < http://usinfo.state.gov/is/Archive/2006/Jun/12-171805.html>

United States Department of State, USINFO (2006), "State Department Targets Stores of Shoulder-fired Missiles," (March 30); at <http://www.fas.org/asmp/campaigns/MANPADS/2006/Hillen30mar06.htm>

United States Mission to the United Nations (2004), "Statement by Ambassador Stuart Holliday, United States Alternate Representative for Special Political Affairs to the United Nations, on Small Arms/Light Weapons, in the Security Council" (January 19); at <http://www.un.int/usa/04_006.htm>

Wassenaar Arrangement (2002), "Best Practice Guidelines for Exports of Small Arms and Light Weapons (SALW)," (December 11–12); at <http://www.wassenaar.org/docs/best_practice_salw.htm>

Wassenaar Arrangement (2003), "Public Statement, 2003 Plenary Meeting of the Wassenaar Arrangement on Export Controls for Conventional Arms and Dual-Use Goods and Technologies"; at <http://www.wassenaar.org/2003plenary/public_statement2003.htm>

Chapter 7

Terrorists and the Internet: Crashing or Cashing In?

Sean S. Costigan

Reports of cyber-terrorism are a regular feature of today's news. While such accounts are commonplace, to the best of our knowledge no computer attacks carried out by terrorists against critical infrastructure have occurred to date.[1] Though data collection on cyber-terrorism is fraught with obstacles, by and large media, industry, and government reports have yet to reveal substantial evidence that terrorists are systematically exploiting weaknesses in information systems. Yet, despite all the talk about cyber-terrorism, scant attention has been given to the seemingly mundane—though most definitely actual and disquieting—use of the Internet and currently available information technologies by terrorists. By examining the background and trends in cyber-crimes, and detailing what is presently known about terrorist uses of information technologies and the Internet, a surprising picture emerges: terrorists use information technologies but, at least for now, not as weapons. Nonetheless, the incessant drive to connect myriad aspects of our increasingly digital lives and infrastructures has, as a by-product of perceived and real efficiencies, created new vulnerabilities that allow for enterprising actors to potentially wreak havoc on a wide scale. The costs of ignoring such new vulnerabilities could be quite high.

Definitions and Data Collection

Any study of computer terrorism and other criminal computer-enabled behavior would be incomplete without first establishing a working definition of cyber-terrorism and discussing the data collection problems associated with distinguishing between cyber-terrorism and cyber-crime. *Cyber-terrorism* is simply a portmanteau of *cyberspace* and *terrorism*. Beyond that simple construction, problems of taxonomy arise, resulting in many definitions that typically hinge either on the intent of the attacker or the effects of the attack.

---

1   Experts agree that there have been no cyber-attacks by terrorists as of yet: "While there is no published evidence that terrorist organizations are currently planning a coordinated attack against computers, computer system vulnerabilities persist worldwide and initiators of the random cyberattacks that plague computers on the Internet remain largely unknown" (Wilson, 2005). "However, to date, there is no published evidence linking a sustained or widespread attack using CNA with international terrorist groups" (Arquilla and Ronfeldt, 2001). Although cyber-attacks have caused billions of dollars in damage and affected the lives of millions, few if any can be characterized as acts of terrorism—fraud, theft, sabotage, vandalism, and extortion, yes; but terrorism, no.

One of the most widely used definitions of cyber-terrorism was penned by Dorothy Denning, a professor in the Department of Defense Analysis at the Naval Postgraduate School, in which she merges intent and effect while focusing on the notion of an attack or a threat. It defines cyber-terrorism as, "Unlawful attacks and threats of attack against computers, networks, and the information stored therein when done to intimidate or coerce a government or its people in furtherance of political or social objectives" (Denning, 2002). Elsewhere, she has elaborated further, stating that:

> to qualify as cyber-terrorism, an attack should result in violence against persons or property, or at least cause enough harm to generate fear. Attacks that lead to death or bodily injury, explosions, plane crashes, water contamination, or severe economic loss would be examples. Serious attacks against critical infrastructures could be acts of cyber-terrorism, depending on their impact. Attacks that disrupt nonessential services or that are mainly a costly nuisance would not (Denning, 2000).

Investigations during and after cyber-attacks are arduous, due in part to the clever way in which the Internet was built to keep data flowing, even in the event of failures in one or another part of the network. Tracing back various packets of information to their source is laborious and often not possible, due both to technical and (as we shall see) jurisdictional concerns. Given the speed of cyber-attacks and the ability of attackers to hide their identities and locations, difficulties in post-attack data collection only serve to further compound the definitional problem by ensuring that the attackers are obscured and their actions hard to characterize. In other words, it can be virtually impossible to answer two crucial questions of any investigation: who was the attacker and what was their intention? (Wilson, 2005, 6) The complexity of data collection is further confounded by troubles in information sharing, as cooperation among law enforcement agencies on cyber-crimes typically involves many jurisdictions and, often, coordination between sovereign nations.

Without doubt, insufficient international cooperation and limited enforcement against computer crimes in many regions of the world allows cyber-criminals the space to work with relative impunity, at little risk to themselves. For the Islamist terrorist, this free and safe electronic space has allowed for the transmission of techniques and ideas through virtual training camps, helping to offset the loss of actual training camps destroyed in Afghanistan and elsewhere. As related in an often-quoted *Washington Post* account, "With laptops and DVDs, in secret hideouts and at neighborhood Internet cafes, young code-writing jihadists have sought to replicate the training, communication, planning and preaching facilities they lost in Afghanistan with countless new locations on the Internet" (Coll and Glasser, 2005). The October 2001 war against the Taliban and Al Qaeda in Afghanistan (Operation Enduring Freedom) gave the United States and its allies a glimpse into how computers had revolutionized the work of terrorists, particularly in their planning and operational support activities.

Given what we now know about how terrorists use information technology, it is time to amend current definitions of what constitutes cyber-terrorism. While acts of cyber-terrorism resulting in damaged infrastructures or lost lives may not yet have occurred, terrorist use of information technologies for intelligence, planning, communication, propaganda, psychological warfare, disruption, and funding is ongoing. Such uses may well presage the form of cyber-terrorism that so many have feared, and so a new definition of cyber-terrorism should include, at the very least, psychological warfare conducted through the Web.

Background, Budgets, Costs

Early events that have been labeled instances of cyber-warfare or cyber-terrorism (the two are often conflated) were generally of low technical quality—essentially the "digital equivalent of graffiti," coming in the form of defacement or other light damage (Lewis, 2002). However, with the continued expansion and increasing sophistication of the Web and its technologies, cyber-attacks have become more frequent and, in some instances, more powerful.[2] Cyber-threats and computer warfare have been a serious concern of the US Department of Defense since at least the 1980s, with current and former defense officials expressing the need for defense restructuring to meet the threat (Hildreth, 2001; Gansler, 2003). In response, considerable funds have been allocated in pursuit of defensive measures against the hazards posed by cyber-threats. In 2003, President Bush included a USD 1.7 billion increase in cyber-security spending in his proposed defense budget—a 68 percent increase over the previous year's budget—bringing the total allocated for computer security in the US defense budget to USD 4.2 billion. FY 2004 saw the budget request for Department of Homeland Security IT funds increase to USD 4.9 billion, and for funds for cyber-security to USD 4.7 billion (Millser, 2003). However, given that the mission to secure America's critical infrastructure is spread out across many agencies—and, in actuality, most of the costs are shouldered by the private sector—it is difficult to accurately gauge how much the government spends on cyber-security.

Since the advent of the Internet, substantial disruptions in Internet traffic have occurred, with the overwhelming majority of attacks and outages attributed to viruses and other malware (software designed to infiltrate or damage computer systems). Most such outages have been historically attributed to lone hackers, so-called hacktivists, or small groups of enthusiasts or criminals. Malware attacks have grown from relatively simple pieces of software launched by individuals to more complex technologies deployed by organized groups, though one constant has remained: the attacks and the resulting network outages often have astonishing, worldwide consequences. One often cited example of malware that caused unanticipated damage is that of the worm dubbed "Slammer," which struck at a weakness in Microsoft's popular SQL database on 24 January 2003. Slammer created immense quantities of data through infected servers, essentially obstructing the information pipelines of networks worldwide. The effects were widespread and unforeseen. By

---

2   According to 2002 Congressional testimony given by Richard D. Pethia, Director of the CERT Centers Software Engineering Institute at Carnegie Mellon University, "Reported attacks against Internet systems are almost doubling each year and attack technology will evolve to support attacks that are even more virulent and damaging. Our current solutions are not keeping pace with the increased strength and speed of attacks, and our information infrastructures are at risk" (Pethia, 2002).

seizing up bank networks, some ATMs, corporate telecommunications systems, emergency response networks, and other services that had been using the *public* Internet, Slammer showed how poor design and human error, coupled with software security flaws and a little ingenuity on the part of the malware designer, can have cascading effects. Since Slammer, a considerable number of viruses and worms have been released, some resulting in spectacular "soft-dollar" costs. According to the cyber-terror analyst John Arquilla, claims paid by insurers for "cyber disruptions" exceed USD 40 billion annually (Arquilla, 2006).

Measuring the cost of known computer malware attacks is quite challenging. Given that the calculation typically involves measuring lost productivity *worldwide*— and often includes the acquisition of additional resources to limit the damage— such estimates are often referred to as "soft-dollar" losses. According to a 2002 interview of Steven Trilling, Symantec's vice-president for research and advanced development, "The numbers certainly differ across the various organizations evaluating them. Clearly there is some cost, and it's significant. Whether it was $10 billion or $100 billion last year, it's hard to say" (quoted in Lyman, 2002). Many media reports of soft-dollar losses come from estimates done by the California firm Computer Economics (computereconomics.com), which has been criticized by many for lacking transparency in its methodology and sources. It has been suggested that, instead of attempting to estimate the monetary losses associated with malware attacks, analysts should create a severity index to rank attacks in terms of their impact (Delio, 2002).

While debate continues on how to measure the true cost of computer viruses, even if we reduce existing publicly reported estimates by a factor of ten it becomes evident that considerable economic losses occur through the deployment of sometimes relatively easy-to-create malware. Such damage—whether in time, money, or damaged hardware—can be vast. For example, the "Love Bug" virus, which was released in 2000, is estimated by the United States General Accounting Office to have cost computer users around the world USD 3 billion to 15 billion (cited in Wilson, 2005). Setting aside the issue of measurement of losses, it is crucial to note that the Love Bug virus was created and launched by a single university student in the Philippines employing commercial, off-the-shelf (COTS) and other easily downloaded technologies (cited in Wilson, 2005). Governments are often favored targets of cyber-attackers, too, and often have the same weak defenses and frailties of corporations. For example, in 2004, after a series of break-ins perpetrated by an insider using freely downloaded password-cracking programs, the FBI was forced to shut down much of its internal network at a cost of thousands of man-hours and millions of dollars (Weiss, 2006).

However costly, malware—such as worms (self-propagating malware) and viruses (small executable programs)—typify only a portion of current attacks and cyber-security difficulties. According to a recent survey from IBM, for-profit attacks, particularly bot attacks, now appear to be on the upswing, and will perhaps overtake the previous lone-wolf/small group malware development model (IBM

Report, 2006).[3] In addition to a marked upswing in for-profit attacks like cyber-extortion bot attacks, targeted e-mails, spear phishing, phishing, and pharming, malware is becoming increasingly complex and more difficult to detect and control.[4] In the United Kingdom, the Department of Trade and Industry reports that computer crime has grown 50 percent over the last two years. In the case of cyber-extortion, an undetermined number of victims are choosing to pay the extortion, which may seem to be a relatively small sum in comparison to legitimate computer protection services.[5] Furthermore, the FBI's Computer Security Institute has reported that, based on its survey of 700 US government, public, and private-sector institutions, the reporting of cyber-attacks is declining. Citing the fear of negative publicity, only 20 percent of respondents reported cyber-attacks, and a scant 12 percent sought legal counsel (Greenemeier, 2005). While damaging terrorist computer attacks appear to have not yet occurred, untold billions are lost annually to cyber-crime and other threats. In 2006, the FBI estimated that industry lost over USD 400 billion annually from all forms of cyber-crime (Jones, 2006).

Are terrorists behind any of these developments and, if not, will they be in the future? Studies of how terrorists and other organized criminals are currently using computer technologies have shown increasing sophistication on their part. As with the adoption of new communication technologies everywhere, younger terrorists appear to be driving the implementation of information technologies for the cause (Arquilla, Ronfeldt and Zanini, 1999). Furthermore, forensic evidence from captured hardware has revealed evidence of planning that has (or could) lead to damaging physical and economic computer attacks, and of technologies that have been used to make the detection of the planning stages of physical attacks more difficult.

Cyber-armageddon, Media Bias, and Uncontrolled Spaces

The media is fascinated with cyber-crime and cyber-terrorism. However, their reporting proclivities and biases have resulted in a proliferation of articles that, in the main, essentially hype the threat of terrorist-generated computer network attacks. A Lexis-Nexis search on "cyber-terror" and its search term variants typically reveals over 150 articles on the topic in any given month, at least half of which represent hypothetical threats—that is, those with no historical basis.

---

3   Botnets, or bot attacks, are collections of software robots that allow a computer to be controlled without the owner's knowledge. Such botnets can number in the thousands, and the collective computing power is often used in distributed denial of service (DDoS) attacks. In a typical DDoS attack, bots will be directed to fill out a form online or otherwise cause the server under attack to perform some activity beyond its capability, resulting in system crashes, data loss, and interruptions of business.

4   For useful definitions of these techniques, see <http://www.symantec.com/avcenter/cybercrime/>

5   According to John Pescatore, an analyst at Gartner, Inc, anti-DDoS services from AT&T and MCI cost around USD 12,000 per month. From what is currently known, cyber-extortionists often ask for sums ranging from USD 1000 to USD 100,000, most often on the lower end in the hope that payout will occur (Pappalardo and Messmer, 2005).

Much like the doomsday news surrounding Y2K, the media seem fixated on the potential for catastrophic collapse of the information infrastructure despite the fact that cyber-terrorism, like cyber-warfare, has not yet shown its full potential. That the "Millennium Bug" itself—the most hyped computer "bug" of all time—did not in fact paralyze the world's information technologies has not served to temper the media's fascination with the topic.

Furthermore, many of the cyber-threats and cyber-crimes as reported by the media appear to emanate from Eastern Europe and Russia; such attention could be due to real-world facts, but could also be prejudice in the form of common thinking that Eastern Europe is the home to great programmers, mafia organizations, criminality, and lawlessness. The Internet is undoubtedly a global service. Even though masking an attacker's location is a relatively straightforward effort, particularly for a savvy computer user, actual evidence from virus trackers reveals malware activity originating in many far-flung and, importantly, nearby locales. However, an in-depth study on cyber-extortion conducted at Carnegie Mellon University in 2004 has revealed that, while the majority of external cyber-extortion threats have not been geographically pinpointed, North America represents the largest source of known threat origins (Bednarski, 2004).

In addition, more sophisticated utilities that mask the origin of attacks help ensure that the already tedious effort to trace attacks back to their points of origin is steadily becoming more difficult. As one report notes, "while the number of random Internet cyber-attacks has been increasing, the data collected to measure the trends for cyber-attacks cannot be used to accurately determine if a terrorist group, or terrorist-sponsoring state, has initiated any of them" (Wilson, 2005, 7). Finally, as we have seen, off-the-shelf technology coupled with easily downloaded scripts and other tools has proven effective at disabling Internet traffic and commerce.

Terrorist Uses of the Internet

Several analyses of terrorist uses of the Internet have been completed.[6] To date, however, most concentrate on jihadis and their websites. As the information infrastructure has not yet been attacked by terrorists nor, to our knowledge, have terrorists weaponized information technologies, what follows is a discussion of how terrorists use such technologies.

Communications

Through the use of simple but powerful encryption programs that can be easily downloaded from the Internet, terrorists are able to communicate in secure environments; and such encryption methods are being taught in virtual training camps (Kelley, 2001). Not only does such encryption make the work of monitoring messages more difficult, if not impossible, it also allows for the creation of "virtual safe houses,"

---

6   Most notable among these studies are: "Al Qaeda Online," 2006; Anti-Defamation League, 2002; and DCSINT Handbook, 2005.

which are hard to detect. "Uncrackable" encryption allows Al Qaeda members "to communicate about their criminal intentions without fear of outside intrusion," former FBI Director Louis Freeh told a US Senate panel. "They're thwarting the efforts of law enforcement to detect, prevent and investigate illegal activities," he warned (Kelley, 2001). Richard Clarke stated that, "Seized computers belonging to Al Qaeda indicate its members are now becoming familiar with hacker tools that are freely available over the Internet" (*Cyberwar!*, 2003).

So-called virtual dead drops have also been used by terrorists, whereby a terrorist planner opens an e-mail account through a free service like Yahoo! or Hotmail, writes a message, saves it in draft form, and then transmits the account information through another forum or vehicle, allowing the recipient to read the message without it ever having been sent, thus avoiding e-mail monitoring. According to intelligence sources, and as reported in the media, Khalid Sheik Mohammed, a key planner of the 9/11 attacks later arrested in Pakistan, used this virtual dead letter box technique (Coll and Glasser, 2005). Instant Messenger (IM) has also become a tool for terrorist communication (Gruen, 2006, 357).

Yet another concern is the possibility of plans or messages being embedded in images, a practice known as steganography. While it is unclear whether terrorist groups have resorted to such advanced methods, some analysts argue that terrorists need not be so sophisticated in their use of computer technology, when coded language sent in plain text or the traditional tactic of placing advertisements in newspapers or websites might suffice to send signals to operatives.

Planning, Research, and Operational Support

Like modern-day students of any type, terrorists and their supporters do considerable planning and research on the Web. Given the amount of publicly available information, for terrorists involved in preparing an attack, investing time in research on the Web is likely to prove much more valuable than developing a sophisticated cyber-attack portfolio. After seized computers in Afghanistan revealed that terrorists had been using the Web for research and planning, Secretary of Defense Donald Rumsfeld issued a memo to the US Department of Defense ordering changes in cyber-security in which he quoted from the so-called Manchester Manual (an Al Qaeda training primer), that "Using public sources openly and without resorting to illegal means, it is possible to gather at least 80 percent of all information required about the enemy" ("Citing Al Qaeda Manual," 2003). In addition, captured equipment and literature has revealed that Al Qaeda operatives are well versed in technology and engineering (Wilson, 2006). Support cells have sprung up across the Web, and sites and chat rooms have been used by such cells to gain information about targets, American interests, and training (Gunaratna, 2005). For now, at least, it appears that computer attacks by terrorists are to be feared less than the benefits that terrorists gain from using computers for research and knowledge sharing.

Propaganda and Psychological Warfare

As a tool for grass-roots organization and information dissemination and propaganda, the Web is unrivalled. Rapid, cheap, and effective propagation is its strong suit, and propagandists of all stripes, particularly modern terrorists, have used it to great advantage. As Timothy L. Thomas puts it, "We can say with some certainty, Al Qaeda loves the Internet" (Thomas, 2003). In addition to rapid and cheap dissemination, the Web allows terrorists to bypass traditional media and get their message out without editors or others controlling it. Whereas traditional media vet sources and some governments censor, terrorists are able to do and say what they want in the dark and hidden corners of the Web, offering often compelling accounts, dramatic footage and, of course, outright fictions that compete with more reliable sources. For example, the rumor that 4,000 Jews were notified of the impending attacks against the World Trade Center on 9/11 and, hence, failed to come to work, was started by Hezbollah on the website of its TV station, *Al Manar* (Anti-Defamation League, 2002, 4). Thousands of such examples of dissemination, both of useful and misleading information, exist on jihadist and terrorist websites. Hezbollah and Hamas have achieved considerable benefits from their use of the Internet and Web, but Al Qaeda may have been the first terrorist organization to fully grasp its importance (Hoffman, 2006, 214). Al Qaeda realized the value of disseminating its views and actions through news networks, as is exemplified by the May 1996 quote of bin Laden: "God willing, you will see our work on the news" (quoted in Bowman, 2002). Nonetheless, while self-publicizing on the Web has its virtues, the traditional news media remain the best outlet for Al Qaeda and other terrorist groups.

Whereas violence attempts to coerce, propaganda aims to persuade (Schmid, 2004). Beheadings have historically been used as a punishment and, ostensibly, as a deterrent (Jones, 2005, 3). Videos of beheadings have considerable shock value, and their psychological impact certainly appears to intimidate populations and, on occasion, governments.[7] Disturbing images have been credited with changing foreign policy in the past, particularly when the US withdrew its troops from Somalia after images of mutilated American soldiers being paraded through the streets of Mogadishu were shown on television. The late Musab al Zarqawi undoubtedly realized this, and may well have been the jihadis' leading proponent of webcasting when he posted video of the beheading of the American contractor Nicholas Berg on 11 May 2004 on the website of *Muntada al-Ansar al-Islami*, or the Forum of the Islamic Supporters. According to one account, the beheading video was "initially sent from a computer that was probably somewhere in Iraq … was copied onto Internet sites [and] within twenty-four hours had been downloaded half a million times … Al Zarqawi's success was possible because he had anticipated the importance of the Internet—an increasingly important weapon in the global terrorist arsenal" (Labi, 2006). As further evidence of the incredible reach that the Web offers terrorists, and the appetite for their communiqués, it is claimed that immediately

---

7   At least one government appears to have been persuaded by the prospect of a beheading; when Iraqi insurgents threatened to decapitate a hostage unless the Philippines withdrew its troops from Iraq, the government chose to withdraw.

after the Berg beheading video went online it was the most popular search on the Web (Al-Marashi, 2004). University of Michigan political science professor Juan Cole has suggested that one possible motive for the Berg beheading video was to scare the non-governmental private contractors in Iraq (quoted in Stannard, 2004).

Other jihadis and terrorists have also recognized the value of the Web as a tool for psychological warfare, chief among them being Ansar Al Sunna ("The List," 2006). Just as bin Laden was quick to adopt high-quality video production techniques, other individuals have played a decisive role in adopting new media strategies, moving from bin Laden's analog world to the digital one of today. As Jarret Brachman, director of research at the Combating Terrorism Center at West Point, convincingly argues, the Syrian Al Qaeda ideologue Abu Mus`ab al Suri was extremely influential in promoting media campaigns as part of a new arsenal to win the jihad.[8]

Recruiting and Encouraging Sympathy for the Cause

For Islamic terrorists, the Web has proven critical for growing a sympathetic audience through regular communications and indoctrination, and maintaining a regular flow of new recruits (Hoffman, 2006, 225; Gruen, 2006, 352). Video games have been developed by jihadist programmers to help reach out to the next generation of potential recruits (Gruen, 2006, 261; Hoffman, 2006, 209).

Gabriel Weimann, a professor of communications at the University of Haifa, points to the case of Ziyad Khalil. According to Weimann and other sources, Ziyad Khalil was recruited online and became an Al Qaeda procurement operative and activist, as well as one-time webmaster of the official Hamas site in the United States (Kohlman, 2003). As one report claims, "Khalil bought satellite telephones, computers, and other electronic surveillance technologies for Al Qaeda" (Cherry, 2005).

Intelligence sources assert that a number of cases have been uncovered in which jihadist cells appear to have formed among like-minded strangers who met online, and there appear to be many other cases in which relationships built in the real world have been sustained and nurtured by the Internet (Coll and Glasser, 2005). Additionally, as we have seen, the Web has served as a virtual replacement for physical training camps and as a repository of jihadist thinking ("Al Qaeda Online," 2006; *NewsHour with Jim Lehrer*, 2005). The Web has helped Al Qaeda grow both its network and its finances. According to Rita Katz of the SITE Institute, which monitors jihadist websites, "If you want to conduct an attack, you will find what you need on the Internet" (quoted in Coll and Glasser, 2005).

---

8   "Propagandists, Suri states, will play the pivotal role in generating the 'global Islamic resistance.' They can do this by pursuing aggressive media campaigns and using technology like satellite television and the Internet to communicate the movement's objectives and justify its use of violence to the public, particularly to the young Muslim men around the world in search of ways to participate" (Brachman and McCants, 2006).

Fund-raising/Finance/Crime

Before 9/11, dozens of websites purportedly from Muslim charities allowed money to be funneled to terrorist organizations. After 9/11, fund-raising and money transfers for terrorists moved to different vehicles, but still employed ostensible charity websites. Law enforcement agencies in the United States, Saudi Arabia, and elsewhere have investigated and shut down many such organizations. However, Al Qaeda, Hamas, Hezbollah, and other groups continue to use the Internet to blend legitimate and terrorist purposes.

According to the Anti-Defamation League and other sources, one such charitable trust website was run by the Benevolence International Foundation (BIF), based in Illinois, a group that described itself as "a humanitarian organization dedicated to helping those afflicted by wars which provides short-term relief such as emergency food distribution, and then moves on to long term projects providing education and self-sufficiency to the children, widowed, refugees, injured and staff of vital governmental institutions." The website provided bank details and suggestions for stock donations, much as legitimate charities do. The BIF was an offshoot of the Benevolence International Corporation, which was created in 1988 by Osama bin Laden's brother-in-law Mohammed Jamal Khalifa as an "import-export" company. Khalifa was arrested in California in 1994 for funding a subsequently foiled terrorist plot; he was deported to Jordan, where he was acquitted of charges against him there.

Given the ease with which they can be perpetrated, targeted e-mail attacks and cyber-extortion may soon capture the imagination of terrorists worldwide. The allure of relatively easy money combined with a low chance of being punished, along with the prospect of inflicting economic damage to an enemy state, might serve as a calling all its own. Perhaps, as IBM's *Global Business Security Index Report 2005* suggests, the current rise in such attacks is already, at least in part, the work of politically motivated parties.[9]

Operations, Disruption, and Destruction

There is clear evidence that Al Qaeda and its offshoots are also using the Internet for tactical and intelligence purposes. According to recent reports from the Critical Infrastructure Protection Board (CIPB), which operates under the Department of Homeland Security, computers "from the Mideast are probing American electric, water, and energy systems, and seem especially interested in gaining access to nuclear-power plants" (Robbins, 2002). Such reports mesh with earlier concerns

---

9   "Targeted Email Attacks—In 2005, approximately two to three targeted email attacks were intercepted each week. This number was almost negligible in 2004, marking a shift in the nature and purpose of the attacks. These attacks, which are often financially, competitively, *politically or socially* motivated, were often directed at government departments, military organizations and other large organizations, particularly in the aerospace, petroleum, legal, and human rights fields. Several high profile cases hit the headlines in 2005 but it is believed many more attacks go undetected by businesses" (emphasis added) (IBM Report, 2006).

uncovered by law enforcement agencies in California of probes against Silicon Valley companies and Bay Area infrastructures, also originating from computers in the Middle East and South Asia (Gellman, 2002). Remedial and defensive measures are complicated by a lack of standard network architectures; vendor mistakes that result in poor security (in the case of commercial software); and, of course, human errors, all of which increase the probability of terrorists finding a weakness worth exploiting.

The CIPB has rated Al Qaeda's current cyber-capabilities as low. However, many specialists consider the probability of a combined computer and physical attack—what the FBI calls a "swarming attack"—to be within the abilities of some terrorist groups.[10] Such an attack, if viable, would serve as a force multiplier, perhaps by attempting to disrupt emergency services during a physical attack.[11] In his 2003 Congressional testimony, Richard Pethia suggested that such an outcome is likely:

> Most threatening of all is the link between cyber space and physical space. Supervisory control and data acquisition (SCADA) systems and other forms of networked computer systems have for years been used to control power grids, gas and oil distribution pipelines, water treatment and distribution systems, hydroelectric and flood control dams, oil and chemical refineries, and other physical systems. Increasingly, these control systems are being connected to communications links and networks to reduce operational costs by supporting remote maintenance, remote control, and remote update functions. These computer-controlled and network-connected systems are potential targets of individuals bent on causing massive disruption and physical damage (Pethia, 2003).

The possibility is not remote. In one case in March 2005, hackers gained power over the electronic control systems of portions of the US power grid and, though no damage was done, it underlined the potential risk of exposing such critical infrastructure to attackers (Hoopes, 2005).

Conclusions and Recommendations

For the foreseeable future, the Web will remain a safe place for terrorists to operate. To dissuade or render impossible attacks against critical infrastructure, the maintenance of "air gaps" for the most sensitive equipment and critical infrastructure elements should remain common practice. For those systems that do have to be connected

---

10 In his March 2004 report, Gabriel Weimann wrote, "One captured Al Qaeda computer contained engineering and structural features of a dam, which had been downloaded from the Internet and which would enable Al Qaeda engineers and planners to simulate catastrophic failures. In other captured computers, U.S. investigators found evidence that Al Qaeda operators spent time on sites that offer software and programming instructions for the digital switches that run power, water, transportation, and communications grids" (quoted in Cherry, 2005).

11 "The only new element attributed to Al Qaeda is that the group might use cyber-attacks to disrupt emergency services in order to reinforce and multiply the effect of a physical attack. If cyber-attacks were feasible, the greatest risk they might pose to national security is as corollaries to more traditional modes of attacks" (Lewis, 2002, 9).

to the public Internet, extreme diligence should be employed to ensure that as few vulnerabilities as possible exist. While standardization of SCADA and other systems associated with critical infrastructure may reduce operating costs, such technical trajectories are likely to attract hacker activity and also increase the risks of terrorist attacks. Though costly, mixed environments with different protocols and proprietary hardware may help reduce incursions and the risk of damage. In addition to the above, a number of steps will help dissuade terrorists from developing sophisticated information technology attacks, while simultaneously giving law enforcement and counter-terrorist forces the upper hand, including:

- Training computer network administrators on the latest techniques
- Increasing software developers' knowledge of vulnerabilities
- Providing incentives for better security features in hardware and software
- Creating disincentives for security flaws, especially in software and technologies used in critical infrastructure
- Encouraging the use of strong encryption for data associated with key infrastructure
- Pursuing better industry and government partnership strategies, such as the Cyber Incident Detection & Data Analysis Center (for more on CIDDAC, see Greenemeier, 2005)
- Monitoring terrorist use of the Internet and Web
- Enacting smarter cyber-crime laws
- Encouraging debate on the merits of powers to shut down or attack known terrorist support sites or sites used for psychological warfare
- Empowering national and international criminal investigative bodies
- Encouraging closer cooperation between governments to facilitate information exchange on cyber-crime and terrorism
- Promoting an open dialogue for editors and those working in the media to consider their role in analysis, reporting, and transmission of terrorist communications
- Expanding the definition of cyber-terrorism to include psychological warfare
- Using the Web and information technologies to counter ideological support for terrorism.

Whereas in the United States there are laws against certain types of pornography being distributed through the Internet, there are currently no legal tools to stop the distribution of beheading videos, which some have likened to so-called snuff films. In many European countries, hate speech is banned, allowing for the possibility that law enforcement agencies might be within their rights to dismantle websites that incite or depict certain crimes. Recently, British police have asked the government of the United Kingdom for powers that would enable them to dismantle terrorist websites, sometimes with just the same cyber-warfare techniques as discussed above (Ilett, 2005). However, for most democracies, the decision of whether to host or attack such terrorist websites is less a question of policy than morality (Walker, 2004).

While cyber-terrorism of the sort that causes major damage or death through computer attacks has apparently not yet materialized, terrorists have taken advantage of the strengths of the Internet and Web to communicate, plan, recruit, fund-raise, and frighten. Definitions of cyber-terrorism and criminal investigative work should account for this understanding. Intelligence analysts, both governmental and open source, are on the lookout for changes in online behavior by terrorists, but better efforts—such as those outlined above, both technical or otherwise—must be made to uncover terrorist plans and, critically, to distinguish between criminal, hacktivist, and terrorist online activities. Waiting for attacks to occur is not a strategy.

References

Al-Marashi, Ibrahim (2004), "Iraq's Hostage Crisis: Kidnappings, Mass Media and the Iraqi Insurgency," *Middle East Review of International Affairs* 8: 4 (December).

"Al-Qaeda Online: Understanding Jihadist Internet Infrastructure," *Jane's Intelligence Review* (1 January 2006); at <http://www.nupi.no/IPS/filestore/Lia2005Al-Qaeda_online__und_75416a.pdf>

Anti-Defamation League (2002), "Jihad Online: Islamic Terrorists and the Internet"; at <www.adl.org/internet/jihad_online.pdf>

Arquilla, John (2006), "Waging War through the Internet: America is far more vulnerable to terrorists who hack systems than missions to blow things up," *San Francisco Chronicle* (15 January).

Arquilla, John and Ronfeldt, David (2001), "The Advent of Netwar (Revisited)," in *Networks and Netwars: The Future of Terror, Crime and Militancy*, eds. Arquilla and Ronfeldt (Santa Monica, CA: RAND).

Arquilla, John, Ronfeldt, David and Zanini, Michele (1999), "Networks, Netwar and Information-Age Terrorism," in *Countering the New Terrorism* (Santa Monica, CA: RAND).

Bednarski, Gregory (2004), "Enumerating and Reducing the Threat of Transnational Cyber-extortion Against Small and Medium Size Organizations," *InformationWeek* (1 September).

Bowman, Marion (2002), Testimony before the Senate Select Committee on Intelligence, Hearings on the Foreign Intelligence Surveillance Act (31 July); at <http://www.fbi.gov/congress/congress02/bowman073102.htm>

Brachman, Jarret and McCants, William (2006), "Stealing Al Qaeda's Playbook," *Studies in Conflict and Terrorism* 29: 4 (June).

Cherry, Steven (2005), "Terror Goes Online," *IEEE Spectrum Online* (January); at <http://www.spectrum.ieee.org/jan05/2472>

"Citing Al Qaeda Manual, Rumsfeld Re-Emphasizes Web Security," InsideDefense.com (15 January 2003); at <http://www.insidedefense.com/>

Coll, Steve and Glasser, Susan (2005), "Terrorists Turn to the Web as Base of Operations," *The Washington Post* (7 August).

Cyberwar! (2003), Frontline (PBS), interview with Richard Clarke (April); at <http://www.pbs.org/wgbh/pages/frontline/shows/cyberwar/vulnerable/alqaeda.html>

DCSINT Handbook No. 1.02 (2005), "Cyber Operations and Cyber-terrorism" (Fort Leavenworth, KS: US Army Training and Doctrine Command); at <http://www.fas.org/irp/threat/terrorism/sup2.pdf>

Delio, Michelle (2002), "Find the Cost of (Virus) Freedom," Wired News (14 January); at <http://www.wired.com/news/infostructure/0,49681-1.html?tw=wn_story_page_next1>

Denning, Dorothy (2000), "Cyberterrorism," Testimony before the Special Oversight Panel on Terrorism, Committee on Armed Services, US House of Representatives (23 May); at <http://www.cs.georgetown.edu/~denning/infosec/cyberterror.html>

Denning, Dorothy (2002), "Is Cyber Terror Next?" in *Understanding September 11*, eds. Craig Calhoun, Paul Price and Ashley Timmer (New York: Social Science Research Council/New Press); at <http://www.ssrc.org/sept11/essays/denning.htm>

Gansler, Jacques (2003), "Next Steps in Defense Restructuring," *Issues in Science and Technology* 19: 4 (Summer).

Gellman, Barton (2002), "Cyber-Attacks by Al Qaeda Feared," *The Washington Post* (27 June).

Greenemeier, Larry (2005), "New Cybersecurity Center to Warn Law Enforcement of Critical Infrastructure Attacks," *InformationWeek* (24 August); at <http://informationweek.com/story/showArticle.jhtml?articleID=170000319>

Gruen, Madeleine (2006), "Terrorist Indoctrination and Radicalization on the Internet," in *Terrorism and Counterterrorism*, eds. Russell D. Howard and Reid L. Sawyer (Dubuque, IA: McGraw-Hill Publishers).

Gunaratna, Rohan (2005), "Responding to the Post 9/11 Structural and Operational Challenges of Global Jihad," *Connections* (Spring).

Hildreth, Stephen (2001), *Cyberwarfare*, Congressional Research Service Report for Congress, Report 30735 (Washington, DC: Library of Congress/Congressional Research Service); at <http://www.fas.org/irp/crs/terror/RL30735.pdf>

Hoffman, Bruce (2006), *Inside Terrorism* (New York: Columbia University Press).

Hoopes, Nathaniel (2005), "New Focus on Cyber-Terrorism," *The Christian Science Monitor* (16 August).

IBM Report (2006), "Surge in Criminal-Driven Cyber-attacks Anticipated in 2006" (23 January); at <http://www-03.ibm.com/press/us/en/pressrelease/19141.wss>

Ilett, Dan (2005), "U.K. Cops Want to Attack Terrorism Web Sites," CNET News.com (25 July); at <http://news.com.com/U.K.+cops+want+to+attack+terrorism+Web+sites/2100-7348_3-5803380.html>

Jones, Matthew (2006), "Cyber-crime Becoming More Organized," Reuters (15 September); at <http://www.wired.com/news/technology/internet/0,71793-0.html?tw=rss.index>

Jones, Ronald (2005), "Terrorist Beheadings: Cultural and Strategic Implications," Carlisle Papers in Security Strategy (Carlisle, PA: US Army War College); at <http://www.strategicstudiesinstitute.army.mil/pubs/display.cfm?PubID=608>

Keizer, Gregg (2006), "Cybercrime Feared 3 Times More than Physical Crime," TechWeb News (January 25); at <http://www.techweb.com/wire/security/177103798>

Kelley, Jack (2001), "Terror Groups Hide Behind Web Encryption," *USA Today* (5 February).

Kohlman, Evan (2003), "'Axis of Evil': Indicted Hamas Leader Linked to Al Qaeda Activist in Midwest," *National Review Online* (2 January); at <http://www.nationalreview.com/comment/comment-kohlmann010203.asp>

Labi, Nadya (2006), "Jihad 2.0," *The Atlantic Monthly* (July/August).

Lewis, James (December 2002), "Assessing the Risks of Cyber-terrorism, Cyber War and Other Cyber Threats" (Washington, DC: Center for Strategic and International Studies); at <http://www.securitymanagement.com/library/CSIS_Cyberthreat0303.pdf>

"The List: The Future of the Insurgency," *Foreign Policy* (June 2006); at <http://www.foreignpolicy.com/story/cms.php?story_id=3517>

Lyman, Jay (2002), "In Search of the World's Costliest Computer Virus," Newsfactor.com (21 February); at <http://www.newsfactor.com/perl/story/16407.html>

Millser, Jason (2003), "IT Budget Request Focuses on Homeland Defense, Cybersecurity," Government Computer News (20 January); at <http://www.gcn.com/online/vol1_no1/20903-1.html>

NewsHour with Jim Lehrer (2005), "Online Terrorism," discussion with Neil Doyle and Paul Davies (2 August); at <http://www.pbs.org/newshour/bb/terrorism/july-dec05/online_8-02.html>

Pappalardo, Denise and Messmer, Ellen (2005), "Extortion via DDoS on the Rise," Network World (16 May); at <http://www.networkworld.com/news/2005/051605-ddos-extortion.html>

Pethia, Richard (2002), "Information Technology—Essential But Vulnerable: Internet Security Trends," Testimony before the House Committee on Government Reform, Subcommittee on Government Efficiency, Financial Management, and Intergovernmental Relations, US House of Representatives (19 November); at <http://www.cert.org/congressional_testimony/pethia-11-02/Pethia_testimony_11-19-02.html>

Pethia, Richard (2003), "Cyber Security—Growing Risk from Growing Vulnerability," Testimony before the House Select Committee on Homeland Security, Subcommittee on Cybersecurity, Science, and Research and Development hearings on "Overview of the Cyber Problem: A Nation Dependent and Dealing with Risk" (25 June); at <http://www.cert.org/congressional_testimony/Pethia_testimony_06-25-03.html>

Robbins, James (2002), "The Jihad Online: Mouse Clicking Your Way to Martyrdom," *National Review Online* (30 June); at <http://www.nationalreview.com/robbins/robbins073002.asp>

Schmid, Alex (2004), "Terrorism as Psychological Warfare," *Democracy and Security* 1: 2.

Stannard, Matthew (2004), "Beheading Video Seen as War Tactic," *San Francisco Chronicle* (13 May).

Thomas, Timothy (2003), "Al Qaeda and the Internet: The Danger of 'Cyberplanning,'" *Parameters* (Spring); at <http://carlisle-www.army.mil/usawc/Parameters/03spring/thomas.htm>

Walker, Duncan (2004), "Who Watches Murder Videos?" BBC News Online Magazine
    (12 October); at <http://news.bbc.co.uk/2/hi/uk_news/magazine/3733996.stm>
Weiss, Eric (2006), "Consultant Breached FBI's Computers," *The Washington Post*
    (6 July).
Wilson, Clay (2005), *Computer Attack and Cyber-terrorism: Vulnerabilities and
    Policy Issues for Congress*, Congressional Research Service Report for Congress,
    Report 32114 (Washington, DC: Library of Congress/Congressional Research
    Service); at <http://www.fas.org/sgp/crs/terror/RL32114.pdf>
Wilson, Clay (2006), "Terrorist Capabilities for Cyber-attack," in *International CIIP
    Handbook 2006*, Vol. 2, eds. Myriam Dunn and Victor Mauer (Zurich: Center for
    Security Studies).

Chapter 8

Preventing Terrorist Best Practices from Going Mass Market: A Case Study of Suicide Attacks "Crossing the Chasm"

Rockford Weitz and Stacy Reiter Neal[1]

Introduction

Over the last 15 years, Al Qaeda has leveraged various aspects of globalization, particularly communication technologies, to become the preeminent terrorist threat to the United States and its allies. The events of 11 September 2001 established Al Qaeda as the world's premier Islamist terrorist organization—a leadership role accompanied by considerable "pride of place" benefits that help attract new personnel, secure financial backing, and build legitimacy and societal support for the organization. Simultaneously, however, Al Qaeda's success has subjected it to enormous pressure from the United States and the international community, which has forced it to adapt to a new set of challenges, including the loss of its sanctuary in Afghanistan.

Authors like Peter Bergen, John Arquilla, and David Ronfeldt believe that Al Qaeda anticipated this pressure and, prior to 9/11, began to redirect its efforts toward galvanizing Islamic support for reestablishing the Caliphate across the greater Muslim world (see Bergen, 2001; Arquilla and Ronfeldt, 1996). These writers posit that Al Qaeda (and particularly Osama bin Laden, given his international business background) has leveraged many of the latest business principles, enabled by the globalization of technology, to support this redirection. Consequently, Al Qaeda has become a lethal amalgamation of multiple organizations that, although independent and maintaining unique and often regional agendas, view the United States and its allies as a common enemy and share a common interest in cooperating to limit US influence throughout the world. Al Qaeda in this sense constitutes a global network that is able to take advantage of the opportunities that such an organizational structure offers.

To realize its full potential, a network-based terrorist organization must develop the capability to identify potential new technologies, weapons, or know-how successfully employed by individual terrorist nodes; and evaluate them for wider use and exploitation by other terrorist nodes across its network. The adoption of

1   The authors wish to thank the Jebsen Center for Counter-Terrorism Studies at the Fletcher School of Law and Diplomacy, Tufts University for supporting the creation of this chapter. The authors also wish to thank Assaf Moghadam for his assistance in researching and editing this chapter. The work greatly benefited from his knowledge and expertise. The authors remain responsible for any errors contained herein.

best practices—from stolen shoulder-fired missiles to innovative money laundering techniques—provides Al Qaeda with synergistic benefits and adds new tools to its toolbox. A successful transfer of these practices from regional terrorist nodes to other elements within the network will result in a multiplier effect, increasing the overall threat posed by the wider network.

Contagion theory supports the idea that "terrorist groups learn from each other, and successful operations in one country are imitated by groups elsewhere" (Lia and Skjolberg, 2004, 18). Moving beyond imitation, network-based terrorist organizations try to foster the diffusion of best practices and technologies across their affiliated terrorist groups. This process shares many characteristics with technology adoption patterns among business customers of high-technology companies, a commonality that could shed new light on how technology adoption influences patterns of terrorism.

Theories developed by high-tech companies and venture capitalists posit that the technology adoption process typically originates among a select group of tech-savvy clients, then proceeds to a slightly larger group of technology-focused customers and, for certain technology products, reaches a tipping point at which the technology extends to the wider mass market. Terrorist networks such as Al Qaeda exhibit a similar process when they share best practices among their affiliated terrorist groups. Applying the analytical tools that high-tech companies use to understand technology adoption could benefit counter-terrorism professionals worldwide.

Using the adoption and spread of suicide attacks as a case study, this chapter aims to illustrate how the theory of technology adoption by business customers utilized by high-tech companies provides a helpful tool for analyzing the proliferation of best practices by networks of affiliated terrorist organizations. To better understand the potential for Al Qaeda to encourage the diffusion of effective terrorist techniques across its network, and to identify methods counter-terrorism professionals might use to slow down the adoption process, this chapter will:

1. Provide a framework for understanding how high-tech companies encourage the mass-market adoption of new technologies by their business customers

2. Use that framework to evaluate how Hezbollah, the Liberation Tigers of Tamil Eelam (LTTE), Hamas, and Al Qaeda invented or adopted the "technology" of suicide attacks, and how Al Qaeda might accelerate its further adoption

3. Identify ways for counter-terrorism professionals to inhibit the further adoption not only of suicide attacks, but other terrorist best practices that threaten global stability, such as improvised explosive devices.

Within the context of global jihad and "netwar"—a state of conflict in which antagonists are loosely affiliated, leaderless networks rather than rigidly hierarchical organizations—terrorist entities such as Al Qaeda may consider encouraging the mass-market adoption of best practices as an important step toward accomplishing their core missions. By spreading effective terrorist techniques across its network, Al Qaeda's ability to wage asymmetric warfare against the United States and other targets around the world could grow exponentially, thus dramatically increasing global terrorist capabilities. This chapter will use technology adoption theory to shed light on the proliferation of best practices by network-based terrorist organizations.

"Crossing the Chasm" to the Mass Market[2]

In the mid-1990s, the "Technology Adoption Life Cycle" gained considerable attention among executives in the high-tech industry and the venture capitalists who largely funded new start-up businesses within the industry. The theory builds upon the simple idea that most people and organizations do not like change. Individuals perceive change as inconvenient, complicated, often costly and, depending upon the function of the product, perhaps even dangerous. Business organizations like change even less than individuals do.

A business organization's technology orientation relates directly to its willingness to invest in technology and, more importantly, to make the behavioral changes required to fully leverage a new technology for its intended purpose. Figure 8.1 illustrates the Technology Adoption Life Cycle (Moore, 1999, 12).

Figure 8.1 Technology Adoption Life Cycle

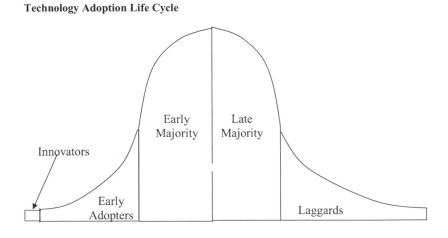

In the Technology Adoption Life Cycle, the market segments demonstrate an increasing skepticism of new technologies as one moves from left to right along the curve. Innovators are technology enthusiasts. They tend to be smaller organizations, led by well-educated and forward-thinking management. Although

---

2   This term was coined by Geoffrey Moore; see Moore, 1999.

they represent a negligible portion of the potential market, innovators are willing to help "debug" a technology, so their input is invaluable to developers (Moore, 1999, 12).

Early adopters are visionary organizations that find profitable applications for new technologies and develop business models that support further adoption. Although they also buy technologies in early stages of development, they do so seeking a competitive advantage and are adept at evaluating technologies and then leveraging them in new and unique ways. They represent a very small but essential part of the potential market (Moore, 1999, 12).

Early majority organizations are pragmatists. Although they are somewhat comfortable with technology, practicality drives their adoption behavior. They expect new products to be fully "debugged," and often require a business case or application before purchasing a new technology. Although they are a difficult group to penetrate, in most cases they represent a full third of the entire market potential (Moore, 1999, 12–13).

Late majority organizations are conservative. They share the early majority's concerns but, unlike the early majority, they are uncomfortable with technology. This means that the late majority will wait until a technology becomes standard, support infrastructure is available, and large, well-established firms are using the technology (Moore, 1999, 13).

Laggards are technology skeptics. They will generally only accept "new" technology if it is buried deep within an existing product. By this stage, the innovators and early adopters have moved on and are busy working a new technology through the cycle (Moore, 1999, 13).

Although the Technology Adoption Life Cycle seems to indicate that new technologies would naturally progress along the curve, many good new technologies with vast amounts of venture capital supporting them never progress through the full life cycle; in fact, most new technologies never even make it to the early majority segment. The difficulty of technology adoption raises two important caveats to the Technology Adoption Life Cycle: the natural "gaps" between all segments, and the "chasm" that often separates early adopters from the early majority, which is considered by the high-tech industry to be the most important gap to cross (Moore, 1999, 16). "Crossing the chasm" refers to technologies that make the transition from early adopters to the early majority, eventually leading to mass-market adoption. Figure 8.2 illustrates the chasm and the other gaps (Moore, 1999, 17).

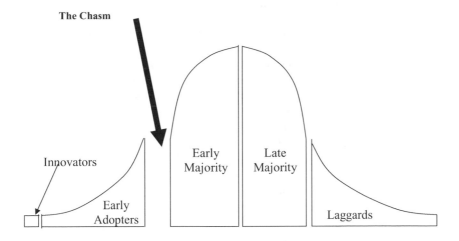

Figure 8.2 The chasm

The chasm is relevant to this analysis because it is where many "good" technologies experience early deaths—not because they are not revolutionary or effective, but because, without valid customer references, no technology can proceed from one segment to the next. Moore's research indicates that when early majority organizations will not naturally accept early adopter references, forward progress can be halted and momentum lost. Then the new technology and the company promoting it become increasingly vulnerable to negative market forces, including intense competition, financial constraints, decreased brand recognition, and even bankruptcy (Moore, 1999, 19–23).

In analyzing the adoption of new technologies, weapons, and know-how by disparate terrorist organizations, the gaps are even greater than those presented above. Regional terrorist organizations are often isolated from groups in other parts of the world and, due to their operational tempo, only the most committed and professional terrorists devote much time to studying the tactics of other organizations. Even then, security considerations prevent the few committed professional terrorists from communicating with other terrorist organizations to share lessons learned without risking detection by counter-terrorism professionals. The linguistic, cultural, and religious divisions within the terrorist world further inhibit the cross-pollination of complex concepts and approaches across terrorist groups.

Some new technologies, weapons, and know-how achieve wide-scale adoption, but many more do not. Suicide attacks are one terrorist technique that has achieved a significant level of adoption in some parts of the world. As will be discussed below, this *modus operandi* provides a case study of the adoption process of best practices across different terrorist organizations.

Technology Adoption of Suicide Attacks

Al Qaeda could dramatically increase the threat it poses to global security if it addressed the natural gaps and challenges inherent in its own terrorist "market" and focused its resources on ensuring that new, deadly technologies cross the chasm and achieve mass-market adoption throughout its terrorist network. This section uses suicide attacks as a case study to explore the applicability of the Technology Adoption Life Cycle to the adoption of best practices by network-based terrorist organizations. In particular, it traces the evolution of suicide attacks among Hezbollah, the Liberation Tigers of Tamil Eelam (LTTE), Hamas, and Al Qaeda, and assesses the risk of Al Qaeda spreading this tactic across its network of affiliated terrorist groups.

Suicide attacks represent a flexible and valuable tactic in the terrorist arsenal. Although terrorist groups use suicide bombings to engage in asymmetric warfare against military targets, civilian targets tend to be even more attractive because they tend to be much "softer" and easier to attack. As Bruce Hoffman has explained, "The fundamental characteristics of suicide bombing, and its strong attraction for the terrorist organizations behind it, are universal: suicide bombings are inexpensive and effective" (Hoffman, 2006, 337).

The modern era of suicide bombing began with the attack on the US Marine barracks in Beirut in 1983 (Cronin, 2003b, 4). Hezbollah, the Islamist terrorist organization responsible for this attack, and later the LTTE in Sri Lanka, were generally considered to be the leading practitioners of suicide attacks from 1983 through the mid-1990s. In the last ten years, successful suicide bombing campaigns by Hamas have elevated it into these ranks as well. To better understand how terrorist best practices can proliferate across different groups, this section will explore these three organizations, as well as the likelihood of Al Qaeda diffusing this tactic among its affiliates.

Hezbollah

Founded in 1982, Hezbollah is a Shi'ite terrorist group with its primary base of operations in Lebanon (see MIPT, 2006b). Historically supported by Syria and Iran, Hezbollah has sought the destruction of Israel and the elimination of US influence in the Middle East. Hezbollah attained international notoriety in April 1983 with its suicide bombing of the US embassy in Beirut, which killed 63 people, including 17 Americans.[3] This event helped to transform the typical terrorist operational model away from hijackings and hostage negotiations, such as the Palestinian airplane hijackings in the 1970s (Kitfield, 2002).

Just six months later, in October 1983, Hezbollah struck again with simultaneous suicide car bomb attacks on the US Marine barracks and the French paratrooper barracks in Beirut, killing 241 US servicemen and 58 French paratroopers. The sheer

---

3   It is important to remember the context within which this attack took place. At the time, the size of the bomb and the resulting loss of life made this the single greatest terrorist attack on a US target to date.

scale of the physical destruction—and the graphic video footage of that devastation, displayed to an unsuspecting American public—dealt a significant blow to US efforts to stabilize Lebanon, and precipitated the evacuation of the Marines shortly thereafter.

Following these bombings against US and French targets, most suicide attacks in Lebanon were directed at the Israel Defense Forces and their allies, the South Lebanon Army. Hezbollah perpetrated at least 13 confirmed suicide attacks between 1983 and 2000. The actual number of Hezbollah-executed suicide operations, however, is probably higher; during that period, 14 unclaimed suicide attacks were staged, the majority likely carried out by Hezbollah (Shay, 2004, 42).[4] Hezbollah's innovative tactic was soon emulated by a number of secular terrorist organizations within Lebanon, which began to adopt suicide tactics in an effort to outdo Hezbollah (Kramer, 1998, 148). Between 1985 and 1987, these secular organizations—many of them pro-Syrian—managed to surpass Hezbollah in their use of suicide attacks.

Hezbollah's creative genius in systematically devising and implementing suicide attacks as a simple and effective weapon significantly altered US Middle East policy in less than eight months. This conceptual advance constituted a significant step forward in asymmetric warfare. Irrespective of Hezbollah's other operational successes, the adoption of the particular terrorist "technology" of suicide attacks may prove to be the organization's greatest contribution to fomenting regional instability.

Overall, Hezbollah's suicide attacks in Lebanon succeeded as a tactic by substantially raising the costs of maintaining a foreign military presence, particularly for France and the United States, as suicide attacks had their clearest success against these two powers, constituting the main factor leading to the withdrawal of their troops. Suicide attacks may also have contributed to Israel's withdrawal from Lebanon to its self-proclaimed "security zone."

In terms of the Technology Adoption Life Cycle, Hezbollah acted as the innovator of modern suicide attacks. It illustrated suicide bombing's effectiveness in wounding both the occupying forces and the public's sense of security. Hezbollah's suicide attacks also marked the beginning of an era in which non-state actors could use asymmetric tactics to undermine the authority and military capability of nation-states.

The Liberation Tigers of Tamil Eelam

The Liberation Tigers of Tamil Eelam grew out of a secular movement in Sri Lanka in the 1970s to provide the Tamil Hindu minority with a stronger political voice in the predominantly Sinhalese Buddhist country (see MIPT, 2006c). Unlike the religiously motivated Hezbollah, the LTTE's mission revolves around nationalist goals, thus demonstrating the utility of suicide attacks across many different causes and cultures.

---

4   Robert Pape's data cite over 40 suicide attacks by Hezbollah. However, it appears that many suicide attacks included in Pape's database that he cites as executed by Hezbollah were actually carried out by other organizations. See Pape, 2005.

If Hezbollah provided the conceptual leap to using suicide attacks, then the LTTE can be credited with a number of advances that operationalized the concept. As Rohan Gunaratna stated in *The New York Times*: "Of all the suicide-capable terrorist groups we have studied, they are the most ruthless, the most disciplined" (quoted in Waldman, 2003). Indeed, until the turn of the twenty-first century, the LTTE was one of the most dominant and effective groups to employ this tactic. Between 1987 and 2001, the LTTE planned and executed an estimated 200 suicide attacks—a number that, until 2003, accounted for more suicide attacks than those by all other organizations combined.[5]

The Black Tigers (the LTTE's elite suicide squad) and the Sea Tigers (the Black Tigers' maritime counterparts) are LTTE segments that have carried out the majority of suicide attacks since the group first adopted the tactic in May 1987. The LTTE specifically recruits and trains individuals for suicide missions; their preparations include intense physical and psychological training.

Over the years, the Black Tigers have made significant advances in the technical aspects of suicide attacks, including the development of innovative explosives belts and concealment methods that enable the squad to approach their targets and detonate bombs at extremely close range. One such example is the 1991 assassination of former Indian Prime Minister Rajiv Gandhi by a member of the "Birds of Freedom," the Black Tigers' female suicide squad. Outfitted with a specialized explosive belt around her waist, the suicide bomber was seen on videotape moving through a crowd surrounding Gandhi and leaning forward as if in deference when the bomb was remotely detonated, killing Gandhi instantly (Dalrymple, 1991).

The LTTE innovated in other ways as well, perfecting seaborne suicide attacks and, consequently, destroying one-third of the Sri Lankan Navy's vessels. By strategically targeting suicide attacks against Sri Lankan political, military, and economic leaders, the LTTE decimated the leadership of the country and undermined its ability to properly function or respond effectively to the ongoing security threat (Waldman, 2003).

The degree to which the Black Tigers have elevated the concept of suicide attacks within both the organization itself and the wider Tamil community represents one of the LTTE's most unsettling advances. The Tamil community has immortalized the man known as Captain Miller, who emerged as the first LTTE suicide bomber in his 1987 attack against an army camp, which killed 40 soldiers (Jayasinghe, 2006). Each year on July 5—the anniversary of Miller's attack—communities with an LTTE presence celebrate "Black Tiger Day" to commemorate the more than 260 Black Tigers who have sacrificed themselves in the last 15 years (Jayasinghe, 2006). Orphanages have been named after other "successful" Black Tigers.

Today, the LTTE is recognized as representing the political leadership of the Tamil liberationists, and has agreed to a cease-fire with the Sri Lankan government that grants it de facto authority within much of Sri Lanka's Jaffna province. LTTE leader Velupillai Prabhakaran, who drove the adoption of suicide attacks by the Black Tigers squad, has achieved many of the LTTE's goals by employing suicide

---

5   See Hoffman and McCormick, 2004, 256. There are no precise data on the number of attacks perpetrated by the LTTE. For a discussion, see 275, note 52.

tactics over the last 15 years (Cronin, 2003b, 5). In the Technology Adoption Life Cycle, the LTTE played the role of an early adopter because it implemented many technical advances in suicide bombing and encouraged wider societal acceptance of the practice within the Tamil community.

Hamas

Sheikh Ahmed Yassin founded Hamas, a group whose leaders and ideology were derived from those of its predecessor, the Palestinian Muslim Brotherhood (see MIPT, 2006d). Since its early days, Hamas focused on providing social services to Palestinians in the occupied territories and filled a void left when the Palestine Liberation Organization (PLO) was forced to relocate to Lebanon and then to Tunis. Increasingly disillusioned with the Arab–Israeli peace process and the PLO leadership, Hamas published its charter in 1988, which declared its intent to establish an Islamic state for Palestinians, destroy Israel, and supplant the secular PLO in the process (ICT, 2006).

A crucial development for Hamas came in 1992, when Israel expelled approximately 450 Islamist activists, including many Hamas members, to Lebanon, where they reportedly received training from Hezbollah at camps in the Bekaa Valley. In addition to proving that Sunni and Shi'ite Muslims could work together, this training appears to have resulted in a dramatic increase in their level of operational effectiveness during the second *Intifada*, where the ratio of Palestinians to Israelis killed dropped from 25:1 during the first *Intifada* to 3:1 (Kitfield, 2002).

Through the 1990s and the first few years of the twenty-first century, Hamas utilized suicide bombings systematically against Israel. Hamas' focus on suicide attacks made three significant contributions that will likely accelerate the adoption rate of this terrorist tactic throughout the world. First, by deploying waves of suicide bombers in Israel, Hamas has undeniably forced itself into the political arena as a power to be reckoned with in the Arab–Israeli conflict. In that context, the successful use of suicide attacks by Hamas helped derail peace negotiations between Israel and the PLO, while subverting the will of the international community, which overwhelmingly supported the peace process. Suicide attacks have given Hamas political significance, and have provided much of its newfound momentum.

Second, Hamas has cultivated widespread support for and acceptance of suicide attacks from within the communities that provide the bombers. Hamas provides an elaborate array of social services and infrastructure to the Palestinian people, including mosques, orphanages, and schools. It uses these social services to identify and recruit fighters and to provide logistical support for its suicide operations within the territories (see Levitt, 2006). Hamas' success in striking Israelis began to resonate with Palestinians, particularly in the occupied territories. The suicide attacks were so successful both in killing Israelis and in striking terror into the hearts of the wider Israeli public that they became a source of pride for many Palestinians. Ramadan Bitta, the Jenin district governor, said in reference to Jenin's reputation as a suicide bomber factory, "It is something people have begun to take pride in. We are not second to Nablus or Gaza in struggle" (quoted in Williams, 2001).

Suicide attacks have also helped Hamas gain additional support from the Palestinian people at the expense of the PLO (Bloom, 2004). While the PLO was directly associated with the failing peace talks, and began to be characterized by its evident inability to influence Israeli policies, many Palestinians viewed Hamas as a dedicated and feared enemy of Israel—a threat the vaunted Israel Defense Forces struggled to address. In reference to trainee motivation, a trainer of suicide bombers for Islamic Jihad, another Palestinian terrorist organization, said, "The competition is clear and the people are the judge. ... If the PLO's way worked, [the Palestinian people] would stay with them. But [the Palestinian people] are coming to us" (quoted in Williams, 2001).

The power of its image among the Palestinian people supports Hamas' third contribution to the potential adoption of suicide attacks around the world. Unlike the LTTE's relatively regional impact, Hamas has used suicide attacks to great effect on what is perhaps the world's most visible geopolitical stage—the key flashpoint in the volatile Middle East. Hamas attacks and their impact are reported frequently by the major Western media outlets, with vivid videos of the victims, heated reactions from Israeli leaders, and direct condemnation by the President of the United States. The media attention, and the power implied by it, has transformed Hamas into a global player. The role of suicide attacks in increasing Hamas' notoriety will not be lost on marginalized groups around the world that are seeking a means through which to gain visibility for their causes. Finally, Hamas' 2006 victory over Fatah in the Palestinian parliamentary elections indicates the level of success Hamas has achieved in conditioning its constituency to accept the use of its terrorist tactics.

In terms of the Technology Adoption Life Cycle, Hamas constitutes either another early adopter or part of an emerging early majority. In the latter case, suicide attacks have "crossed the chasm" to the mass market, and will start to become a more prevalent tactic of terrorist organizations around the world.

Al Qaeda

Al Qaeda has its own record of successful suicide attacks, including the bombings of two US embassies in East Africa in 1998, the *USS Cole* attack in Yemen in 2000, and the events of 11 September 2001. These complex attacks against multiple targets were of such symbolic importance that Al Qaeda derived immeasurable value in terms of global attention. Two of these attacks utilized the simultaneous targeting of disparate targets, which has become a hallmark of Al Qaeda and is eerily reminiscent of the simultaneous Hezbollah bombings against US Marines and French paratroopers in Beirut.[6]

Bruce Hoffman refers to these Al Qaeda suicide attacks as their "spectaculars," and the group's ability to carry them out drives US policy makers to place a high premium on combating Al Qaeda (Hoffman, 2004). The US security community hopes that denial of sanctuary to Al Qaeda through the war in Afghanistan, combined

---

    6   Al Qaeda operatives involved in the 1998 attacks on US embassies in Africa testified about meetings between bin Laden and Imad Fayez Mugniyah, the suspected head of Hezbollah's "security apparatus." See Kitfield, 2002.

with the arrest and/or killing of the senior Al Qaeda leadership, will significantly undermine the network's effectiveness.

A 2003 Congressional Research Service report entitled *Al Qaeda after the Iraq Conflict* posed the question of "whether Al Qaeda can launch additional major attacks of strategic impact, or whether the organization is now largely relegated to low-level tactical attacks" (Cronin, 2003a). This question fails to consider Al Qaeda's likely intent to move toward a more network-based organizational model. As noted by Bergen, Arquilla, and Ronfeldt, Al Qaeda started morphing into a more network-based organization prior to the attacks of 9/11. With an estimated 20,000 to 50,000 supporters trained in Al Qaeda camps in Afghanistan and now distributed across more than 65 countries, Al Qaeda is arguably well-positioned to make this transition (see MIPT, 2006a).

Hoffman has argued that two distinct but complementary missions drive Al Qaeda today. On one hand, Al Qaeda seeks to continue the "spectacular" attacks that provide it with legitimacy and pride of place among Islamist terrorist organizations. On the other hand, Al Qaeda is expanding its role as a "venture capitalist" by "soliciting ideas from below, encouraging creative approaches, and funding proposals he [bin Laden] finds promising" (Hoffman, 2003, 26–7).

To manage this dual mission, Hoffman has identified four types of personnel within the Al Qaeda network (Hoffman, 2003):

1. *Professional cadres*: The most dedicated and highly trained members of Al Qaeda. These fighters are responsible for the "spectaculars." Hoffman provides Mohammed Atta as an example.

2. *Trained amateurs*: These fighters likely come from other terrorist organizations and are well trained, but not to the same degree as the professional cadres. Hoffman cites Ahmed Ressam, who was arrested in December 1999 attempting to cross the US–Canada border with explosives in his car to attack the Los Angeles airport.

3. *Local walk-ins*: These potential fighters have local agendas and ambitions, but seek the venture financing Hoffman mentions. They see some synergy between their goals and Al Qaeda's objectives. Their levels of training vary widely, but some may be quite professional. If Al Qaeda's reputation grows, this group will increase in number.

4. *Like-minded guerrillas and terrorists*: This level consists of insurgent or terrorist groups with historical ties to bin Laden, some of whose members have received training in Afghanistan or elsewhere. These groups represent nodes in the Al Qaeda network. They have operations in places as diverse as the Philippines, Indonesia, Kashmir, Uzbekistan, Chechnya, and Bosnia.

Applying the Technology Adoption Life Cycle to its use of suicide attacks, Al Qaeda's network of terrorist groups may constitute an emerging early majority adopting this terrorist tactic. If so, suicide attacks have "crossed the chasm" to the mass market, and will continue to proliferate among Al Qaeda-linked organizations. By helping the technology of suicide bombing cross the chasm, mass-market adoption across the Al Qaeda network could result in thousands of simple, efficient, but deadly suicide attacks around the world. Different groups within Al Qaeda's network can be viewed as innovators, early adopters, early majority, and late majority segments. Using marketing tools to assess Al Qaeda's potential helps frame its strategies and capabilities in a new way.

To follow the Technology Adoption Life Cycle, Al Qaeda will have to decide which terrorist nodes to develop next. The prioritization process has many inputs, including the availability of a suitable professional cadre, and security concerns regarding the ability of the professional cadre to enter certain countries to engage various terrorist nodes. Al Qaeda will also need to assess each terrorist node's leadership, capabilities, and goals, and the likely success of a suicide bombing campaign against the terrorist group's targets.

Conclusions and Recommendations

The Technology Adoption Life Cycle provides another way to understand the challenges and opportunities faced by Al Qaeda as it tries to encourage the proliferation of best practices across its network of affiliated terrorist groups. It builds upon contagion theory and applies analytical techniques from the high-technology industry to shed new light on how network-based terrorist organizations share knowledge across their constituent nodes. Most importantly, the Technology Adoption Life Cycle—and the case study of suicide attacks progressing through that cycle—illustrates the importance of preventing terrorist tactics from crossing the chasm to extend to the mass market.

This chapter aims to encourage the counter-terrorism community to engage the high-tech industry to seek new ways to prevent terrorist organizations from making this transition. For example, the Technology Adoption Life Cycle, when applied to the case of suicide attacks, illustrates that counter-terrorism professionals should target the professional cadre of highly trained terrorists, because eliminating them has a disproportionate effect in curbing the proliferation of best practices among affiliated terrorist groups. Limiting the impact of these "innovators" will prevent the adoption of effective tactics by other terrorist nodes in the network, and will halt the natural progression of the Technology Adoption Life Cycle.

Al Qaeda faces immense challenges in moving best practices along the Technology Adoption Life Cycle. Security surveillance will inhibit Al Qaeda's ability to interact with its terrorist nodes. Cultural, linguistic, and religious differences among Al Qaeda's growing network of terrorists will also impede the spread of best practices. However, if Al Qaeda can gain crucial early successes, and identify some innovators and early adopters among its terrorist nodes to help drive this adoption curve, the resulting momentum may become irreversible.

Suicide attacks provide a dramatic example of a terrorist tactic that has proceeded along the Technology Adoption Life Cycle. Similarly, the improvised explosive device (IED) represents another possible terrorist technique that could cross the chasm and go mass market. In fact, the IED may have already made this leap; according to Norwegian defense researchers, "[r]ecent investigations into the use of IEDs in cars by Islamist groups suggest 'a global bomb-making network,' as the same designs for car bombs have been found at terrorist attack sites in Africa, the Middle East, and Asia" (Lia and Skjolberg, 2004, 18).

In addition to asymmetric warfare tactics, Al Qaeda has developed other, non-violent technologies that could be replicated and used to strengthen terrorist organizations. For example, Douglas Farah highlights Al Qaeda's development of a new money laundering technique that establishes partnerships with leaders in weak, poorly governed states, such as Liberia's Charles Taylor, and leverages the unique black market diamond trade that takes place in Liberia and Sierra Leone (see Farah, 2004). Money laundering is an important resource for any terrorist organization requiring significant funds to purchase weapons and build social infrastructure to engender community support. The innovation of this new money laundering technique and other advances in material support strategies present additional sources of terrorist know-how that could be diffused among Al Qaeda's network of terrorist organizations.

The ability to recognize this adoption process, and to then disrupt and inhibit further adoption, will be of strategic importance to the US in the future, as effective terrorist tactics, such as suicide attacks, either fail to progress and fall into the chasm or, more ominously, receive wider adoption throughout Al Qaeda's growing global terrorist network. The following recommendations are offered to help counter-terrorism professionals use the Technology Adoption Life Cycle to predict, prevent, and preempt the activities of Al Qaeda and other network-based terrorist organizations.

Prediction

- Use the Technology Adoption Life Cycle to establish a better understanding of how Al Qaeda and other network-based terrorist groups have the potential to accelerate the adoption of effective terrorist tactics throughout their networks.
- Map Al Qaeda's network to identify those nodes that consistently act as innovators and early adopters. Focus efforts on the early identification and eradication of these particular groups, as their efforts represent a key catalyst to the adoption of best practices across the wider Al Qaeda network.

Prevention

- Once members of the professional cadre have been identified and monitored, target them aggressively, as they are critical players for transmitting best practices among the various nodes composing terrorist networks, and are difficult for network-based terrorist organizations to replace.
- Focus regional counter-terrorism efforts on innovator and early adopter nodes, as they are catalysts, and thus pose the greatest threat to stability. By eradicating these nodes, other groups in terrorist networks may hesitate to adopt similar tactics.

Preemption

- Identify and eliminate Al Qaeda's cadre of highly trained professionals because of the crucial direct support they provide to affiliated terrorist groups in the network. As the most skilled members of Al Qaeda, the impact of their elimination will be disproportionate to their numbers.

Since it takes a network to fight a network, the recommendations above require a high level of international coordination. The risk of network-based terrorist organizations, like Al Qaeda, further adopting best practices requires counter-terrorism professionals to build networks with international partners to prevent effective terrorist tactics from "crossing the chasm" to a wider mass market. The Technology Adoption Life Cycle provides a helpful tool for understanding how successful techniques spread throughout network-based terrorist organizations, and for devising innovative responses by the counter-terrorism community to slow down such a proliferation process.

References

Arquilla, John, and Ronfeldt, David (1996), *The Advent of Netwar* (Santa Monica, CA: RAND Corporation).

Bergen, Peter L. (2001), *Holy War Inc.: Inside the Secret World of Osama bin Laden* (New York: Free Press).

Bloom, Mia M. (2004), "Palestinian Suicide Bombing: Public Support, Market Share and Outbidding," *Political Science Quarterly* 119: 1.

Cronin, Audrey Kurth (2003a), *CRS Report for Congress: Al Qaeda after the Iraq Conflict* (Washington, DC: Library of Congress/Congressional Research Service); at <http://fpc.state.gov/documents/organization/21191.pdf>

Cronin, Audrey Kurth (2003b), *CRS Report for Congress: Terrorist and Suicide Attacks* (Washington, DC: Library of Congress/Congressional Research Service); at <http://fpc.state.gov/documents/organization/24049.pdf>

Dalrymple, William (1991), "After the Gandhis: Dignity and Death with the Freedom Birds," *Independent* (London) (26 May).

Farah, Douglas (2004), *Blood From Stones: The Secret Financial Network of Terror* (New York: Broadway Books).

Hoffman, Bruce (2003), "The Leadership Secrets of Osama bin Laden: The Terrorist as CEO," *The Atlantic Monthly* 291: 3 (April 2003).

Hoffman, Bruce (2004), "Plan of Attack," *The Atlantic Monthly* 294: 1 (July/August 2004).

Hoffman, Bruce (2006), "The Logic of Suicide Terrorism," in Howard and Sawyer, eds, *Terrorism and Counter-Terrorism: Understanding the New Security Environment*, Second Edition (Dubuque, IA: McGraw-Hill).

Hoffman, Bruce and McCormick, Gordon H. (2004), "Terrorism, Signaling, and Suicide Attack," *Studies in Conflict and Terrorism* 27: 4.

International Policy Institute for Counter-Terrorism (ICT) (2006), "Hamas"; at <www.ict.org.il/inter_ter/orgdet.cfm?orgid=13>

Jayasinghe, Amal (2006), "Sri Lanka Steps Up Alert as Tigers Honour Suicide Bombers," Agence France-Presse (4 July).

Kitfield, James (2002), "The Hezbollah Model," *The National Journal* (17 May), at <http://nationaljournal.com/about/njweekly/stories/2002/0517nj1.htm>

Kramer, Martin (1998), "The Moral Logic of Hizballah," in Reich, ed., *Origins of Terrorism: Psychologies, Ideologies, Theologies, States of Mind* (Washington, DC: Woodrow Wilson Center Press).

Levitt, Matthew (2006), *Hamas: Politics, Charity, and Terrorism in the Service of Jihad* (New Haven, CT: Yale University Press).

Lia, Brynjar, with Skjolberg, Katja (2004), "Causes of Terrorism: An Expanded and Updated Review of the Literature," *Forsvarets Forsknings Institutt/Rapport-2004/04307* (Kjeller, Norway: Norwegian Defence Research Establishment); at <http://rapporter.ffi.no/rapporter/2004/04307.pdf>

MIPT Terrorism Knowledge Base (2006a), "Group Profile: Al Qaeda"; at <www.tkb.org/Group.jsp?groupID=6>

MIPT Terrorism Knowledge Base (2006b), "Group Profile: Hezbollah"; at <www.tkb.org/Group.jsp?groupID=3101>

MIPT Terrorism Knowledge Base (2006c), "Group Profile: Liberation Tigers of Tamil Eelam"; at <www.tkb.org/Group.jsp?groupID=3623>

MIPT Terrorism Knowledge Base (2006d), "Group Profile: Hamas"; at <www.tkb.org/Group.jsp?groupID=49>

Moore, Geoffrey A. (1999), *Crossing the Chasm: Marketing and Selling High-Tech Products to Mainstream Customers*, rev. ed. (New York: HarperBusiness).

Pape, Robert (2005), *Dying to Win: The Strategic Logic of Suicide Terrorism* (New York: Random House).

Shay, Shaul (2004), *The Shahids: Islam and Suicide Attacks* (New Brunswick, NJ: Transaction Publishers).

Waldman, Amy (2003), "Masters of Suicide Bombing: Tamil Guerrillas of Sri Lanka," *The New York Times* (14 January).

Williams, Daniel (2001), "Where Palestinian 'Martyrs' Are Groomed; West Bank City of Jenin Emerges as Suicide Bomb Capital," *The Washington Post* (15 August).

Chapter 9

Free Trade and Terrorism

Katherine Barbieri and Swapna Pathak

People remain divided about the consequences of international trade and globalization for peace, prosperity, and security. The divisions should be expected, since societies have always debated the wisdom of opening one's borders to outsiders, their goods, ideas, and possible influence. Despite being a champion of free trade, the United States has always regulated foreign trade for security purposes. After the terrorist attacks on Washington and New York on 11 September 2001, the United States government introduced a new series of regulations designed to enhance trade security; their goal was to address potential threats at each stage of the global supply chain. Yet, the question remains: has the US adopted the most effective trade security regime? Is the system based on faulty assumptions about the actors involved in trade security and their interests?

The Connection Between Free Trade and Terrorism

Scholars remain divided over whether the expansion of free trade will lead to a more peaceful world or whether it will increase the likelihood that state and non-state actors will engage in different manifestations of violent conflict.[1] Supporters of free trade stand on one side of the debate, describing the peaceful, prosperous, and harmonious world that results from the creation of a global economy. On the other side of the debate are the critics and protectionists, warning of the dangers of open borders, free markets, foreign influences, dependence on outsiders, and the expansion of global markets. Each side provides reasonable arguments for its respective position.[2]

In the post-9/11 world, more attention has been devoted to security concerns in all areas, including international trade. Policy makers have debated how best to balance the quest for profits and security. The controversy that erupted over the Dubai World Ports deal in early 2006 brought new life to debates about foreign influences tied to trade. The arguments presented in that situation reflect the same concerns over trade and security advanced during the Cold War and other periods.

Free trade exposes states to threats from terrorism for several broad reasons. It may provide the motivation or cause grievances that lead groups to adopt terrorist strategies. It might also provide the funds and instruments needed to wage war. Finally, the porous borders required by free trade systems might provide the opportunity for terrorists to penetrate a state and launch an attack. We focus our attention primarily

---

1   The literature on trade and conflict is too extensive to cover here. For reviews, see Mansfield and Pollins, 2001; and Schneider, Barbieri and Gleditsch, 2003.

2   See Baldwin, 1985; Spiegel, 1991; Viner, 1937; and Irwin, 1996 for summaries of economic nationalism and liberalism.

on the opportunities that the system of free trade offers to terrorists, in order to understand whether the US has gaps in its trade security regime.

Free trade facilitates the entry of both desirable and undesirable goods and services into the marketplace; by its nature, it does not discriminate. It provides a diverse set of goods and services for its buyers, and generates revenue for sellers. The expansion of markets across national borders leads to other ties between states, including increased communication. But the benefits of increased revenue and communication do not accrue solely on the side of legitimate business interests. The money earned from international trade could help support terrorists, whether it was earned through legal or illegal sales. In addition, for example, customers in the global market may be interested in purchasing weapons for waging war. Improved communication might facilitate the spread of terrorist ideology, or it could aid in recruitment, training, and the transfer of funds.

On the other hand, the goods, services, and funds that the free market provides can also be used to protect states and ports from terrorist and other threats. Free markets facilitate innovation. This can spur the creation of products and technologies needed to deal with new threats, including terrorism. For example, some of the information technology products and processes designed to aid business in conducting complex global operations could be harnessed to monitor terrorists' activities.

The United States' goals for free trade and national security often require contradictory policies. The US policy of promoting free trade requires it to lower barriers to the movement of goods, labor, capital, and technology across borders. It must develop policies that lower transaction costs, including the time it takes to move products from their point of origin to their destination and to complete the financial exchanges involved in the transaction. Trade is not simply the exchange of goods, as most people realize. Instead, it includes all the inputs that go into the creation of a product, from the first steps of raw materials production or extraction to the process of delivery to its ultimate destination. This requires considering all the actors that are involved in the making, buying, selling, packaging, marketing, and transporting of a product.

If we consider instead the proclaimed US policy of fighting a "war on terror," however, the priorities quickly shift from reducing barriers to entry to increasing these same barriers. Rather than speeding up the transaction process, the new regulations threaten to slow it down. The issue of the weight given to security considerations in business decisions will certainly differ depending upon the type of business one conducts, the importance of cross-border trade, the diversity of ports used, the relative costs of different ports, and so on. Finally, one needs to consider a given firm's position with respect to security. Is the firm in question paying for security measures, or otherwise providing security for itself? The goals of a private security firm are different from those of firms being taxed to use a port, and can influence the decisions that businesses ultimately make.

Research Approach

There have been few efforts to systematically examine the impact of expanded commerce on the frequency or ease of execution of terrorist incidents. Aside from the problem of data availability, there are other challenges involved in studying this relationship. The theoretical arguments concerning where one should focus one's attention are ambiguous—should attention be given to the connections between trade and peace, or those between trade and conflict? How one answers that question will significantly influence the conclusions one draws. One might look at global trends in trade and terrorism; one might consider whether a state's trade activities and policies affect the likelihood that the state will be either a target or producer of terrorists. Whichever strategy one adopts, data limitations pose serious problems to any research design.

It is also difficult to assess the impact of expanded commerce on terrorism, particularly trans-national terrorism. For example, trade relationships—and trade in general—might have differential effects on countries, and on groups within countries, from which a terrorist group derives support. It seems more plausible to argue that a domestic terrorist group's grievances may be tied to how the income within a society or the gains from its trade are distributed than to argue that their grudge would be against free trade *per se*. In this respect, one could make the same arguments about how trade might affect terrorist groups as one would make about any rebel group within a state.[3]

Scholars interested in examining questions about port security, compliance with trade security laws, illegal trade, terrorism, and other sensitive areas confront major hurdles that may be impossible to overcome. It is difficult to collect accurate data about illegal trade, terrorist groups, and other criminal activities. When governments compile data relevant to sensitive topics, they are unlikely to share the information with the general public, including academics lacking any connection to the intelligence community.

Competing Interests: Private versus Public Interests

The war on terror has been portrayed as a united effort on the part of all Americans to combat terrorism. There are always problems with portraying nation-states as unitary actors, but it is particularly problematic in the area of international trade relative to other foreign policies. Within the field of international and comparative political economy, there is a rich literature on the domestic determinants of trade. Scholars attempt to explain why some groups within society support free trade while others oppose it; these scholars view trade policy as the product of a highly political process, where actors with vested interests in open versus closed trade lobby to influence the degree to which the government enacts protectionist or liberal policies (for examples, see Goldstein, 1988; Grossman and Helpman, 1994; Hiscox, 2002a, 2002b; Rogowski, 1987, 1989). If one considers this literature, it becomes clear that

---

3   See Barbieri and Reuveny, 2005, for a review of trade's impact on civil war.

there are problems with the underlying assumptions of the current trade security regime.

In the case of trade security, another dimension of complexity is added by introducing agencies and actors in the national security community. Therefore, we have divisions across trade and security communities as well as within them. Compliance with any given policy will be tied to the various interests involved in foreign trade and security. In particular, compliance and enforcement will be affected by the interests of the actors involved in foreign trade, and of those who are faced with bearing direct and indirect security costs. There are clear tensions that exist between the imperatives of maximizing security and maximizing profit. A terrorist attack would harm business in general, but it is unclear that most individual businesses would consider it worthwhile to pay regular security bills for what many might believe is a low-probability event—a terrorist attack.

Most people assume that the federal government wants to maximize security, while businesses (in general) want to maximize profits. These are ideal types, with different groups (private and public) falling along a spectrum, with one end placing ultimate priority on security, and the other placing ultimate priority on profits. In addition, it is important to consider that not all governments have the same objectives. It is important to have some idea of where agencies sit along this spectrum, and to understand what responsibilities they bear in ensuring trade security. In trade and port security, much of the burden of providing security falls on the private sector, where profit maximization is the goal. This is a serious weakness in the US trade security program.

Those on the business end tend to focus on the logistics associated with moving a good or service from one place to another and lowering the transaction costs associated with it. The government, on the other hand, wishes to address any security gaps that might exist along the route that a particular product travels to its destination. It would be difficult to argue that any actor in the United States would like to see a terrorist attack (other than those supporting terrorism). Nevertheless, should such an attack occur, some firms will profit from it. These firms will include competitors of firms that offered customers flawed security solutions, who have seen their product proven superior under fire, as well as firms that have addressed a previously unidentified security threat in their preparations, whether intentionally or not.

In some respects, the same calculus applies to other actors with a stake in trade security. No one wants their port destroyed or their nation attacked, but each risk assessment will vary depending upon the actor involved, what its role is in relation to the port and the community, and how often it uses the port. Businesses must calculate the risks of a terrorist attack at a given port and determine whether it is worth paying the higher price of using one port rather than another because of the promise of higher security. Many businesses might look at the incidence of terrorist attacks on commercial vessels or US ports and conclude that the risks of a terrorist attack on a port are low.

In their overall approach to trade security, in fact, businesses may recognize that, in aggregate, the risk of a terrorist attack is extremely slight. While people tend to overestimate the likelihood of rare events, businesses conducting in-depth cost–benefit analyses are likely to conclude that profit maximization is preferred to higher security standards (Sunstein, 1994). Some scholars have even argued that government expenditures for homeland security are not worth the money, if one considers the relatively low risk of attack (Becker and Rubinstein, 2004).

One might expect large businesses, vessel owners, and terminal operators to be more risk-averse, and therefore more willing to pay high premiums for security. The problem is that paying for greater security may involve far more costs than the security fee alone. It often means paying the indirect costs associated with heightened barriers to trade that slow down business and diminish profits further. US policies have tried to change this equation by providing economic incentives to firms who voluntarily upgrade their security measures, as will be discussed below. They pay higher costs for security, but gain greater profits through participating in "fast-lane" trade. This is the type of policy that recognizes the competing interests of business and government, and attempts to reconcile them, instead of claiming that they share the same interests.

Despite the design of such a policy, one will easily see that this approach to trade security creates some rather serious security gaps. The upgraded security measures that some companies choose to pay for may not offset the time consumed by the stages of inspection that other vessels face. The key concern of business is not a terrorist attack, but faster turn-around time at customs and in port. Given most firms' priorities of cutting costs, and their tendency to view a terrorist attack as highly improbable, the majority of small businesses are unlikely to want to pay to increase security measures, or to implement security standards above and beyond federal guidelines. Large businesses and vessel owners may view the situation differently. The problem is that much of the responsibility for ensuring trade security falls on the shoulders of private security firms.

US public ports are expected to monitor the businesses operating within their domain, and to gauge the potential security threats that the port faces. All ports must meet some minimal level of security standards as outlined in federal regulations. Beyond that, ports vary in what they provide users, what they charge for it, and in how such decisions are made. It is difficult to determine whether one port is more effective than another in providing security, since data are not systematically reported. One serious problem is that ownership and control of ports and different security configurations differ by state and port.[4] The absence of a standard policy across the United States makes it difficult both to adopt standard security policies and to assess the effectiveness of those policies.

Ports as Actors

What often gets lost in most analyses of ports is the fact that the ports themselves generally have their own goals that may or may not be consistent with those of other actors in the trade and security communities. When a city or state government controls a port, its goals are generally tied to economic growth, such as attracting

---

4   For more information about variations among ports, see the American Association of Port Authorities website dealing with port security, at <http://www.aapa-ports.org/Issues/USGovRelDetail.cfm?itemnumber=1056>

business, providing jobs, generating income, and collecting tax revenues. Ports are able to transfer their operating costs to businesses that use the port. But charging high prices for port use may drive businesses to a nearby port whose usage fees are less onerous. Thus, the cost of providing security for businesses involved in trade may be lower for firms doing business at ports that have lower security standards, or by virtue of economies of scale.

When low security costs at ports are associated with lower security provisions, the potential of problems associated with security threats increases. Nevertheless, if firms are motivated by profit, they are likely to divert their transportation business to those ports that have lower costs. Some ports are introducing new regulations that include high taxes on ship containers, with the proceeds being used to heighten security measures. It is difficult to determine whether or not variations in security costs such as these surcharges on containers will lead to trade being diverted to other ports. Part of the problem in determining the effects of such policies resides in the fact that we have not had much time to witness the results of the post-9/11 security regime, which brought changes that are still being digested by many of the firms involved in international trade.

US Trade Security

Prior to 9/11

The United States, like most nations, has always regulated trade for security purposes. It has done so during times of both war and peace, involving both strategic and non-strategic goods, and in relations with both friends and adversaries. Even the World Trade Organization (WTO), whose mission is to eliminate tariff and non-tariff barriers to trade, recognizes a state's right to guard against trade that may threaten its national security. In fact, the WTO outlines a list of national safeguards that includes political, economic, and social threats to society that permit protectionist policies (see World Trade Organization, 2005).

Prior to 9/11, the main concerns of most businesses involved in international trade were maximizing efficiency and profits. Large firms engaged in significant international enterprises were concerned about security only to the extent that it affected the theft of property, including intellectual property. These businesses were also concerned with corruption and organized crime. Smaller firms were primarily interested in penetrating markets overseas and in buying low-cost goods for import. During this period, the US government took steps to expand its programs to aid firms interested in establishing export businesses. Here, the focus was not on security (with the exception of exports of defense-related and other sensitive technologies). While the federal government had some security concerns, most of them centered on smuggling, illegal trade, and capturing revenue, state and local governments were mainly concerned with economic development, increasing revenue and growth, attracting new business (and all that entails), enhancing competitiveness relative to other states, and conforming to federal regulations.

Government efforts to keep strategic goods and sensitive products out of the hands of enemy nations that might use them to wage war have existed for centuries. What we know less about, however, is the economic impact of war itself. Several scholars have examined the impact of war on trade, and find mixed results on whether or not trade declines significantly during wartime. Barbieri and Levy argue that, during nearly every war, traders are willing to cross enemy lines, and frequently place profits ahead of patriotism (Barbieri and Levy, 1999; Levy and Barbieri, 2004). There may be other reasons for engaging in such trade, including providing humanitarian assistance to those in need. The same uncertainties likely apply to the impact on trade of the war on error. The problems and challenges that beset those involved in international trade before September 2001 now seem minor in comparison with those that have emerged in the post-9/11 climate.

The US Bureau of Industry and Security (BIS) regulates with whom United States businesses trade and regulates the products that are traded. A US firm engaged in international trade is responsible for making sure that it engages in "secure trade." What this means in practical terms is that a US business thinking about buying rugs, for example, must be certain that the supplier of those rugs has no ties to terrorism. Theoretically, the firm must determine whether the goods it buys will provide money that might fund terror (for example, the rug maker might buy materials that are produced by a firm that finances terrorist groups). In the same way, a US citizen interested in exporting to a foreign state must be certain that the product being sold does not end up in enemy hands.

BIS also maintains a list of those traders for which it was unable to carry out full investigations. US exporters are supposed to check with BIS before exporting to people or firms on this so-called "Unverified List." However, other prohibitions on trade are issued by other parts of the government as well. For example, the US Department of Commerce also maintains an "Entity List," which is tied to activities related to the proliferation of weapons of mass destruction. The Treasury Department maintains a list of "Specially Designated Nationals and Blocked Persons," which is updated regularly and includes individuals and organizations that represent restricted countries or are themselves involved in terrorism or narcotics trafficking.

One might argue that the same agencies that oversaw trade security in the Cold War period would have been sufficient to address the new conditions posed by the war on terror. These groups have had experience dealing with other international threats, and are familiar with most of the players involved. BIS has been at the forefront of the United States' efforts to guarantee that businesses comply with national security goals. They have not always been successful at preventing violations to the US trade security regime, but perfection is an unrealistic expectation.

Post-9/11

The events of 9/11 initiated a number of changes in the realm of trade security, both for businesses in the United States and their trading partners abroad. The passage of the Maritime Transportation Security Act (MTSA) of 2002 (P.L. 107–295) was one of the most important changes for trade-related security issues. MTSA placed responsibility for different security tasks on several groups, with the goal of overhauling the port security system in the United States to more effectively prevent the importation of materials that could be used in terrorist attacks, particularly those used in weapons of mass destruction.

Owners of ships and port facilities were required to conduct a self-assessment of their security measures, identify the gaps, and develop a program to address those gaps. The adjustments they made to their security procedures differed depending upon their individual security assessments. Although the US Coast Guard had to approve and monitor the plan, the structure of the program placed a large share of the responsibilities on the ports themselves. If we view the port and the vessel facilities as profit maximizers, rather than security maximizers, the problem with self-assessment is clear. Admittedly, the private sector polices itself in many ways but, as we have seen, many people were quick to point to the problems of privatizing airport security. In addition, it is unclear that all actors involved in securing the port, including local law enforcement agencies, are trained and equipped to guard and defend US borders.

MTSA required ports to set up an Area Maritime Security Committee (AMSC), or else utilize a Port Security Committee or the Coast Guard's Port Security Committee to bring together federal, state, and local law enforcement agencies involved in securing the port. This included the local fire and rescue agencies, local and state crisis management and emergency response agencies, maritime industry representatives (vessel owners or shipping companies, facility owners, labor organizations), any territorial or tribal governments that may have a stake in the port, and any other port stakeholders affected by security practices.

The Coast Guard attempts to deter threats and respond to them before they reach US shores. As part of this work, it prepares National Maritime Security Initiatives, designates area Federal Maritime Security Coordinators, and establishes area maritime security. Vessel owners and operators must develop processes within their organizations and onboard their vessels that address security issues. They must also designate and provide contact information for a Company Security Officer (CSO) and a Vessel Security Officer (VSO) for each vessel, and identify how those officers can be contacted at any time.

The Customs-Trade Partnership against Terrorism (C-TPAT) is an initiative introduced by US Customs and Border Protection in collaboration with carriers, brokers, and warehouse operators to improve the security of ports. It includes guidelines to enhance maritime security and improve the performance of port facilities while mitigating the risk of loss, damage, theft, and the introduction of potentially dangerous materials into the supply chain. Many US importers and their suppliers have joined C-TPAT. The Department of Homeland Security claims that, with this "first-of-its-kind global supply chain security initiative, companies will ensure a more secure supply chain for their employees, suppliers, and customers."[5] The firms participating in C-TPAT stand to gain from having the processing of their cargos expedited, while those who refuse to join may be subject to security checks that raise the costs of trade. C-TPAT is a voluntary program that requires companies

---

5   For related information, see <http://www.customs.gov/xp/cgov/import/commercial_ enforcement/ctpat/>

to guarantee that their supplies are "secure." In addition, US Customs has offices overseas to supplement their activities in securing import shipments. C-TPAT is designed to allow customs personnel to exert greater control over the movement of goods, while encouraging the private trade community to secure its own supply lines.

Research on these issues suggests that it is easier to gain compliance from existing trading partners on security issues than it might be to expand markets to include new partners at the requisite level of security. It also suggests that the international community should do more to minimize the influence that vessel owners and third-party flags might have on minimizing responsibility for vessel security. The goal should be reducing the number of actors in the supply chain.

The Role of Business

Businesses must guarantee that their trade is secure. The individual business must identify whether it needs a license to export a particular product. It must also determine whether it may trade with a particular country, and whether it is able to trade with the particular person or firm with whom it hopes to transact business. This places a heavy burden on US firms. Small firms interested in expanding overseas are likely to have difficulty complying with the proliferation of security regulations. The same may be true of large firms with a diversified set of partners.

Firms must also determine whether their trade partners are linked to terrorism in any way. In addition, US businesses are responsible for determining whether goods will be shipped to a third party that might be tied to terrorism. The same is true of importing businesses. There are usually several other actors and organizations that are involved in any international exchange between Buyer A and Seller B. There is the vessel owner who will transport the goods; there may be intermediaries in sales, shipping, financing, and more. Banks are expected to investigate whether a company has terrorist links, but it may be difficult to determine whether the party borrowing the funds or depositing funds from an overseas firm has questionable relationships.

The problem with this approach is that it places almost all of the responsibility on the private sector. This might be reasonable if a business is a large company that participates in a good deal of international trade. If, on the other hand, there is a case of a small business that wants to take advantage of programs designed to stimulate exports, it is unlikely that the small firm will be familiar enough with the system to adequately navigate the thicket of regulations. In fact, many businesspeople seem unaware that the responsibility for ensuring that they do not do business with individuals or businesses or states involved with terrorism rests with them. If the goal is to prevent incidents of non-compliance, the government might do a better job by shifting the burden for security checks onto the federal government.

Vessel owners also play a role in the overall plan. They are responsible for providing the US Customs office with the vessel's manifest, which describes the approved cargo. The vessel itself is not expected to check on whether a particular business deal seems questionable. It simply acts as the intermediary in the process. If we consider the interests of vessel owners, several contradictions seem obvious. First, vessel owners seek to maximize their profits but, given the cost of their ships, they have an interest in maximizing security. In this respect, the vessel owner generally has more incentive to see that the businesses using its cargo space are legitimate and pose no security risk. At the same time, if a vessel is detained for closer inspection, the vessel may be able to increase its shipping rates with little addition to its operating costs.

Violations to trade security laws occur more frequently than most people realize.[6] During nearly all wars, there are some people or firms who are willing to trade with the enemy (Barbieri and Levy, 1999; Levy and Barbieri, 2004). Some large firms might be willing to take the risk and violate security laws, because the potential costs involved may be far less than the potential profits.

International Concerns

The United States' multi-layered approach also applies overseas, where it relies upon numerous governmental and private-sector actors to help provide trade security. This poses serious problems for the US strategy of ensuring trade security. The US must rely heavily on foreign governments to identify which firms, goods, parties, funds, transactions, business agreements, and so on may have links to terrorism. One should simply think about any cargo ship and the money associated with the many transactions tied to each business deal represented in the goods carried by that single ship—this is the investigative burden that the US government is counting on foreign governments to shoulder. The US relies upon overseas financial intelligence units and foreign governments to monitor finances and money laundering activities. The US strategy seems to assume that anyone who signs on to be a partner in the war on terror maintains a fundamental harmony of interests with the United States. Yet, it is not always clear which actors overseas are exerting control over which stages of the process.

The International Maritime Organization (IMO) strives to improve the safety and security of international shipping, and to prevent marine pollution from ships. As part of the United Nations, when the IMO first began operations its chief concern was to develop international treaties and other legislation concerning safety and marine pollution prevention. But this work was by and large completed by the 1970s, and since then its emphasis has been on trying to ensure that these conventions and other treaties are properly implemented by the countries that have accepted them. Since 9/11, just like many other actors around the globe, the IMO has been trying to deal with the terrorist threat to national and international security. Some of the major initiatives taken by the IMO and other agents regarding seaport security and trade are discussed below.

The International Ship and Port Facility Security (ISPS) code is the international body responsible for improving the safety and security of international shipping, and to prevent marine pollution from ships. The principal objectives of these guidelines are to strengthen maritime security and prevent and suppress acts of terrorism against shipping. The IMO updated the ISPS code after 9/11 to require port, carrier, and

---

6   Listings of violations are available through BIS.

vessel security personnel to delegate responsibility for security arrangements. The code provides a standardized, consistent framework for evaluating risk, enabling governments to offset changes in threat levels with changes in security for ships and port facilities. Functional security requirements spelled out by the ISPS code require ports to put in place security plans, security officers, and certain security equipment. The code also requires ports to monitor and control access and the activities of people and cargo, and to ensure that security communications are readily available.

The problem with the ISPS code is that there is no external authority empowered to implement it. The onus is on the contracting governments to make sure that their ports are secure; thus, it is up to individual member states to enforce the required security arrangements. The IMO hopes that "market forces and economic factors will drive compliance" (International Maritime Organization, 2006). Here it is assumed that the international community would not wish to trade with non-compliant countries out of fear for their own national security.

The Container Security Initiative (CSI), another international endeavor, was introduced in 2002 to protect container cargo from terrorist threats. In this instance, the US attempted to expand its zone of security outward, so that American borders are the last line of defense instead of the first. It is a strategic program aimed at securing what is believed to be the most vulnerable link in the global supply chain—the ocean-going shipping container. It entails inspection of high-risk containers by US Customs officials at foreign ports before they are shipped to the US. The pertinent question to raise here is whether the United States has enough manpower to deploy its officials at foreign ports. Another related question is whether the United States has a jurisdictional mandate to carry out such inspections.

In addition to IMO-initiated security measures covering ports and ships, the World Customs Organization (WCO) looks into the overall maritime security framework pertaining to cargo (see World Customs Organization, 2005). This set of institutional frameworks forms the core structure responsible for monitoring and ensuring the overall security of the global supply chain.

However, since all the initiatives and organizations mentioned above rely heavily on individual states to implement enhanced security measures to combat terrorism, the gap in the security of the global supply chain could persist because of the structure of implementation and not necessarily because of lack of will. Just as there are vested interests in the United States that could compromise national security for the sake of profits or other objectives, there are vested interests in other countries that could do the same. With no central monitoring authority and limited power for the US government to implement its strategies overseas, the security of the supply chain for US maritime trade seems muddled at best.

Conclusions

Businesses share a good deal of the burden in ensuring the security of the goods and services that are imported to and exported from the United States. One would like to believe that private firms are motivated to protect national security. However, private firms often have differing interests from the nation as a whole. The US government must recognize this if it hopes to confront issues of trade security. In addition, the federal government must recognize that different levels of government may have different priorities when it comes to balancing profit maximization and security. The further one moves from the federal level for national defense, the more priorities are likely to shift away from security maximization and toward profit maximization and economic growth. Ports must also be seen as actors, with their own interests. The lack of standardization in port ownership and control across states in the US makes it difficult to evaluate the effectiveness of particular policies to improve port security.

In evaluating the costs and benefits of these policies, government analysts should try to put themselves into the shoes of business owners. Those who run for-profit private-sector firms will make every effort to minimize their expenses, on security and otherwise. While the government assumes that its rules regarding trade security will not be violated, it should not rest secure that no firms will try to circumvent these regulations if doing so will allow it to substantially increase its profits. Violations of trade laws tied to security concerns occur with greater regularity than most assume. Given that, even in wartime, some firms are willing to conduct trade with enemy states if the profits are sufficiently high, we cannot blithely assume that firms will not pursue their financial interests as vigorously during peacetime, or during ill-defined times such as the present war on terror.

The government must recognize the differences between the average business that utilizes a port for trade activities and a private military or security firm. The latter recognizes that maximizing profits is best achieved by maximizing security. One loses business to competitors and risks profits if the security strategy fails. This is something that other businesses and even the military do not experience. Therefore, if the government wishes to rely on the private sector for trade security, the greatest hope may be found in private military firms.

In order to clarify this uncertain picture, future research must consider the ways in which the costs and duties of security are distributed. In addition to the total funds expended on security, who pays for and who provides security are equally important considerations. Current trade policies do not adequately consider the divisions that exist within society between public and private-sector actors. More needs to be done to examine the variation in security standards that exist across US ports.

In addition, more research is needed to determine ways in which the allocation of particular responsibilities to various government agencies might be coordinated to take advantage of the strengths and weaknesses of some groups over others. The tasks assigned to different groups, and the regulations that these groups adopt, must include some recognition of the variations in interests that exist within US society. The government must also recognize that actors are motivated by economic incentives and disincentives. There are obvious interests at stake when one considers the impact of security costs on profits.

References

Anderton, Charles and Carter, John (2001), "The Impact of War on Trade: An Interrupted Times-Series Study," *Journal of Peace Research* 38: 4.

Baldwin, David (1985), *Economic Statecraft* (Princeton, NJ: Princeton University Press).

Barbieri, Katherine (2002), *The Liberal Illusion: Does Trade Promote Peace?* (Ann Arbor: University of Michigan Press).

Barbieri, Katherine and Levy, Jack (1999), "Sleeping with the Enemy: The Impact of War on Trade," *Journal of Peace Research* 36: 4.

Barbieri, Katherine and Reuveny, Rafael (2005), "Economic Globalization and Civil War," *The Journal of Politics* 67: 4 (November).

Becker, Gary and Rubinstein, Yona (2004), "Fear and the Response to Terrorism: An Economic Analysis," Working Paper, University of Chicago (1 August); at <http://www.econ.ku.dk/CAM/Files/Autumn%202004/beckerrubinstein_0801.pdf>

Goldstein, Judith (1988), "Ideas, Institutions, and American Trade Policy," *International Organization* 42.

Grossman, Gene and Helpman, Elhanan (1994), "Protection for Sale," *American Economic Review* 84: 4.

Haverman, Jon, Shatz, Howard and Vilchis, Ernesto (2005), "U.S. Port Security Policy after 9/11: Overview and Evaluation," *Journal of Homeland Security and Emergency Management* 2.

Hiscox, Michael (2002a), "Class Versus Industry Cleavages: Inter-Industry Factor Mobility and the Politics of Trade," *International Organization* 55 (Winter).

Hiscox, Michael (2002b), *International Trade and Political Conflict: Commerce, Coalitions and Mobility* (Princeton, NJ: Princeton University Press).

International Maritime Organization (2006), "IMO Adopts Comprehensive Security Measure"; at <http://www.imo.org/home.asp>

Irwin, Douglas (1996), *Against the Tide: An Intellectual History of Free Trade* (Princeton, NJ: Princeton University Press).

Levy, Jack and Barbieri, Katherine (2004), "Trading with the Enemy during Wartime," *Security Studies* 13: 3.

Mansfield, Edward D. and Pollins, Brian, eds (2001), *New Perspectives on Economic Exchange and Armed Conflict* (Ann Arbor: University of Michigan Press).

Ortiz, David and Willis, Henry (2004), "Evaluating the Security of the Global Containerized Supply Chain," RAND Technical Report (Santa Monica, CA: RAND Corporation).

Rogowski, Ronald (1987), "Trade and the Variety of Democratic Institutions," *International Organization* 41: 2.

Rogowski, Ronald (1989), *Commerce and Coalitions: How Trade Affects Domestic Political Alignments* (Princeton, NJ: Princeton University Press).

Schneider, Gerald, Barbieri, Katherine and Gleditsch, Nils, eds. (2003), *Globalization and Armed Conflict* (Lanham, MD: Rowman and Littlefield).

Spiegel, Henry (1991), *The Growth of Economic Thought*, 3rd ed. (Durham, NC: Duke University Press).

Sunstein, Cass R. (1994), "Well-Being and the State," *Harvard Law Review*, 107: 6 (April), 1303–27.

Sunstein, C.R. (2003), "Terrorism and Probability Neglect," *Journal of Risk and Uncertainty* 26 (March).

Viner, Jacob (1937), *Studies in the Theory of International Trade* (New York and London: Harper and Brothers).

World Customs Organization (2005), "The WCO's Framework of Standards To Secure and Facilitate Global Trade" (24 June); at <http://www.wcoomd.org>

World Trade Organization (2005), "Understanding the WTO" (Geneva: WTO, Information and Media Relations Division); at <http://www.wto.org>

PART 3
Policies

Chapter 10

Institutionalized Responses to 9/11

Rico Carisch

Overview

By the time the 19 Al Qaeda attackers crashed jets into the World Trade Center towers and the Pentagon on 11 September 2001, the financing of international terrorism had already been on the radar screens of law enforcement and intelligence agencies across the international community for some years. Identifying the precise beginning of the international community's attempts at interdicting funds intended for terrorist groups does not really matter as much as the nature of these responses, since these responses have always—both before and after 9/11—been very politicized. As a consequence, these efforts have been sometimes ill-considered, often inconsistent, and mostly devoid of any resolve to respond not only to the security and military but also to the cultural, socio-economic, humanitarian, and historical challenges presented by the new forms of international terrorism. Certainly, the war against terrorism financing never squarely addressed the fact that the 9/11 hijackers had established regular bank accounts in Western financial institutions in several countries, even after they had already been identified as terrorist suspects by the intelligence services of several nations. As the report of the National Commission on the Terrorist Attacks upon the United States—also known as the 9/11 Commission—made abundantly clear, the tragedies of 9/11 were made possible not because the possible perpetrators remained unrecognized, but because no coordination of analysis and interdiction took place.

The successful suppression of terrorism by discovering and tracking terrorists' sources of financing can result only once all the relevant political and bureaucratic processes are tuned to each other and cooperate fully. This requires more than simply a few strokes of the legislative pen or international conventions; it requires the identification and surgical removal of terrorist nodes from a densely networked, fully globalized financial industry, through which immense sums of money are being pumped every day at cyber-speeds. This is a task of global scope, one in which the sheer number of interactions between various national private and public sectors has apparently rendered helpless the established political thinking and the customary level of governmental supervision. Some of this difficulty is understandable, because effective tracing of terrorist funds represents not only a major intellectual challenge, but also tends to be an extremely costly endeavor (ITAC Presents, 2006).

Politicians have not spent enough time on such laborious endeavors, and have instead left this struggle to nameless technocrats, both at the UN and other multilateral bodies and in their own governments. In this uncertain multilateral space, and in the absence of any clear political will that articulates a concise plan of action, a clutter of UN Security Council resolutions, conventions, and treaties have been created—all founded on the basic notion that those who will not comply can actually be sanctioned.

Faced with the critical need to protect itself against unintentional entanglements with financiers of terrorism, however, the private sector needed to act fast, and thus simply developed a prevention system on its own. The semi-conscious motivation for this quick and costly development work is of course the fear of being overregulated— a fear that, in the minds of many CEOs of the world, represents the biggest threat to business growth. (PricewaterhouseCoopers, 2005).

The general thrust of the many political responses and actions that so far have been taken against the financing of terrorism has been focused on the production of conventions and treaties and resolutions. But these legal instruments, worthwhile as they may be, are not proportionate to the problem we are facing, and are by a wide margin unequal to the creation of a dedicated institution that is designed to effectively suppress the financing of terrorism.

The Institutional Response

1267 Committee

To this day, the most important multilateral tool in existence in the fight against terrorism is one that was created in the aftermath of Al Qaeda's attacks against the US embassies in Nairobi and Dar es Salaam and other strikes that occurred during the years 1998 and 1999. On 15 October 1999, under the forceful leadership of the United States, the UN Security Council adopted Resolution 1267 under Chapter VII of the UN Charter (see <http://www.un.org/Docs/sc/committees/General. Information.pdf>). A whole host of unusually coercive measures against Al Qaeda and its host, the Taliban government of Afghanistan, became part of the international community's arsenal against terrorism. The key point of Resolution 1267 was to insist that the Taliban comply with previous resolutions, in particular with those regarding providing sanctuary and training for terrorists. The Taliban were put under extreme duress by demands from the UN that they immediately ensure that their territory would no longer be used for terrorism installations and camps, as well as for preparations for terrorist acts. The biggest challenge was presented in paragraph 2, in which the Security Council demanded:

> that the Taliban turn over Osama bin Laden without further delay to appropriate authorities in a country where he has been indicted, or to appropriate authorities in a country where he will be returned to such a country, or to appropriate authorities in a country where he will be arrested and effectively brought to justice.

Because an indictment had already been handed down by a US Federal Court against Osama bin Laden, this paragraph signaled the extent to which the US was in full control of the war against terrorism. To further ensure immediate compliance from the Taliban, it was decided that on 14 November 1999 measures would be imposed to deny take-off and landing permission to any Taliban-controlled aircraft, and to freeze funds and financial resources controlled by the Taliban.

The Security Council also wanted to assure everybody that this catalogue of punitive measures would not simply be a paper tiger. It decided to establish a committee that would:

- Seek information from all states concerning their implementation of these measures
- Consider information provided by all states regarding violations of these measures, and to recommend measures in response thereto
- Report periodically on the impact, including humanitarian implications, of the sanctions
- Report alleged violations of the measures, and identify persons or entities reported in such violations
- Designate aircraft and funds in order to facilitate the implementation of the sanctions
- Consider exemptions from the sanctions
- Examine reports submitted by all states regarding their compliance with the measures.

Methods Versus Success

This committee is now commonly referred to as the "1267 Committee." But subsequent resolutions—particularly UNSC Resolution 1373, of 28 September 2001—created other committees. Most notably, Resolution 1373 was the basis for the formation of the Counter-Terrorism Committee (CTC), which also obtained a broad mandate to supervise the implementation of measures against terrorism by all member states. Given these circumstances, the 1267 Committee should have become unusually powerful. But the truth is that Resolution 1267 was established long before 9/11, when many UN member nations considered compliance not necessarily obligatory, and the committee's work was impeded from the start. By the time the Al Qaeda terrorists struck the World Trade Center and the Pentagon, many nations were used to the idea that passive resistance to UN resolutions carried no political costs. All of this changed after 9/11, when a shocked world backed the United States and allowed it to drive ahead with an anti-terrorism agenda that included aggressive prodding of reluctant or non-compliant states. At this point, the CTC should have become the hub of the wheel that drove all international actions against financing of terrorism.

After a brief phase of cooperation and solidarity with the US, many nations started to resent the heavy hand of the American terrorist hunters. Once the integrity of US-obtained investigative results proved to be flawed, the willingness of other states to comply dropped dramatically. Soon the feeling emerged that UN resolutions were being driven too far and too fast by US interests, that these interests were taking a decidedly undemocratic turn, and that many citizens of the Western democracies would simply not tolerate this undermining of what they consider their essential values. For the 1267 Committee and the CTC, this devolution translated into a fight about how to confront terrorism, rather than actually fighting terrorism.

In response to these criticisms, members of the United Nations attempted to internationalize the effort by creating the Counter-Terrorism Committee Executive Directorate (CTED) in 2004. The intention was to strengthen and revitalize the much-maligned Counter-Terrorism Committee by discreetly balancing the role of the US with other members, who might stand more for measures consistent with democratic principles. The way to accomplish this goal was to create the CTED, a directorate that included 40 member states. So far, however, it is unclear what the CTED has been contributing, either in enhanced analytical or intelligence capabilities or to the cohesiveness of the international effort against terrorism.

In October 2004, the UN Security Council created yet another working group, this one to formulate measures against terrorists who do not belong to Al Qaeda and are therefore not covered by existing resolutions against Al Qaeda. This working group consists of delegates from the 15 member states of the Security Council. To date, the group has not agreed on sanctions against relevant individuals.

Non-UN Institutions

While the creation of political structures and the strengthening of compliance with international rules and UN resolutions in the fight against terrorism were supposed to take place through these UN bodies, the actual fighting of terrorist financing was left to other institutions. All of these institutions were in existence long before 9/11, and all of them came into being with a mandate to fight money laundering. They have since been retooled to fit the new task of cutting off the funding sources of international terrorists.

Foremost among these is the Financial Action Task Force (FATF), which was created by the G-7 members in 1989 with the intention of confronting money laundering in tax evasion schemes (see <http://www.fatf-gafi.org>). In October 2001, FATF expanded its original 40 recommendations against money laundering by eight additional suggestions, and in October 2004 by one additional recommendation, in order to deal with terrorism financing. The FATF 40+9 recommendations are now considered to be the conceptual gold standard of measures against the financing of terrorism.

One expression of this leadership role is the International Monetary Fund's (IMF) decision in March 2004 to initiate assessments of its member states' efforts to combat money laundering and the financing of terrorism (measures known as AML/CFT). The assessment is largely based on an analysis of compliance with the FATF 40+9 recommendations (IMF, 2005).

Building on FATF's pioneering work, the Egmont Group became another critical player in the fight against money laundering and terrorism funding. Cross-border sharing between national law enforcement agencies—usually called Financial Intelligence Units (FIU), which are in charge of collecting and analyzing data on suspicious or unusual financial activities—has traditionally not been carried out with the necessary expedience to match the speed and fluidity of trans-national criminal enterprises. Thanks to the protocols that serve as the foundation of the interactions between the members of the Egmont Group, sharing relevant information across national borders has become much more informal and more pragmatic. Today,

Financial Intelligence Units in 101 countries are recognized by the Egmont Group as operational. It is noteworthy that the Egmont Group too was started in 1995 for the purpose of combating money laundering (see <http://www.egmontgroup.org/>).

The Problem with Money Laundering

There is an unresolved problem in the deployment of specialists in the fight against terrorism financing who in actuality have been groomed in the fight against money laundering networks that are operated to benefit criminal enterprises. The differences between terrorism and organized crime are fundamental, and can lead to difficulties for operatives trained in one area but expected to work in the other.

For criminals, illicit acts are the means to an end, which is wealth. For terrorists, the illicit act *is* the goal: the exploding bomb. Criminals resort to violence only if it is an expedient method to gain wealth; terrorists must by definition be violent. Criminals are satisfied with accumulating and maximizing material gains, whereas terrorists pursue material interests only to enable them to cause more violence.

Additional distinctions need to be made that separate the category of well-established, organized terrorism—groups such as Hezbollah, Hamas, the IRA, ETA, and so on—from that of small, ad hoc groups of terrorists who operate with very little institutional support, and that distinguish both of these forms from organized crime groups. They all may to some degree depend on money laundering operations, and therefore must make certain investments in order for their illicit ambitions to proceed smoothly. The difference is that, for criminals, these investments not only make sense—they are mandatory. After all, their ultimate goal is merely to convert illicit gains to licit wealth. Sometimes—and if they are able to repeat this conversion frequently and easily enough—they or their offspring may prefer to mutate into law-abiding citizens. The better their money laundering schemes operate, the closer criminals come to their ultimate goal. The logic is that significant investments that ensure the working of money laundering operations make good sense to criminals. And since safe and efficient money laundering operations are an ongoing need, they build solid structures staffed with committed allies who can provide investment advice, legal counsel, and know-how to maintain a screen of corporate entities that enable them to legitimize their illegal profits.

Terrorists require funding only to the extent that a steady flow of cash helps them to maintain a sufficiently consistent and menacing threat level. They require a ready supply of attackers and supporters, and sometimes they have to cover relatively small operational costs. To finance these needs, some terrorist groups may have a choice between legitimate and illegitimate funding. In many ways it is easier and safer for them to operate as long as possible with as much legitimacy as possible. The appearance of legitimacy helps to maintain the security of an operation until the point when the funding is leveraged into acts of death and destruction. It relieves terrorists from having to maintain cumbersome and costly money laundering operations. Most importantly, illicit acts may increase the risks of premature discovery, thus preventing terrorists from carrying out the violent act that is their ultimate goal.

But such an ideal may not in all cases be achievable. Although many of the recent terror attacks could have been financed with an average-size US or UK consumer loan, sufficient funding from unsuspecting sources is not always that easy to come by. Sometimes, terrorist organizations have to engage in criminal activities to finance the overhead necessary to maintain training camps, conduct surveillance operations, acquire weapons and counterfeit documents, and pay for living allowances. These are all necessary steps if an organization intends to remain a constant and menacing threat to society.

The obvious conclusion of these observations and experiences is that a conventionally trained investigator of money laundering organizations may look in all the wrong places. The public should not feel reassured in the absence of any visible confirmation that law enforcement and intelligence agencies have systematically adjusted their internal training. An important signal of such fine-tuning would be to see a close level of cooperation between those who man the frontlines in the fight against terrorism. On the one hand, these are law enforcement and intelligence specialists, and on the other hand there are those employees who are responsible for risk mitigation in financial service companies and in other industries, such as transportation. All these private sector employees represent the true first contact points for a potential financier of terrorism.

With such measures, one might win the fight against terrorism financing for a short, interim period. But the international community has to recognize that the interdiction of financial flows necessary to support large terrorist organizations addresses only half the problem, and it may actually complicate the solution to the entire problem. The eradication of organized terrorism does not automatically mean that the root causes of terrorism have also been eliminated. Yet, as long as the root causes of terrorism persist, a small percentage of highly violent individuals will always find ways to express their rage.

The real danger is the fight against unknown enemies. With the elimination of Hezbollah, Hamas, and other groups like them, new threats will mushroom through small, ad hoc groups of deeply radicalized individuals. They will launch small and cheap attacks from an information void. Such ad hoc groups may operate with legitimate funding, which would be virtually undetectable by virtue of their small size and their lack of any connection to well-recognized terrorist organizations.

The Regulatory Response

In the aftermath of the September 11 attacks, the US benefited from the existence of experienced law enforcement and intelligence structures. The debates about how well the relevant agencies worked revealed major weaknesses in their structures and capabilities, but they were thought to be correctable once appropriate oversight and regulations were established. Not surprisingly, with the passage of the Patriot Act, the United States developed the first major regulatory regime in response to terrorism financing. Since these new laws were developed under extraordinary time pressures, the Patriot Act represents a clumsy body of laws and rules that have required many improvements and revisions. Unfortunately, because of the global reach of the US financial industry, the Patriot Act was not just imposed on Americans, but on the whole world. Compliance with some stipulations of the Patriot Act is a particularly challenging and costly task.

The private sector has very pragmatically merged Patriot Act compliance and commensurate due diligence measures with its pre-existing risk management provisions. Bundled into one massive compliance response to a multitude of risks, the private sector has internalized all the risks and the due diligence needs that arise from protecting themselves against involvement in financing terrorism, along with responses to the implications of being inattentive to the demands of the Sarbanes-Oxley Act, and many more such needs. No major publicly traded company can afford to operate without a fully functioning system that prevents failures in these areas.

The pertinent parts of the Patriot Act are an elaborate implementation of the International Convention for the Suppression of the Financing of Terrorism, which the United Nations General Assembly adopted on 10 January 2000. The International Convention, drawn up and adopted in the pre-9/11 era, obligated every UN member state to strengthen its efforts like never before in the fight against terrorism financing. As a typical example of the sincerity with which the world was now confronting any proximity to terrorism financing, Article 2.3 is instructive: "For an act to constitute an offence set forth in paragraph 1, it shall not be necessary that the funds were actually used to carry out an offence referred to in para 1, subpara a) or b)."

In Article 2.5, a treacherous problem rears its ugly head, one that will plague the international community for a long time to come. Since many Islamic organizations engage in a wide range of activities, including both perfectly acceptable social aid programs and providing funding for deadly terrorist attacks, the question is addressed of how to assign culpability:

Any person also commits an offence if that person:

c) Contributes to the commission of one or more offences as set forth in para 1 or 4 of this article by a group of persons acting with a common purpose. Such contribution shall be intentional and shall either:
i) Be made with the aim of furthering the criminal activity or criminal purpose of the group, where such activity or purpose involves the commission of an offence as set forth in para 1 of this article; or
ii) Be made in the knowledge of the intention of the group to commit an offence as set forth in para 1 of this article.

The last stipulation bears potential for abuse, such as in cases when a state determines via sanctions that one group—for example, Hamas—is criminal. Therefore, anybody donating funds to Hamas may be considered culpable for attacks for which Hamas claims responsibility. Yet the donation to Hamas may not have been intended for a branch engaged in terrorism, but for the ones providing social services, an area in which Hamas performs extensive work in the West Bank.

The Post-9/11 Reactions

Resolution 1373

Rather than reassessing the international community's response and developing a fundamentally new strategy after the attacks on New York and Washington, after 9/11, reactions to the financing of this new form of terror were simply stacked on top of the existing approaches, which had started with the very first terrorism-related convention, dating from 1963. The only really new act taken immediately after 9/11 was a substantial consolidation of all existing efforts, which was established under UNSC Resolution 1373 and was adopted, under Chapter VII of the UN Charter, in late September 2001.

Among other provisions, this resolution called upon all states to implement appropriate legislation concerning countering terrorism financing. Resolution 1373 contained no new sanctions, but it strengthened UNSC Resolution 1267 from October 1999, whose "smart sanctions" against the Taliban and Al Qaeda involved the freezing of those groups' financial assets. Another important decision contained in Resolution 1373 was the language that created the Counter-Terrorism Committee and activated a Monitoring Group, whose principal mandate was to monitor and report to the 1267 Committee on compliance with UNSC resolutions by member states.

The Backlash

These regulatory responses against terrorism were cobbled together from a menu of traditional coercive mechanisms that the UN Security Council had developed over the past years in its struggles with African warlords and other recalcitrant actors. They consist of arms embargoes, economic sanctions, diplomatic restrictions, targeted financial sanctions, and individual travel bans. All these measures were brought to bear against Al Qaeda and the Taliban, with the exception of economic and diplomatic sanctions.

These measures fell on already compromised soil, since at precisely the same time that they were passed a debate about the effectiveness of UN sanctions was raging full force. Shortly after the attacks of 9/11, the Working Group on General Issues on Sanctions within the Security Council came to a stalemate in its attempts to develop general recommendations on how to improve the effectiveness of United Nations sanctions (see UN Press Release SC/7187, 25 October 2001). Some member states argued that studies proved that sanctions were not effective. Evidence was cited that a number of states continued to defy the observance of sanctions, and that some states lacked the capacity to enforce them. Others pointed out the extent to which the unintended economic and humanitarian costs of sanctions often outweighed the corrective effect they had on the intended target.

There was simply no space for such bureaucratic finesse in the days after the US embassies in Nairobi and Dar es Salaam had been destroyed, and there was even less interest in introspective analysis once the World Trade Center lay in smoking ruins. The language of UNSC Resolutions 1267, 1333, 1363, and 1373 was now being written with an uncompromising intention to sanction anybody who was not going to comply. These resolutions also conveyed with palpable urgency and pragmatism to UN member states the importance of maintaining a state of vigilance and war-readiness that would be reviewed at regular intervals by the Security Council's suddenly stringent Monitoring Group.

Both the coercive measures against terrorist suspects and the compliance pressures on member states soon revealed themselves as a flawed strategy. Initially, some UN member states submitted a significant number of terrorist suspects and terrorist funding networks for inclusion on the UN's consolidated lists of Taliban and Al Qaeda associates. Individual sanctioning was soon perceived to be a flawed approach, however, because of poor adherence to tolerable evidentiary standards. These lapses led to the premature blacklisting of entities such as Al-Barakat or Al-Taqwa, or the sanctioning of individuals whose personal information such as surname, first name, date of birth, or domicile were so poorly researched that no practical action was possible. If nothing else, the premature blacklistings preempted potentially critical intelligence gains that might have resulted from more orderly investigative efforts. UN member states who oppose sanctions on principled grounds, or whose self-interest places them in opposition to certain anti-terrorism measures, used the excuse of insufficient due process procedures for their lack of compliance with UNSC resolutions.

This much was glaringly obvious: the denial of effective due process had turned the UN's confrontation of terrorism into an offensively undemocratic exercise. Citizens in many member states simply could not accept the idea that their countries would be associated with a global effort that was led by a nation—the United States—who dropped Al Qaeda suspects into a legal vacuum at the Guantanamo Bay facility, who rendered suspects to states with non existent or insufficient human rights protections for prisoners, and who seemed unable to prevent massive prisoner abuses in Iraq and Afghanistan. The lack of due process became the battle cry for all those who oppose US leadership in general, and in particular the domineering version of the US war against terrorism.

Unfortunately, despite widespread agreement in the opposition against the US, the opposing camp never produced a coherent regulatory alternative. The final evidence that the international community had no substance behind its posturing for democratic values revealed itself in the successive reports of the Monitoring Group. The catalogue of conclusions by its long-time chairman Michael Chandler explains in unusually clear language how fighting terrorism most often was relegated to the second rank of concerns, while the debate over the methods of *how* to fight was always at the top of the agenda of UN members. Some of Chandler's conclusions were:

- Less and less useful information resulting from investigations by member states was shared with the UN Sanction Committee
- Even less information was reported about terrorism suspects, therefore significantly decreasing the deterrence effects that it was hoped that international cooperation would achieve
- Significant lack of means, resources, and know-how in too many states

prevented effective collaboration
- Financial and technical assistance that was promised in the UN resolutions remained scarce; the assistance that was provided resulted from general bilateral considerations rather than from the overarching multilateral commitment
- Rather than addressing the flaws in its approach to countering terrorism, the international community merely further bureaucratized badly needed improvements by creating more Security Council committees, which by their nature rely on UN staff to fulfill their mandate
- The Monitoring Group was disbanded, and eventually an analytical support team was created that is far less aggressive in pursuing non-compliant member states.

The Effectiveness of Targeted Financial Sanctions and Travel Bans

The Elements for Assessing Success

While institutionalizing comprehensive global counter-terrorism efforts never succeeded—in fact, such an attempt was never seriously made—because most member states could not adjust to the scale of the threats, those narrow measures on which the international community was able to agree require special consideration. These measures have always been limited to sanctions, of which targeted financial sanctions and travel bans are usually considered to have the most piercing effect. Although it should be understood that no solid data confirms the effectiveness of sanctions in general, it is generally assumed that they work … somehow. This point must remain provocatively tentative until some additional issues are fully understood.

One has to assume that no accurate assessment of UN-approved sanctions is possible as long as it is conducted in isolation from a consideration of other sanction regimes, of multi- and bilateral pressures, and without consideration of the very substantial role of the rapidly growing compliance and due diligence industry. However, one fundamental reality of UN sanctions can be stated with certainty: they are only as effective as the resolve of member states to enforce them is strong (Lopez, 2006). In fact, one might very well take this statement a step further, and assert that the presence of strong political will behind financial sanctions and travel bans, along with the normative pressures for compliance that the private sector is building, probably represent the best guarantee for success.

In the US-led war against terrorism, the initial round of successful financial sanctions was directed against the Taliban and their corporate entities and organizations. The Taliban were of course a secondary target because of their support of Al Qaeda. They took the initial brunt both in terms of broad sanction regimes and in terms of military action. The fact that these actions were successful are best demonstrated by the fact that the corporate entities associated with the regime—such as Da Afghanistan Bank; Afghan Export Bank; Agricultural Development Bank of Afghanistan (ADB); Banke Millie Afghan (aka Afghan National Bank; aka Bank E. Millie Afghan); and the Export Promotion Bank of Afghanistan—were the first corporations to be delisted under the economic sanctions. These positive signs of course do not imply that the remnants of the Taliban may not have been able to create new funding sources.

The overall scenario concerning financial sanctions against terrorism is far more debatable. The actual dollar amounts that have been frozen under the sanctions regimes are surprisingly small (see Table 10.1 below). One has to question whether these funds offer an accurate sense of the true size of the global funding network of terrorist organizations, or whether these freezing actions resulted from the need to provide politicians with evidence of success. For example, it is unclear whether some frozen assets from the coffers of Hamas or Hezbollah are related to these organizations' terrorist activities, or whether they are part of the funding for their much more elaborate social service programs. Another complicating factor is the lackadaisical nature of the reporting habits of UN member states, which have played a large role in preventing the publication of reliable UN statistical data about the quantity of funds frozen and the identity of the blocking nation. Consequently, one has to depend on the publications of the US government's Office of Foreign Asset Controls (OFAC) on this issue.

Table 10.1   Blocked funds in the United States relating to SDGT, SDT, and FTO programs

Organization/Related Designees	Blocked as of 2005 (USD)	Blocked as of 2004 (USD)
Al Qaeda	7,457,579	3,889,655
Hamas	6,201,874	5,893,101
Mujahedin-E Khalq Organization	108,255	90,073
New People's Army	3,750	3,750
Palestinian Islamic Jihad	18,795	17,746
Kahane Chai	201	201
Taliban	2,648	1,809
Total assets of SDGTs, SDTs and FTOs	**13,793,102**	**9,896,335**

Source: OFAC

Coordinated Naming and Shaming

While most freezing of assets was undertaken on the initiative of the U.S. and the European Union, the UN can take credit for a far higher rate of success with "naming and shaming" actions. Once a target becomes subject to targeted financial sanctions or a travel ban issued by the UN Security Council, this action represents a worldwide condemnation. The damage to these targets' reputations is enormous. Nevertheless, in some instances naming and shaming has its limitations, too. It works best against targets that:

- Do most of their business in well-regulated nations
- Have substantial economic interests in maintaining a sound reputation because their survival and funding depends on respect within the international capital markets.

Those who work with sanctions regimes in African crisis zones have experienced that targeted financial sanctions have little effect if the target:

- Operates exclusively in unregulated or poorly regulated states
- Does not depend on capital markets, but conducts business with private or stolen capital
- Its government ignores or is opposed to international and UN policy objectives.

If the basic premises for success are met, however, the long-term experience is that targeted financial sanctions and travel bans help to frustrate violators of sanctions, and thus they contribute to a shortened time-span of violations. The process can speed up considerably once the international community fully synchronizes its actions. Then, in addition to the UN sanctions, violators find themselves facing a barrage of additional actions. These may include:

- Unilateral sanctions imposed by the US
- Unilateral sanctions imposed by the EU
- Prosecutions by the International Criminal Court or other special international jurisdictions
- Local prosecutions.

The fact that the UN serves merely as the lead sanction agency, and that others can and do define much more detailed ways to deal with sanctionable activities, is expressed by the fact that, of the more than 20,000 individuals, corporations, and other entities that are currently under some form of unilateral or multilateral financial sanction or travel ban somewhere in the world, the share imposed by the UN accounts for less than one-tenth, as reflected in Table 10.2.

Table 10.2 Current targets of financial sanctions and travel bans

Targeted Regimes/ Organizations	Financial Sanctions	Travel Bans
Individuals and entities belonging to the Taliban	143	143
Individuals and entities belonging to Al Qaeda	334	334
Cote d'Ivoire	3	3
Democratic Republic of the Congo	16	16
Iraq	288	None
Sudan	4	4
Liberia	58	59
Sierra Leone	None	30
Total UN	**846**	**589**
Total EU	**3322**	**n/a**
Total US-OFAC	**20,000 (estimated)**	**n/a**

(data as of 30 April 2006, collected by the author)

The Role of the Private Sector

By far the most important element of the success of sanction regimes is the full cooperation of the private sector. Once again, targeted financial sanctions offer the most relevant case studies, and the United States, with its early lead in imposing targeted financial sanctions and the creation of the OFAC list, is the relevant reference point for all others who wish to impose sanctions. The OFAC list came into existence with the introduction of the US Narcotics Trafficking Sanctions. From that moment on it was no longer practical for members of the financial industry to continue the laissez-faire practices of the past. Banks had to pay attention to who they did business with, and needed to protect themselves if they wanted to prevent an unpleasant imbroglio with the government. Publicly traded banking firms could simply not face risks for which the international capital markets had no tolerance, and at the very top of the list of these intolerable risks were scandals resulting from banking relationships with Latin American drug barons. Consequently, most US and eventually other international banking groups made some investments to establish compliance departments. In the eyes of the investing public, the OFAC listings offered an institutionalized prerogative allowing each bank manager to prevent relationships with ill-suited clients.

Based on this attractive concept, the listing of sanctionable entities has mushroomed within the United States' bilateral policy structure, as well as within the UN and eventually the EU. This trend toward internationalization is beneficial to all issuers of sanctions. The more collaborative the spirit behind a sanction regime, the fewer safe havens are left for the sanctioned entity to flee to, and the more successful the overall exercise becomes. An additional benefit results from the US and the EU's demonstrated willingness and ability to not only seize violators' assets but sometimes impose stiff penalties on financial institutions that have aided and abetted violators.

After 9/11, this well-functioning international system was dealt a serious blow. In Washington, DC, it was no longer expert investigators who led in the determination of who should be added to the OFAC list. Representatives of the National Security Agency and the White House took over the identification of sanctionable entities. Under their direction, the listings proliferated, and so did the shoddiness of the data leading to the listings. Spelling mistakes or incomplete names for listed entities were the most obvious signs of a breakdown in the system. One of the most grievous consequences was that individuals and entities were added to the list with virtually no evidence existing to support the listing. Another was the cluttering of the sanction list with individuals who in all probability have neither cash nor any other attachable assets. Obviously, including these listings under a targeted financial sanction regime made no sense. They place unnecessary additional administrative burdens on the financial industry, and they tend to weaken all other sanction cases.

Outside a small circle of political operators in Washington, nobody believed any longer that the justifications for listings were based on proper methodologies. This presented the private sector with a conundrum. On the one hand, there was no point in opposing an agenda that was driven by extremist political ambitions. On the other hand, no responsible corporate CEO was going to err on the side of chance in the difficult post-9/11 climate. As much as they resented it, in the end, management was left to draw the only possible conclusion: sacrifice clients and business as soon as a whiff of a problem was raised. Clearly, for business leaders, this could not be a long-term solution.

Radical Solutions from the Private Sector

For business to prosper, rules are needed. It is not important whether these rules are right or wrong, whether they are just or unfair—as long as the rules are dependable guides, and are enforced consistently, businesses can accommodate to them and make profits. Complying with the Patriot Act in the US was just such an exercise. It was accomplished by most banking enterprises within a short period of development time, but it required substantial investments. The estimates for such extra costs vary from industry to industry, but on average they amount to about an additional 40 percent added to corporate budget lines for auditing and technology (Speech by the Chairman of the Association of Financial Professionals to the Japan CFO Association, 14 July 2005, citing data from AuditAnalytics). The entire due diligence efforts of the industrialized world's financial systems, as well as systems in many other industries, were substantially strengthened, not only by the addition of qualified staff but also by very sophisticated technologies.

All major corporations had to undergo a fundamental rethinking of their risk mitigation provisions. It was no longer merely a task of avoiding relationships with confirmed terrorists or criminals. Now, proper risk management required forward thinking that helped protect a company against threats that lurk beyond the horizon. As difficult as it seems, responsible management teams must now protect against relationships with individuals or entities who in the future could turn out to be related to terrorism, organized crime, political corruption, environmental pollution, problematic workplace conditions, and many other potential reputation killers.

These wholesale protection mechanisms required that banking groups have fully automated databases of potentially problematic individuals, companies, or organizations at their disposal. Once such databases became available, data related to all relationships that an enterprise maintains must be scanned and monitored on a regular basis. Only through this extensive scrutiny can hidden problems be detected.

Assembling fully automated databases of potentially problematic individuals, companies, or organizations could only be accomplished by a few specialized firms. Among the biggest large-scale consolidators of due diligence data are Reuters/ Factiva, Thompson Financial Systems, and the global market leader, Worldcheck, a privately held venture that was originally supported by Swiss banking groups. These providers offer commercially available data collections containing 250,000 to over 450,000 entries of PEPs (Politically Exposed Persons). These lists include not only everybody who has ever been sanctioned by anybody, but everybody UN investigators and monitors have ever mentioned in their reporting. Also included is everybody non-governmental organizations, activist groups, and journalists have mentioned (in reporting and investigations that are admittedly not always highly credible). Of course, any publicly reported individual who has been indicted in any country is reflected in these databases, as are politicians, senior public servants, or military officers from as many countries as possible.

By now, virtually all leading financial institutions around the world are utilizing such due diligence software. These products are integrated to the extent that compliance departments of financial institutions can monitor client activities for potentially sanctionable actions continuously, automatically, and in perfect synchronization with the publication of the latest investigatory results.

These advancements represent substantial gains in the confrontation with many forms of terrorism financing. Even though they will not absolutely prevent new financing schemes, such due diligence efforts certainly raise the costs significantly for anybody who wishes to provide sustained financial support to terrorist organizations. But this is a two-edged sword. A truly professional money launderer now must merely gain access to the due diligence software products to have a pretty good idea of what to watch for in order to remain undetected. Automated compliance monitoring can easily be abused. In the hands of a skillful operator, potential violators now have real-time information available about who is and who is not on the radar screens of investigators. For those who have organized their economic livelihoods around sanction-busting, it is easy enough to detect when it is time to change banks, liquidate assets, or simply shift assets to another corporate front.

After all, the global prevention systems against terrorism financing are based on a strictly formalized check-point process. The actual investigative efforts that lead to new insights and eventually to new listings are still under the strict control of national investigative authorities. Experience shows that, in every nation, law enforcement and intelligence organizations are not likely to give up their turf in order to serve a multilateral ideal that is still very vague, especially one whose applications are pursued by most nations in a very tentative manner, and only then if their national interests do not happen to block their participation.

Conclusion

The establishment of the 1267 Committee and its wide-ranging mandates, along with other UN Security Council committees, such as the one established under Resolution 1540 (2004), are encouraging signals of a world that is attempting to organize itself against an incalculable threat. Organizations such as the Egmont Group, and steps like the creation of the nine additional FATF recommendations, are important contributions in the harmonization and tightening of global efforts against terrorism financing. However, if the goal is to effectively eliminate terrorism, regardless of which brand, then, while these efforts may be commendable, unfortunately they remain entirely insufficient. The primary reason is that the international community has not been able to move ahead toward a more substantial and formalized response, as it has done when faced with other global crises.

So far, the international community has chosen only one of many available measures: highly politicized sanctions regimes. In addition, some nations choose to go to war (whether unilaterally or not), and others prefer to prosecute terrorism in legal courts as if it were a common crime.

The question must be posed whether sanctions are indeed the best way to eliminate terrorism, or at least the financing of terrorism. They can have a devastating effect when applied against individuals or nations, but they do not seem to serve very well in organizing a sustained response to a persistent and multidimensional problem. Sanctions are based on UN resolutions whose language is notoriously imprecise and ambiguous. Sanctions are temporary measures that require frequent review, and are at best reflective of the best efforts the international community is capable of making at that particular moment in time. But in the pressure cooker of the multilateral world, that "best effort" frequently amounts to no more than the lowest common denominator. Sanctions are, ultimately, a political tool. And the financing of terrorism is quite clearly much more than merely a political problem.

Global terrorism is too important and too complex a problem to leave the solution to what is essentially a simple-minded combative approach. In some ways, fighting terrorism with economic sanctions is the equivalent of sending out a few hundred nurses with flyswatters to combat malaria. One would never have seriously considered such pin-point responses to other issues that create recurrent global stress. To confront a global health crisis, the international community mobilizes and gives the lead management responsibility to the World Health Organization (WHO), a specialized agency. And to mitigate food shortages and prevent famine, the global community set up the World Food Program (WFP), fitted with all the necessary skills and equipment. The list of coherent responses to global issues of various kinds goes on and on.

Yet in fighting terrorism, and particularly fighting the financing of terrorism, the international community has abdicated its responsibility. The UN member states have not even attempted to forge a way through the thicket of conflicting interests that would lead to a dedicated institutional response to terrorism. Instead, they have outsourced many of the investigative and monitoring tasks to temporary expert groups. They have created ad hoc groups and given them short-lived mandates. With the terrorism-related Security Council resolutions, the member states have created a patchwork of pseudo-laws that in many cases they themselves have not fully integrated into their own legal systems. And to carry out the new tasks implied by these resolutions, they have agreed that they are forcing responsibilities onto civil servants who have never been prepared for such a task. Finally, the burden of actually operating in this much more risky world falls to the private sector. In order to meet the mounting compliance costs that result from political indecision, the private sector simply bundles them into the prices that consumers ultimately end up paying.

References

International Monetary Fund (2005), "A Fact Sheet: The IMF and the Fight Against Money Laundering and the Financing Of Terrorism" (September).

ITAC Presents (2006), *Terrorism Financing and Financial System Vulnerabilities: Issues and Challenges*, Trends in Terrorism Series (Ottawa: Carleton University); at <http://www.csis.gc.ca/en/itac/itacdocs/2006-3.asp>

Lopez, George (2006), "UN Sanctions After Oil-for-Food: Still a Viable Diplomatic Tool?" Testimony at the Hearings of the Sub-committee on National Security, Emerging Threats and International Relations, House of Representatives, Committee on Government Reform, 109th Congress (2 May).

PricewaterhouseCoopers (2005), Poll presented at the 2005 Financial Services Audit
    Committee Forum in New York; at <http://www.pwc.com/extweb/insights.nsf/
    docid/23B464F0A399DD6785256F8D004EE322>

Chapter 11

Using Sanctions to Fight Terrorism[1]

Gary Clyde Hufbauer and Thomas Moll

We will direct every resource at our command—every means of diplomacy, every tool of intelligence, every instrument of law enforcement, every financial influence, and every necessary weapon of war—to the disruption and to the defeat of the global terror network.

— *George W. Bush*, *Address to a Joint Session of Congress, 20 September 2001*

We will starve terrorists of funding, turn them one against another, drive them from place to place, until there is no refuge or no rest.

— *George W. Bush*, *Address to a Joint Session of Congress, 20 September 2001*

We have developed the international financial equivalent of law enforcement's "Most Wanted" list. And it puts the financial world on notice. If you do business with terrorists, if you support or sponsor them, you will not do business with the United States of America.

— *George W. Bush*, *White House press conference, 24 September 2001*

Introduction

Following the attacks on the World Trade Center and the Pentagon in September 2001, President George W. Bush prepared the country for a "war on terror." As outlined in his speech before the joint session of Congress on 20 September 2001, this is a war that will be fought on many fronts—diplomacy, intelligence, covert action, economic sanctions, law enforcement—as well as on the traditional military front. Speaking from the White House Rose Garden on 24 September 2001, President Bush reiterated the importance of economic sanctions in the war on terror.

Notwithstanding the Bush Administration's enthusiasm for using economic tools to fight terrorism, the history of economic sanctions in the past century reveals very few instances in which these measures, used independently, achieved major foreign policy goals (Hufbauer, et al., forthcoming). In the vast majority of cases, only military force and covert action have proved able to play a decisive role in a battle

---

1   This chapter draws heavily from Hufbauer, et al., 2001.

of this magnitude; at best, economic sanctions can play a supporting role in the war on terrorism.

Nevertheless, the auxiliary role for sanctions is an important one. This chapter will examine the continuous use of counter-terror sanctions strategies dating to the 1970s, as well as the current administration's mixture of sanctions designed to confront the new face of terrorism. Having elevated the role of economic sanctions as part of the war on terrorism, the Bush Administration appropriately realized the need to recalibrate America's toolbox of economic weapons. Indeed, confronting the new terrorist enemy has required the mixing of sanctions strategies according to their intended target: nation-state or terrorist group.

States employ traditional methods of economic diplomacy against other states to induce changes in regime behavior by imposing penalties for harboring terrorists. The Bush Administration has continued to impose punitive economic measures against other nations by using the list of state sponsors of terrorism. Dating to 1979, the state sponsor designation permits the use of trade and financial sanctions against other countries that support or harbor terrorists. Since 9/11, these sanction "sticks" have been complemented with economic "carrots" designed to induce cooperation. These measures include preferential trade measures, favorable loans, and in some cases the removal of existing sanctions as rewards for cooperation in the war against terrorism.

The financial fight against non-state terrorist groups, however, focuses solely on punitive measures designed to fight terrorism by eliminating sources of funding. To this end, the Bush Administration has stepped up efforts to use list-based sanctions against terrorist entities, a strategy that originated in the 1990s when President Clinton began using lists of Specially Designated Terrorists (SDTs) and Foreign Terrorist Organizations (FTOs) to freeze terrorist assets. By expanding these counter-terrorism tactics, the Bush Administration has focused on denying terrorists the means with which to commit atrocities rather than attempting to coerce changes in the behavior of organizations whose raison d'être is committing acts of terror.

The following sections examine the history of US sanctions against both state sponsors of terrorism as well as non-state terrorist entities. A discussion of the Bush Administration's sanctions strategy in the wake of 9/11 will follow.

State Sponsors

In the 1970s and 1980s, US counter-terrorism policy primarily focused on state sponsorship of international terrorism. State sponsors of terrorism are countries that the US Secretary of State has designated as having "repeatedly provided state support for acts of international terrorism."[2] The State Department's *Country Reports on Terrorism 2005* listed six countries as state sponsors: Cuba, Iran, Libya, North Korea, Sudan, and Syria (US Department of State, 2006).[3] This designation triggers a series of economic sanctions under different laws:

---

2   Under Section 6 (j) of the Export Administration Act of 1979.
3   Libya's designation was rescinded on 15 May 2006.

- Restrictions on export licenses (or a general ban) for dual-use items or critical technology (under the Export Administration Act of 1979)
- Ban on sales or licenses for items on the US Munitions Control List (under the Arms Export Control Act)
- Ban on US foreign assistance, including Export-Import Bank credits and guarantees (under the Foreign Assistance Act of 1961)
- Authorization for the President to restrict or ban imports of goods and services from designated terrorist countries (under the International Security and Development Cooperation Act of 1985)
- Prohibition of financial transactions by US persons with the governments of designated terrorist countries (under the Antiterrorism and Effective Death Penalty Act of 1996)
- Requirement that US representatives at international financial institutions vote against loans or other financial assistance to designated countries (under the International Financial Institutions Act of 1977)
- Ineligibility for the Generalized System of Preferences, or GSP (under the Trade Act of 1974).

Although naming a country as a state sponsor of terrorism does not automatically trigger a total economic embargo, all countries (with the exception of Syria[4]) currently designated as state sponsors—Cuba, Iran, North Korea, and Sudan—are also subject to comprehensive trade and financial sanctions imposed by the executive branch under the International Emergency Economic Powers Act (IEEPA). In some of these cases—particularly Cuba and North Korea—US sanctions policy is less determined by concerns over terrorism than by broader foreign policy conflicts.

Iran

In response to alleged Iranian involvement in the bombing of the US Marine barracks in Beirut in 1983, the State Department added Iran to the list of state sponsors of terrorism in 1984. Export controls were subsequently tightened twice. In 1987, under pressure from Congress, President Reagan invoked Section 505 of the International Security and Development Act in order to ban all imports from Iran and prohibit the export of several potentially militarily useful goods. In 1992, Congress passed the Iran-Iraq Arms Nonproliferation Act to prohibit the export of defense items, nuclear material, and certain dual-use goods under the Export Administration Act. This legislation also imposed extraterritorial sanctions on foreign governments and entities that "knowingly and materially" contributed to Iran's efforts to acquire "destabilizing numbers and types" of weapons.

---

4   Sanctions on Syria were tightened under the Syria Accountability Act (2003) and subsequent Executive Orders (2004, 2005). These measures banned all exports to Syria except food and medicine, and barred Syrian aircraft from landing in the United States. President Bush also invoked Section 311 of the Patriot Act to sever US ties with the Commercial Bank of Syria, and the International Emergency Economic Powers Act to freeze the assets of certain Syrian entities.

With a potential USD 1 billion deal between Conoco and the National Iranian Oil Company looming, and amid heightened concerns about Iran's nuclear program and support for terrorist organizations, in 1995 President Clinton preempted a Congressional response by tightening the sanctions regime on Iran. Through a series of executive orders, Clinton eventually barred all US trade with and investment in Iran.

Encouraged by the potential for reforms under moderate President Mohammad Khatami, the Clinton Administration signaled its willingness to improve relations by lifting selected sanctions in 1999 and 2000. In April 1999, the administration modified the trade ban to allow for the sale of food and medicine on a case-by-case basis, and a year later the administration lifted the ban on certain non-oil imports from Iran, such as carpets, caviar, pistachios, and dried fruit.

President Clinton signed the Iran Nonproliferation Act in March 2000, ending a two-year dispute with Congress that began with his veto of the legislation in its original form. The act allows, but does not require, the President to impose sanctions on foreign entities that assist Iran with its weapons programs.

Over more than two decades, US sanctions against Iran have expanded so that nearly all trade and financial dealings between the two countries are banned. Additionally, the US sanctions regime against Iran has incorporated extraterritorial measures designed to prevent other countries from investing in Iran's energy sector and selling sensitive proliferation technologies. Yet, despite these exhaustive sanctions efforts, Iran remains the "most active state sponsor of terrorism," according to the State Department's *Country Reports on Terrorism 2005*.[5]

Iraq

Iraq was placed on the state sponsor of terrorism list in December 1979 and removed in 1982. After invading Kuwait in 1990, Iraq was again placed on the list, where it remained until after the US-led removal of Saddam Hussein from power in 2003. For more than a decade, Iraq had been subject to the most comprehensive US and UN trade and financial sanctions regime mounted since the Second World War. Nevertheless, the supposed futility of sanctions (as perceived by US officials) played a partial role in the decision to intervene militarily against the Hussein regime in 2003. While the multilateral sanctions on Iraq did little to weaken the regime's monopoly on political power—a goal embraced by Washington—the sanctions probably did curb Iraq's ability to revamp its weapons of mass destruction (WMD) programs by reducing the resources available to Saddam Hussein. The regime was not deterred, however, from planning and sponsoring international terrorism focused on Iraqi dissident groups and offering safe haven to various expatriate terrorist groups, such as the Popular Front for the Liberation of Palestine and the Abu Nidal organization.

---

5   Former CIA agent Robert Baer extensively documents Iranian sponsorship of Middle East terrorism (Baer, 2002).

Libya

Libya's long history of sponsoring international terrorism led to its placement on the first state sponsor list in 1979. Export controls preceded a ban on crude oil imports from Libya, restrictions on exports of sophisticated oil and gas equipment and technology, and later a ban on imports of refined oil products. In response to Libyan involvement in the terrorist attacks on airports in Rome and Vienna, President Reagan invoked IEEPA to implement comprehensive trade and financial controls in 1986. The Reagan Administration barred most exports and imports of goods, services, and technology, prohibited all loans or credits to the Libyan government, and froze Libyan government assets held in US banks.

Following the bombings of Pan Am Flight 103 in December 1988 and France UTA Flight 772 in September 1989, US policy toward Libya was dominated by efforts to extradite two Libyan intelligence agents accused of the Pan Am bombing. Libyan intransigence in the face of these extradition demands led to greater multilateral cooperation in exerting pressure on Libya. In 1992, the UN Security Council imposed an arms embargo on Libya and prohibited all travel to and from Libya. A year later, the United Nations banned the sale of petroleum equipment to Libya and froze all non-petroleum-related Libyan government assets abroad.

Eventually, Colonel Muammar Qaddafi began to take steps required for the multilateral sanctions to be lifted. In 1999, Libya secured the suspension of UN sanctions by permitting the extradition of two suspects to be tried for the Pan Am 103 bombing. Libya met the requirements for a permanent lifting of these sanctions in 2003 by accepting responsibility for the actions of its officials connected to the Pan Am bombing, making arrangements to compensate the families of the victims, agreeing to cooperate with any future requests for information relating to the Pan Am investigation, and formally renouncing terrorism in a letter to the UN Security Council. In December 2003, Libyan Foreign Minister Abdel Rahman Shalqam announced that Libya would eliminate all weapons of mass destruction.

These steps led to the gradual lifting of US sanctions throughout 2004, a shift that culminated in September of that year when President Bush terminated the state of emergency declared in 1986 and lifted all sanctions imposed against Libya under IEEPA. On 15 May 2006, the State Department announced its decision to rescind Libya's designation as a state sponsor of terror, omit Libya from the list of countries not fully cooperating with anti-terrorism efforts, and establish an embassy in Tripoli.

Syria

Syria has been on the terrorism list since its inception in December 1979. Although subject to strict export controls and other economic restrictions due to its status as a state sponsor of terrorism, limited trade and investment relations between the United States and Syria otherwise prevailed until late 2003. In December 2003, President Bush signed the Syria Accountability Act, imposing harsher sanctions until Syria ends its support for international terrorism, terminates its occupation of Lebanon, halts its development of WMD, and cuts off support for the Iraqi insurgency. The sanctions include a ban on all exports to Syria except food and medicine, plus a ban on Syrian aircraft in US airspace. According to the State Department's *Country Reports on Terrorism 2005*, although Syria has not been implicated directly in an act of terrorism since 1986, it continues to support Hezbollah and numerous Palestinian terrorist groups, many of which base their external leadership in Damascus.

Sudan

Sudan signaled its willingness to cooperate with international counter-terrorism efforts shortly after the State Department added Sudan to the list of state sponsors in August 1993. In 1994, Sudan extradited the infamous terrorist "Carlos the Jackal" to France. Under US pressure, Sudan also expelled Osama bin Laden in 1996. Nevertheless, the United States imposed comprehensive sanctions on Sudan because of the persecution of Christians in southern Sudan. Preempting Congressional action, President Clinton issued Executive Order 13067 in November 1997, blocking all property of the Sudanese government in the United States, imposing a trade embargo, and prohibiting any financial transactions with Sudan.[6]

The United Nations levied sanctions against Sudan in 1996 to press for the extradition of three suspects in connection with the assassination attempt against Egyptian President Hosni Mubarak the previous year. Punitive measures included reduction of Sudanese diplomatic staff, travel restrictions for Sudanese government and military officials, and a ban on Sudanese aircraft from the airspace of UN member states. While the suspects were never offered for extradition, the United Nations dropped this requirement for lifting sanctions, observing that the three had left the country. In September 2001, the Security Council lifted the sanctions against Sudan, welcoming Sudan's accession to the relevant international conventions for the elimination of terrorism, its ratification of the 1997 International Convention for the Suppression of Terrorist Bombings, and its signing of the 1999 International Convention for the Suppression of Financing of Terrorism.

In May 2004, the State Department removed Sudan from the list of "non-cooperative" countries in the war against terrorism. The United States kept Sudan on the 2005 terrorism list for other reasons, however, including the numbers of foreign nationals who have passed through Sudan to join the insurgency in Iraq, as well as previous instances in which terrorist organizations such as Hamas were allowed to base operations in Sudan.

Cuba

Cuba, which has been under comprehensive US economic sanctions since 1960, was added to the list of state sponsors in 1982, primarily because of its support for the M-19 guerrilla organization in Colombia. Although the Castro regime was very active in providing arms and training to leftist terrorist organizations during the

---

6   Although Congress passed the International Religious Persecution Act in 1998, no additional sanctions were imposed on Sudan. The State Department argued that existing measures met the requirements of the act.

Cold War, Cuba is no longer active in supporting armed struggles around the world. Cuba remains on the list of state sponsors because it continues to provide refuge to international terrorists.

North Korea

North Korea has been subject to comprehensive US sanctions for several decades, since the end of the Korean War. Resulting from its implication in the bombing of a South Korean airliner in November 1987, North Korea was added to the list of countries sponsoring terrorism. Although North Korea has on several occasions publicly condemned all forms of terrorism, it remains on the state sponsor list due to questions surrounding its treatment of Japanese and South Korean abductees.

Afghanistan

The State Department characterized Afghanistan in 1999 as "the primary safe haven for terrorists" in the world. However, the country was never designated as a state sponsor of terrorism in order to avoid granting de facto recognition of the Taliban as the legitimate government of Afghanistan. Instead, President Clinton invoked the Antiterrorism and Effective Death Penalty Act of 1996, thus prohibiting arms sales to Afghanistan by naming it on the list of countries "not cooperating fully with United States antiterrorism efforts." Afghanistan first received this designation in May 1997, becoming the only country on the list that is not also on the list of state sponsors of terrorism.[7]

Because Islamic fundamentalist terrorists continued to train and operate out of Afghanistan, and more specifically because the Taliban continued to harbor Osama bin Laden after his terrorist network was blamed for the bombing of two US embassies in Africa, the Clinton Administration imposed comprehensive sanctions against the Taliban regime in 1999. By executive order, President Clinton banned all trade with Taliban-controlled areas of Afghanistan, froze Taliban assets in the United States, and prohibited financial contributions to the Taliban by US persons. The United Nations supported US efforts, imposed a flight ban, and froze overseas Taliban assets. A year later, the United Nations also imposed an arms embargo and ordered the freezing of the assets of bin Laden and his associates.

After the 9/11 Al Qaeda attacks on New York and Washington, President Bush sent troops to Afghanistan to lead an international coalition that removed the Taliban's grip on power over much of the nation's territory. In May 2002, President Bush issued a proclamation to normalize trade relations with Afghanistan, and in July 2002 he noted the success of the military campaign as reason to revoke Clinton's 1999 executive order. Also during 2002, the United Nations lifted the arms embargo, travel ban, and asset freeze on Afghanistan.

---

7   Afghanistan was certified for the first time under Section 40A of the Arms Export Control Act on 22 May 1997. In 1996, the State Department's Office of Defense Trade Controls amended the International Traffic in Arms Regulations to indicate that the United States would not issue licenses authorizing transactions involving Afghanistan.

Somalia

Although Somalia is not listed as a state sponsor of terrorism, the Bush Administration has expressed concern about terrorist training centers in Somalia, and regards the country as a possible alternative safe haven for Al Qaeda operatives who have been expelled from their enclaves in other countries. Somalia has been without a central government since its last president, Mohamed Siad Barre, fled in 1991, when factional fighting led to national disintegration. The United Nations intervened in 1992, and imposed a weakly enforced arms embargo. The United States closed its embassy and ended its participation in the UN mission in Somalia in 1994. According to US intelligence reports, Somalia has served as a regional base for operations of Al Qaeda since 1993, when bin Laden first provided assistance to the warlord Mohamed Aideed, whose forces killed 18 US soldiers serving in a UN peacekeeping mission. Al Qaeda has also maintained ties with the radical Somali Islamic group Al-Itahaad.

Summary of State Sponsors

This brief review of US policy toward state sponsors of terrorism suggests that unilateral US sanctions have not deterred all target countries from engaging in or supporting terrorist activities. Despite several decades of economic sanctions, the majority of designated state sponsors have continued to shelter and harbor international terrorists and terrorist groups in their territories. In two cases, Iraq and Afghanistan, the United States abandoned sanctions altogether in favor of military intervention directed against the targeted entities. Nevertheless, sanctions did help secure the extradition of the Pan Am bombing suspects from Libya, as well as the dismantling of WMD programs in the same country. Multilateral sanctions also succeeded in convincing Sudan to cooperate with US counter-terrorism efforts. These are the only two terrorism-related cases in which the United States succeeded in garnering multilateral support for economic sanctions. Syria toned down its overt support for terrorism, but it may still support unofficial terrorist organizations.

The modest successes in these two or three cases correspond with general trends we have observed in all US unilateral sanctions episodes since the end of the Second World War. In a survey of more than 60 cases of US unilateral economic sanctions imposed since 1945, we found sharply declining success rates over the last several decades. Between 1960 and 1970, the success rate of US unilateral sanctions dropped from more than 60 percent to roughly 25 percent. These low success rates for all US unilateral sanctions correspond with those of state sponsor of terrorism sanctions throughout the 1980s and 1990s.

US Extraterritorial Sanctions

The United States' approach in dealing with state sponsors of terrorism has differed from the approach favored by its allies. While the European Union has employed "constructive engagement" with countries such as Iran, the United States has shown a proclivity for isolating and punishing these countries. Frustrated by a lack of international cooperation, the US Congress has sought to extend the reach of unilateral US measures by imposing extraterritorial sanctions. In 1996, Congress passed the Helms-Burton Act, which targeted foreign companies that invest in Cuba. A few months later, Congress passed the Iran-Libya Sanctions Act (ILSA), which sought to prevent European companies from investing in the energy sector in either country.[8] The extraterritorial scope of these measures irritated key US allies, and prompted retaliatory legislation in some cases. In order to avoid imposing sanctions against allied industrial nations, Presidents Clinton and Bush have consistently waived key provisions of each bill.

Other secondary measures imposed in the 1990s include an amendment to the Foreign Assistance Act of 1961. The amendment prohibits selected forms of US government aid to any country that provides economic assistance or lethal military weapons to designated terrorist countries. The Iran Nonproliferation Act of 2000 allows the imposition of economic sanctions against entities in third countries that contribute to weapons proliferation in Iran. The threat of secondary sanctions in these instances has not led to greater international cooperation with US counter-terrorism policies.

Specially Designated Terrorists and Foreign Terrorist Organizations

Historically, most major acts of terrorism against American citizens and other targets abroad were supported and, in some cases, instigated by state sponsors. Accordingly, US policy in the 1970s and 1980s focused on state sponsors and the groups they support. However, as the State Department began noting in its annual reports, increasingly, signs point to a declining role for state sponsorship of terrorist activities, and instead indicate a rising threat posed by independent terrorist entities such as Osama bin Laden's Al Qaeda network. In response to these new threats, US counter-terrorism initiatives have been expanded to incorporate list-based restrictions on foreign terrorist groups and individuals.

In 1995, President Clinton began aiming sanctions against individuals and organizations named on the list of Specially Designated Terrorists (SDTs). By executive order, Clinton identified 12 terrorist organizations that threatened to disrupt the Middle East peace process. Clinton also empowered the Secretary of the Treasury and the Attorney General to expand the list (Executive Order 12947, 23 January 1995). All assets of Specially Designated Terrorists were frozen; additionally, transfers of funds, goods, and services to SDT designees were prohibited. The SDT

---

8   Frustrated by President Clinton's inability to gain international support for isolating the regime in Tehran, Congress began drafting legislation to impose extraterritorial sanctions on foreign firms doing business there. The Iran-Libya Sanctions Act, signed by President Clinton in August 1996 in the face of overwhelming Congressional support for the bill, imposed trade and financial sanctions on firms that invest more than USD 20 million in Iran's energy sector. Senator Ted Kennedy (D-MA) added an amendment to the bill to extend the sanctions to firms investing more than USD 40 million in the Libyan energy sector; however, these measures no longer apply to Libya.

sanctions apply to any entity "owned or controlled by, or to act for or on behalf of" any Specially Designated Terrorist.

Sanctions on non-state actors were broadened and codified with the Antiterrorism and Effective Death Penalty Act of 1996. The central legislative initiative with respect to US counter-terrorism policy in the 1990s, this act provides for the designation of Foreign Terrorist Organizations (FTOs) by the Secretary of State, a designation equivalent to that of a state sponsor of terrorism. Once designated an FTO, the terrorist group is prohibited from conducting financial transactions in the US, and all assets are frozen. Section 303 makes it a crime for US residents to knowingly provide material support or resources to a designated FTO. In addition, financial institutions are required to block funds in "which a foreign terrorist organization, or its agent, has an interest" and report the existence of these funds to the Treasury Department (Antiterrorism and Effective Death Penalty Act of 1996, Title III, Section 303, PL 104–132). The Treasury Department may require US financial institutions to freeze assets of a designated FTO.

One provision of the act that received great publicity was the so-called "Farrakhan Amendment."[9] In its broadest interpretation, this amendment prohibits financial transactions between US persons and the governments of designated terrorist countries. The Clinton Administration, in issuing the regulations, chose to interpret the provision more narrowly, as restricting donations or transactions when a US person has reason to believe it will be used to support terrorist acts in the United States.

The 1990s saw the emergence of Osama bin Laden and the Al Qaeda network on the international scene. After the United States successfully pressured Sudan into expelling Osama bin Laden in 1996, he found refuge in Afghanistan. From there, he is believed to have masterminded the bombing of US embassies in Nairobi and Dar es Salaam in 1998, and the suicide attack on the *USS Cole* in October 2000. In response to the 1998 embassy attacks, President Clinton determined that Osama bin Laden and his Al Qaeda network constituted a threat to the Middle East peace process (Executive Order 13099, 21 August 1998). By adding them to the list of SDTs, President Clinton banned US financial transactions with Al Qaeda operatives and froze any bin Laden assets in the United States. Despite this new authority, the Treasury Department was unable to link any assets to either bin Laden or his organization prior to the 9/11 attacks.

Notwithstanding the substantial experience of the Treasury Department's Office of Foreign Assets Control (OFAC) in administering financial sanctions, its pre-9/11 efforts to stop the flow of funds to terrorist organizations were not particularly successful. The 2000 Treasury Department annual report on terrorist assets reveals that only USD 301,146 in assets of designated FTOs or SDTs had been frozen in the years prior to the 9/11 attacks. A major challenge for an asset

---

9   This amendment was named for radical Minister Louis Farrakhan who was offered a USD 1 billion donation, supposedly for charitable purposes, by Colonel Muammar Qaddafi in 1996. The Treasury Department barred Farrakhan from receiving the donation, citing an earlier executive order. To preclude similar circumventions in the future, Congress enacted the "Farrakhan Amendment."

freeze program is to identify funds that belong to the individuals, governments, and organizations targeted. Although the means of tracking financial assets have greatly improved, so have the means of evasion. Even when individual funds can be identified as belonging to specific terrorist entities, secrecy and speed are critical in preventing targets from moving assets to numbered accounts in offshore banking centers. Unfortunately, secrecy and speed are not easily reconciled with the need to coordinate efforts with allies or within the UN Security Council. For example, even if the United States, the European Union, and the United Nations all agree on sanctioning Al Qaeda, the task of matching up lists of targeted individuals can present significant difficulties.

Post-9/11 Initiatives

As President Bush noted in his Rose Garden speech on 24 September 2001, economic sanctions play a prominent role in fighting the war on terror. The Bush Administration has pursued three broad strategies. First, the United States has cast a wide net in sanctioning non-state terrorist entities, both under existing legislation and new legislation. Second, the United States has buttressed multilateral sanctions regimes. Third, the United States has offered incentives in the form of lifting sanctions on countries to induce cooperation in the war on terror.

Targeting Non-state Terrorist Entities under US Legislation

Following the attacks of 9/11, law enforcement agencies focused intently on the financial trails of terrorist networks. Declaring a national emergency with respect to acts of terrorism, President Bush used his power under the IEEPA on 23 September 2001 to broaden existing authorities in several ways. First, the new executive order expanded the scope of past executive orders from terrorism in the Middle East to cover global terrorism. Second, it expanded the class of targeted groups to include all those who are "associated with" designated terrorist groups. Third, it established the ability to freeze US assets (and deny access to US markets) of foreign banks that refuse to freeze terrorist assets. This expansion of authority was modeled after the Specially Designated Narcotics Traffickers (SDNT) program, which has shown modest success in allowing OFAC to target entities providing material, technological, or financial assistance to designated narcotics traffickers.

In the wake of 9/11, the administration worked closely with Congress on broad new anti-terrorism legislation. The USA Patriot Act, passed by Congress in October 2001, expanded the ability of US law enforcement and intelligence agencies to track and detain suspected terrorists. The act also includes several measures to disrupt money laundering and other methods of terrorist financing.[10] The act requires that foreign banks with corresponding accounts in US banks designate a point person to receive subpoenas related to these accounts. Furthermore, US banks are barred from doing business with banks that have no physical facility or operate outside the regulated banking system. The Treasury Department also has the authority to require banks to scrutinize deposits from residents of nations that do not cooperate with US officials. The Patriot Act also includes a provision that allows the Treasury Department to impose sanctions on banks that refuse to provide information to law enforcement agencies.[10]

Multilateral Sanctions

Multilateral UN sanctions to fight terrorism have dovetailed with those imposed by the United States.[11] For example, both parties began targeting the Taliban in the 1990s, and subsequently ratcheted up the pressure. UN measures date to 1999, when the Security Council ordered an asset freeze and flight bans on the Taliban (UNSCR 1267, 15 October 1999). In the same resolution, the United Nations requested that the Taliban deny terrorists access to its territory and turn over Osama bin Laden for extradition. The Security Council broadened these measures in 2000 to include an arms embargo prohibiting sales of weapons to portions of Afghan territory under Taliban control (UNSCR 1333, 19 December 2000). Soon after the 9/11 attacks, the Security Council broadened all of these measures to apply to all terrorist entities (UNSCR 1373, 28 September 2001). In 2005, the Security Council adopted a US-sponsored resolution that further broadened these measures to sanction any entity "associated with" Al Qaeda, Osama bin Laden, or the Taliban (UNSCR 1617, 29 July 2005).

Modest Expectations for Sanctioning Terrorists

Modesty is the proper watchword for attempts to fight terrorism through financial measures. Asset freezes through the SDNT program typically disrupt less than 1 percent of the annual flow of drug-related funds (Hufbauer, et al., 2001). It seems unlikely that the success rate in freezing terrorist assets is significantly higher. Furthermore, measuring total assets frozen may not even be the most accurate way to measure the effectiveness of the sanctions regime. Other authors have suggested using a flow test (sum of assets blocked with each new terrorist entity sanctioned), as opposed to a stock test (total amount frozen or seized) (Reuter and Truman, 2004, 143).

Even assuming a perfectly functioning asset freeze system, terrorists can still utilize unregulated financial instruments outside the formal banking sector. These groups can transfer money through networks that operate far from the watchful eye of governments, using either cash or street-corner money exchange systems. Attempts to stop terrorism through asset freezes are also problematic because of the relatively small sums of money required for terrorist groups to operate. Unlike other

---

10   Section 311 of the Patriot Act was first invoked in 2004 when the Treasury Department designated the Commercial Bank of Syria as a "Primary Money Laundering Concern," thereby prohibiting US financial institutions from all dealings with the bank (Reuter and Truman, 2004, 144).

11   For an account of international efforts to strengthen the anti-money laundering regime after 9/11, see Steil and Litan, 2006, 38–9.

criminal activities that are financed from an accumulated stock of capital, terrorism can be carried out with small, discrete financial flows (Steil and Litan, 2006, 41).

Carrots

In rallying global support for the war on terrorism, the Bush Administration has offered countries a number of financial incentives, including the permanent lifting of economic sanctions. Pakistan, India, China, and Central Asia all illustrate this "carrot" approach.

Pakistan

- Less than two weeks after the 9/11 attacks, the Bush Administration waived sanctions that were imposed when Pakistan conducted nuclear tests in 1998, as well as other restrictions dating back to the early 1990s. We estimate that the average annual costs of US sanctions to Pakistan were about USD 405 million (or 1 percent of Pakistan's 1990 GDP) (Hufbauer, et al., forthcoming).
- In late September 2001, President Bush released an initial USD 50 million in emergency aid to Pakistan, and rescheduled more than USD 12 billion of Pakistan's foreign debt.
- The United States and the European Union have made limited concessions regarding import restrictions on textiles from Pakistan, the country's largest source of manufacturing employment.
- At a 2003 Camp David summit with Pakistan's President Pervez Musharraf, President Bush announced his intention to work with Congress to provide Pakistan with a USD 3 billion assistance package, designed to bolster Pakistan's counter-terrorism capabilities and to fight poverty.

India

- Less than two weeks after the 9/11 attacks, the Bush Administration lifted all remaining nuclear-related sanctions against India. While most sanctions imposed in response to India's nuclear tests in 1998 had already been waived, we estimate that the initial costs of economic sanctions to India were about USD 678 million annually (Hufbauer, et al., forthcoming).
- At a Washington summit in July 2005, Indian Prime Minister Manmohan Singh and President Bush announced a plan for "full civil nuclear cooperation." This plan, if approved by the US Congress, would give India access to a wide range of US nuclear technology.

China

In October 2001, Presidents Bush and Jiang Zemin agreed on their common interest in fighting terrorism, and this shared vision facilitated a partial warming of Sino-American relations. The two Presidents met four times in just over a year following the 9/11 attacks, including a meeting at President Bush's ranch in Crawford, TX. Additionally, the United States froze the assets of the East Turkestan Islamic Movement, an anti-PRC group active in China's Xinjiang region.

Speculation arose that the United States would waive its Tiananmen sanctions to allow China an opportunity to purchase parts for Black Hawk helicopters, but the White House denied the rumors. The United States did waive the Tiananmen sanctions two times during January 2002—once for export of a bomb containment and disposal unit for the Shanghai fire department to thwart terrorist bombings, and again to consider export licenses for equipment to clean up chemical weapons left in China by Japan after the Second World War. Speculation has arisen about the possibility for future waivers to allow Chinese purchases of equipment for security during the 2008 Beijing Olympics.

In sum, however, cooperation with China in the war on terrorism has produced little more than rhetorical carrots from the United States, as bilateral relations are driven by numerous other issues, including Taiwan, negotiations with North Korea, proliferation of WMD, and currency manipulation.

Central Asia: Kazakhstan, Kyrgyzstan, Tajikistan, Turkmenistan, Uzbekistan

As part of a broader effort to fight terrorism, promote security, facilitate domestic reforms, and secure energy interests, the Bush Administration has significantly increased foreign aid to states in Central Asia. Prior to the 9/11 attacks, Central Asia received less than 14 percent of all foreign aid budgeted for Eurasia. This share nearly doubled, to a quarter of all Eurasian aid in 2002, reflecting the Bush Administration's realization of the importance of Central Asia in the war against terrorism. Additional cash flowed into Central Asia from the United States in the form of payments for military base leases, as well as landing and overflight fees.

Due to the lack of democratic reforms and mercurial military relationships (such as the expulsion of the US military from its airbase in Uzbekistan), disbursements of both aid and military payments to Central Asian states have been periodically delayed or canceled. Nonetheless, the broader trend of US policy in Central Asia has been increasing engagement since 9/11, consistently providing incentives for countries willingly cooperating in the war against terrorism. In June 2004, the United States and all five Central Asian countries signed a trade and investment framework agreement.

The United States has worked actively to promote the shipment of Caspian Sea oil through the Baku–Tbilisi–Ceyhan pipeline. This route increases export outlets for key Central Asian energy suppliers by sidestepping Iranian and Russian distribution networks.

Armenia and Azerbaijan

As the United States began preparations to lead a military campaign against the Taliban in Afghanistan, Armenia and Azerbaijan quickly granted overflight rights in support of Operation Enduring Freedom. Soon thereafter, President Bush began lifting sanctions against both countries. In January 2002, he waived Section 907 of the Freedom Support

Act in order to make Azerbaijan eligible for US foreign aid. In April, President Bush lifted restrictions on arms sales to both Armenia and Azerbaijan. These countries had been added to the International Traffic in Arms Regulations (ITAR) list of proscribed destinations for defense articles and services in 1993. The removal of Armenia and Azerbaijan from the ITAR list made these countries eligible to purchase items on the US Munitions List on a case-by-case basis.

Appraisal

In the aftermath of 9/11, the Bush Administration took the proper course in modifying the counter-terror sanctions regime. It used existing statutory powers to the fullest extent, and enlisted multilateral cooperation in freezing the assets of terrorist groups and their supporters. Notably, on 18 November 2001, all G-20 finance ministers (including those from Saudi Arabia and Indonesia) agreed, at urging from the United States, to impose forceful financial measures against terrorist groups. Imaginatively, the Bush Administration used the lifting of preexisting US sanctions as inducements for newly discovered allies-of-convenience. The administration worked diligently to speed other financial assistance for these same allies through the halls of the IMF, the World Bank, and similar institutions.

In spite of these positive steps towards recalibrating the US sanctions regime in the war on terror, it would be illusory to expect that the arsenal of economic sanctions can play more than a modest role in the war against terrorism. There are several reasons to suggest that even the best-conceived measures will have only a limited effect:

- First, the history of sanctions against state sponsors of terrorism shows a very modest record of success in achieving limited goals (Libya and Sudan are the only solid success cases).
- Second, the history of sanctions in the past decade records no instance of success against terrorist groups, such as Hezbollah, Hamas, Abu Nidal, or for that matter, Al Qaeda. Since terrorism is their raison d'être, using economic sanctions to stop these groups amounts to seeking a major policy objective with purely economic tools. Economic sanctions have almost never succeeded in such cases.
- Third, in the financial war against drug lords, probably less than 1 percent of a vast ocean of cash has been captured by various asset freezes. Terrorist groups command a far smaller stream of resources than drug lords, and thus present a more elusive target.

To say that economic sanctions will play an auxiliary role to intelligence, covert action, and military intervention is not to denigrate their importance. In all of America's wars during the past century—the First and Second World Wars, the Korean War, the Vietnam War, and the Gulf War—sanctions made tangible, if secondary, contributions. In the war against terrorism, asset freezes and other sanctions will pinch terrorist organizations, but economic sanctions alone cannot be expected to bring bin Laden and Al Qaeda to heel. Nevertheless, the judicious combination of sanctions and positive measures (including the selective waiver of existing sanctions) can help build support among the frontline states in the global war against terrorism.

References

Baer, Robert (2002), *See No Evil* (New York: Crown Publishers).
Bush, George W. (2001), "President Freezes Terrorists' Assets," Remarks by the President, Secretary of the Treasury O'Neill, and Secretary of State Powell on Executive Order, from the Rose Garden (24 September).
Hufbauer, Gary C., et al. (2001), *Using Sanctions to Fight Terrorism*, Policy Brief 01-11, November (Washington, DC: Institute for International Economics).
Hufbauer, Gary C., et al. (forthcoming), *Economic Sanctions Reconsidered*, 3rd ed. (Washington, DC: Institute for International Economics).
Reuter, P. and Truman, E.M. (2004), *Chasing Dirty Money* (Washington, DC: Institute for International Economics).
Steil, B. and Litan, R.E. (2006), *Financial Statecraft* (New Haven, CT: Yale University Press).
United States Department of State (USDOS), Office of the Coordinator for Counterterrorism (2006), *Patterns of Global Terrorism 2005*. (Washington, DC: United States Department of State).

Chapter 12

The Brittle Superpower[1]*

Stephen E. Flynn

Introduction

The United States has been living on borrowed time—and squandering it. In the five years since the 9/11 attacks on New York and Washington, the Bush Administration has chosen to emphasize the use of military operations overseas over an effort to reduce America's vulnerability to catastrophic terrorist attacks at home. While it has acknowledged in principle the need to improve critical infrastructure protection, in practice it has placed the burden for doing so primarily on the private sector that owns and operates much of that infrastructure. But this delegation of responsibility fails to acknowledge the practical limitations of the marketplace to agree upon common protocols and to make investments to bolster security. As a result, the transportation, energy, information, financial, chemical, food, and logistical networks that underpin US economic power and the American way of life remain virtually unprotected. If the federal government does not provide meaningful incentives to make US infrastructure more resilient and create workable frameworks for ongoing public and private partnerships to advance security, future terrorist attacks—and the resulting profound economic and societal disruption—are inevitable.

It does not have to be this way. The federal government should be taking the lead in engaging the private sector in a collective effort to confront the threat of catastrophic terror events and natural disasters at home. Unfortunately, while the post-9/11 case for homeland security is seemingly a straightforward one, Washington has demonstrated an extraordinary degree of ambivalence about making any serious effort to tackle this mission. Instead, the White House has favored muscular efforts abroad to combat terrorism, and has passed along the mission of emergency preparedness to governors, county commissioners, and mayors. The premise behind the Bush Administration's strategy of the preemptive use of force is that, as long as the United States is willing to show sufficient grit, it can successfully hold its enemies at bay. Throughout the 2004 presidential campaign, the President and Vice President asserted that the war on terror had to be waged at its source. In the words of Vice President Dick Cheney: "Wars are not won on the defensive. To fully and finally remove this danger [of terrorism], we have only one option—and that's to take the fight to the enemy" (Cheney, 2005). On 4 July 2004, President Bush made the point this way: "We will engage these enemies in these countries [Iraq and Afghanistan] and around the world so we do not have to face them here at home" (Bush, 2004).

---

1   * Portions of this chapter were published in Auersald, et al., 2006. The recommendations section is drawn from Flynn and Prieto, 2006. The author retains the copyright for this chapter.

Chasing the Threat

Targeting terrorism at its source is an appealing notion. Unfortunately, the enemy is not cooperating. As the March 2004 attacks in Madrid, the July 2005 attacks in London, the August 2005 attacks in Sharm el Sheikh, Egypt, and the October 2005 attacks in Bali, Indonesia have made clear, there is no central front on which Al Qaeda and its radical jihadist imitators can be confronted and destroyed. Terrorist organizations are living and operating within the jurisdictions of US allies, and do not need to receive aid and comfort from rogue states. According to the US Department of State's annual global terrorism report, the number of terrorist incidents reached a record high in 2004, despite the US-led invasions of Afghanistan and Iraq (US Department of State, 2005).[2] There is mounting evidence that the invasion of Iraq is fueling both the number of recruits and the capabilities of radical jihadist groups (Clarke, et al., 2004).

The reluctance of the White House and the national security community to adapt to the shifting nature of the terrorist threat bears a disturbing resemblance to the opening chapter of the Second World War. In September 1939, the German Army rolled eastward into Poland and unleashed a new form of combat known as *blitzkrieg*, or "lightning war." When Poland became a victim of the Third Reich, London and Paris finally abandoned their policies of appeasement and declared war. The British and French high commands then began to execute war plans that relied on assumptions drawn from their experiences in the First World War. They activated their reserves and reinforced the Maginot Line, heavily fortified defenses of mounted cannons stretching for 250 miles along the Franco-German border. Then they waited for Hitler's next move.

The eight-month period before the fall of Paris came to be known as "the phony war." During this relatively quiet interlude, France and the United Kingdom were convinced that they were deterring the Germans by mobilizing their more plentiful military assets in an updated posture of trench warfare. But they did not alter their tactics to respond to the new form of offensive warfare that the Germans had executed with such lethal results in Eastern Europe. In May 1940, they paid a heavy price for their complacency: Panzer units raced into the lowlands, circumvented the Maginot Line, and conquered France shortly thereafter. The British expeditionary forces narrowly escaped by fleeing across the English Channel aboard a makeshift armada, leaving much of their armament behind on the beaches of Dunkirk.

Instead of a Maginot Line, the Pentagon is executing its long-standing forward defense strategy, which involves leapfrogging beyond US borders and waging combat on the turf of the United States' enemies or allies. Meanwhile, protecting the rear—the United States itself—remains largely outside the scope of the national

---

2   The report does not include the specific figures, but states in its overview: "Despite ongoing improvements in U.S. homeland security, military campaigns against insurgents and terrorists in Iraq and Afghanistan, and deepening counterterrorism cooperation among the nations of the world, international terrorism continued to pose a significant threat to the United States and its partners in 2004." However, *The Washington Post* reported that Congressional aides briefed on the US Department of State statistics confirmed that the number of serious terrorist incidents tripled in 2004; see Glasser, 2005.

security apparatus, even though the 9/11 attacks were launched *from* the United States on targets *within* the United States.

Al Qaeda has demonstrated that, by directing terrorist attacks on major urban areas and the critical foundations of modern life, it can generate a very big "bang for its buck." It has also placed the United States at the top of its target list, and has made clear that it wants to carry out a more devastating attack than those launched on New York and Washington ("Official: Voice on Tape," 2002).

Defenders of the Bush Administration's war on terrorism are quick to point to the absence of another 9/11-style attack on US soil as vindication for the approach of placing overwhelming emphasis on an offense-oriented strategy. To be sure, there is ample evidence that the war in Iraq has been attracting foreign insurgents and Al Qaeda sympathizers to Baghdad instead of to Main Street. However, this is likely to prove to be a short-term reprieve that poses a longer-term danger. Beginning in June 2003, Iraq's energy sector became a primary target for insurgents. By mid-July 2005, nearly 250 attacks on oil and gas pipelines had cost Iraq more than USD 10 billion in lost oil revenue. Successful attacks on the electrical grid have kept average daily output at 5 to 10 percent below the pre-war level, despite the USD 1.2 billion that the United States has spent to improve Iraqi electrical production (Benjamin and Simon, 2005, 37).

In some ways the situation in Iraq is analogous to what happened during the decade-long conflict from 1979–89 during the Soviet occupation of Afghanistan. The foreign participants who joined the *mujahedin* in that conflict became the hardened foot-soldiers who would ultimately transform themselves into Al Qaeda. But unlike Afghanistan, where the combatants waged war in the context of a pre-modern society, in Iraq insurgents are refining the skills to sabotage critical modern infrastructures. Accordingly, when these foreign insurgents eventually return to their native lands, they will do so with the experience of successfully targeting complex systems that support economic and daily life within advanced societies.

Planning Terror

Even if the United States had not chosen to invade Iraq, there is an alternative explanation for why there has not been another attack on American soil besides ascribing success to US counter-terrorism operations abroad. As a practical matter, planning sophisticated attacks on the scale of the 9/11 attacks takes time. Since Al Qaeda has proclaimed that it wants to surpass the destruction and disruption associated with toppling the World Trade Center towers, meticulous planning is required. Deploying the complex organizational structure necessary to carry out those plans can take several years. This is because it typically involves deploying a three-cell structure, where the members of each cell are isolated from one another to provide the best chance of survival should any one cell be compromised.

An Al Qaeda-style operation will involve a *logistics* cell to attend to such things as locating safe houses, providing identity documents, and finding jobs for the operatives so that they can blend into the civilian population. There is also a *surveillance* cell that is charged with scoping out potential targets, probing security measures, and conducting dry runs. Finally, there is an *attack* cell, which may include suicide bombers who are charged with executing the attack (Flynn, 2005).

Establishing this organizational capacity is a painstaking process, particularly within the United States, where Al Qaeda must work from a much smaller pool of operatives and sympathizers than it has in Western Europe or in countries like Indonesia. It is also a resource that must be carefully husbanded, since using it will likely translate into losing it. This is because it is impossible to carry out an attack without leaving some forensic clues that expose terrorist cells to enforcement action. Accordingly, going after what would seem to be a plentiful menu of seemingly soft targets like shopping malls or sporting events can produce plenty of short-term media attention. But if these attacks cannot be sustained over time because the authorities are able to track down and destroy the terrorists' organization, the long-term economic consequences of these attacks are likely to be modest. As a result, terrorists will want to make sure that they pick meaningful targets where the attack proves to be worth all the organizational effort required to carry it out.

Paying for Safety

In short, it would be foolhardy to act as though the 9/11 attacks were an aberrant event where Al Qaeda got lucky simply because America's guard was temporarily down. The sad truth is that the United States' guard was never really up, and despite all the political rhetoric, little has changed in recent years. The most tempting targets for terrorists remain those whose destruction can create widespread economic and social disruption. However, the White House has declared that safeguarding the nation's critical infrastructure is not really a federal responsibility. According to President Bush's 2002 *National Strategy for Homeland Security*, "The government should only address those activities that the market does not adequately provide— for example, national defense or border security. ... For other aspects of homeland security, sufficient incentives exist in the private market to supply protection" (*National Strategy for Homeland Security*, 2002, 64).

Unfortunately, this expression of faith has not been borne out by the facts. According to a survey commissioned by the Washington-based Council on Competitiveness just one year after 9/11, 92 percent of business executives did not believe that terrorists would target their companies, and only 53 percent of the respondents indicated that their companies had increased security spending between 2001 and 2002 (Council on Competitiveness, 2002, 19). With the passing of each month without a new attack, the reluctance of companies to invest in security has only grown.

The lack of enthusiasm on the part of corporate CEOs to provide leadership when it comes to developing the means to safeguard critical infrastructures should not be surprising. This is because survival in the marketplace has required that they be responsive to four imperatives of globalization—how to make critical infrastructures:

- As open to as many users as possible

- As efficient as possible
- As reliable as possible
- As inexpensive to use and operate as possible.

Since the conventional view of security is that it implies higher costs, undermines efficiency, is at odds with assuring reliability, and applies constraints on access, there has been a clear disincentive for the private sector to make it a priority. As a result, we entered the new millennium with networks that have an extraordinary capacity to generate wealth, but with few meaningful safeguards should they come under attack.

The challenge of elevating the priority of protecting critical infrastructure and crafting a tidy division of labor in the security realm between the private and public sectors is complicated by two additional factors. First, safeguards that apply only within US borders will not work, since America's critical infrastructures are dependent on their links to the rest of North America and the world. Second, the United States competes in a global marketplace, and it must be mindful of not unilaterally incurring costs that place US companies and the US economy at a competitive disadvantage.

Private-sector concerns about maintaining economic competitiveness in the face of the growing security imperative are legitimate. Security is not free. A company incurs costs when it invests in measures to protect the portion of infrastructure it controls. If a company does not believe other companies are willing or able to make a similar investment, then it faces the likelihood of losing market share while simply shifting the infrastructure's vulnerability elsewhere. If terrorists strike, the company will still suffer the disruptive consequences of an attack, right alongside those who did nothing to prevent it. Those consequences are likely to include the costs of implementing new government requirements. Therefore, infrastructure security suffers from a dilemma commonly referred to as the "tragedy of the commons."

Take the case of the chemical industry. By and large, chemical manufacturers have a good safety record. But security is another matter. Operating on thin profit margins and faced with growing competition from overseas, most companies have been reluctant to incur the additional costs associated with improving their security. Now let us imagine that the manager of a chemical plant looks around his facility and gets squeamish about the many security lapses he finds. After a fitful night of sleep, he wakes up and decides to invest in protective measures that raise the cost of his product to his customers by USD 50 per shipment. A competitor who does not make that investment will be able to attract business away from the security-conscious plant, because his handling costs will be lower. Capable terrorists and criminals will target this lower-cost operation, since it is an easier target.

In the event of an incident, particularly one that is catastrophic, two consequences are likely. First, government officials will not discriminate between the more security-conscious and the less security-conscious companies. All chemical plants are likely to be shut down while the authorities try to sort things out. Second, once the dust clears, elected and regulatory officials will scramble to impose new security requirements that could nullify the proactive plant owner's earlier investments. Given this scenario, the most rational behavior on the part of the nervous manager would appear to be to keep tossing and turning at night while focusing on short-term profitability during the day.

The only way to prevent the tragedy of the commons is to convince all the private participants to abide by the same security requirements. When standards are universal, their cost is borne equally across a sector. As taxpayers or as consumers, Americans will end up bankrolling these measures, but what they will be paying for is insurance against the loss of innocent lives and a profound level of disruption to their society and the economy.

The problem boils down to this: the design, ownership, and day-to-day operational knowledge of critical systems rest almost exclusively with the private sector. But security and safety are public goods whose provision is a core responsibility of government at all levels. The government is unable to protect things of which it has only a peripheral understanding and over which it has limited jurisdictional reach, and the market will resist providing public goods if doing so puts them at a competitive disadvantage by eroding their profits or diminishing their market share.

Certainly, 9/11 created a general sense among public- and private-sector actors that the security imperative requires far more attention than it had been receiving. But the reality is that there still remain disincentives for the private sector to cooperate with government entities on this agenda. Some of the structures in place, such as the laws and regulations that guide the interaction within and among these sectors, remain static. For instance, antitrust laws put severe constraints on the ability of industry leaders to come together and agree to common protocols. Also, companies that make a good-faith effort to undertake industry-generated anti-terrorist measures potentially risk open-ended liability issues should terrorists succeed at defeating those measures. After the post-mortem, public officials are likely to be at the head of the queue insisting that private-sector entities be held accountable for not having done enough.

While there are practical barriers to having the private sector assume the bulk of the responsibility for the post-9/11 security mandate, leaving it to the public sector alone to map the path ahead holds little promise as an alternative. When the government announces requirements or "best practices" after a lengthy deliberative process with nominal industry input, they almost always miss the mark. More often than not, the proposed or mandated safeguards reflect a poor understanding of the design and operation of critical infrastructures and the real versus the perceived vulnerabilities. This is because many of the most critical issues span multiple agency jurisdictions, and these agencies rarely work well together. The results end up being a mix of unacknowledged gaps and redundant requirements.

Sharing the Burden

If improving homeland security requires that the US government reconsider many of its assumptions and priorities, it also requires a population that acknowledges that security must become everyone's business. The starting point for engaging civil society in this enterprise is a willingness to accept that there will never be a permanent victory achieved in a war on terrorism through overseas military campaigns. Terrorism is simply too cheap, too available, and too tempting to ever be totally eradicated. And US borders will never serve as an effective last line of defense against a determined terrorist. What is required is that everyday citizens develop both the maturity to live with the risk of future attacks and the willingness to invest in reasonable measures to mitigate that risk.

This is not a defeatist position. Improving the United States' defenses and its resilience to withstand acts of catastrophic terrorism has both tactical value in defending against these attacks and strategic value in deterring them in the first place. Radical jihadist groups do not have unlimited resources. When they strike, they want to be reasonably confident that they will be successful. They also want to inflict real damage that will generate political pressure to adopt draconian measures in response to the demands of a traumatized public.

Today's terrorist masterminds know that the main benefit of attacks on critical infrastructure is not the immediate damage they inflict, but the collateral consequences of eroding the public's trust in the services on which it depends. Certainly this lesson has not been lost on Osama bin Laden. In a video tape broadcast on *Al Jazeera* on 1 November 2004, bin Laden claimed: "For example, Al Qaeda spent $500,000 on the event [the 9/11 attacks], while America, in the incident and its aftermath, lost— according to the lowest estimate—more than $500 billion. Meaning that every dollar of Al Qaeda defeated a million dollars by the permission of Allah, besides the loss of a huge number of jobs" (see <http://english.aljazeera.net>).

What if the next terrorist strike were on the American food supply system? The attack itself might kill only a handful of people, but without measures in place to reassure the public that follow-up attacks could be prevented or at least contained, consumers at home and abroad would lose trust in an economic sector that accounts for more than ten percent of US GDP. Similarly, a dirty bomb smuggled in a container and set off in a seaport would likely kill only a few unfortunate longshoremen and contaminate several acres of valuable waterfront property. But if there is no credible security system to restore the public's confidence that other containers are safe, mayors and governors throughout the country, as well as the President, will come under withering political pressure to order the shutdown of the intermodal transportation system. Examining cargo in tens of thousands of trucks, trains, and ships to ensure it poses no threat would have devastating economic consequences. When containers stop moving, assembly plants go idle, retail shelves go bare, and workers end up in unemployment lines. A three-week shutdown could well spawn a global recession.

The Benefits of Preparation

As long as perpetrators of catastrophic terrorism are assured of generating a huge bang for the buck, current and future US adversaries will make it the first weapon they reach for in attacking the country. Their confidence in their ability to inflict real damage on the world's sole superpower will be directly proportional to the unwillingness of private and public leaders to acknowledge the risk of market failures associated with excessive reliance on unprotected networks that are sophisticated, concentrated, and interdependent. Given the futility of taking on US military forces directly, attacking these networks is not irrational. In warfare, combatants always seek to exploit their adversary's weaknesses.

However, if terrorist attacks were likely to be detected, intercepted, contained, and managed without doing any measurable damage to the quality of life of a significant number of Americans, their value as a means of warfare would be depreciated. Since such acts violate widely accepted norms, they will almost certainly invite not just American, but also international, retribution. Most adversaries would probably judge this too high a price to pay if striking civilian targets holds out little chance of causing the desired level of mass disruption.

A focus on critical infrastructure protection can also improve the effectiveness of more conventional counter-terrorism measures. Bolstering the security of critical networks in advance of possible attacks will require adversaries to put together more complex operations to target them successfully. The resultant need for terrorists to raise more money, recruit more expertise, and lengthen planning cycles and rehearsals would be a boon for intelligence services and law enforcement officials. This is because such pre-execution activities elevate the opportunities for infiltration and raise the odds that terrorist groups will attract attention.

There is an added bit of good news that comes from placing greater emphasis on homeland security. The most effective measures for protecting potential targets or making them more resilient in the face of successful attacks almost always have derivative benefits for other public and private goods. For instance, strengthening the tools to detect and intercept terrorists will enhance the means that authorities have at their disposal to combat criminal acts such as narcotics trafficking, migrant smuggling, cargo theft, and violations of export controls. The risk of an avian flu pandemic and diseases such as SARS, AIDS, West Nile, foot-and-mouth, and BSE have highlighted the challenges of managing deadly pathogens in a shrinking world. Public health investments in processes to deal with biological agents or attacks on food and water supplies will provide US authorities with more effective tools to manage these global diseases as well. Likewise, measures adopted to protect infrastructure make it more resilient not only to terrorist attacks, but also to acts of God or human and mechanical error. They also invariably reinforce US values that are respected around the world, whereas reliance on aggressive military measures invariably puts those values at risk.

How much security is enough? Answering that question requires both some clarity about the threat that a security measure is designed to counter and an identification of the appropriate point at which an additional investment in a security measure yields only a marginal return. Asking the private sector to decide independently where this line should be drawn is impractical, both because they lack access to intelligence and because they need "good Samaritan" safeguards, should their efforts fall short of deterring every terrorist incident. Only the federal government has access to the threat information, and only the federal government can establish liability limits.

In the end, the threshold for success will be when the American people can conclude that a future terrorist attack on US soil will be an exceptional event that does not require wholesale changes in how they go about their lives. This means that they should be confident that there are adequate private and public measures in place to confront the danger and manage its aftermath. In other words, homeland security should strive to achieve what the aviation industry has done with safety. What sustains air travel, despite the periodic horror of airplanes falling out of the sky, is the extent to which the industry's long-standing and ongoing investments have convinced the public that it is safe to fly. Public confidence can never be taken for granted after a major jet crash, but private and public aviation officials start from a credible foundation built upon a cooperative effort to incorporate safety into every part of the industry. In the immediate aftermath of airline disasters, the public is reassured by the fact that the lessons learned are quickly compiled and released, and that the government and the industry seem willing to take whatever corrective actions are required.

Ongoing and credible efforts to confront risk are essential to the viability of any complex modern enterprise. Aviation safety provides helpful reference points for how to pursue security without turning the United States into a national gated community. First, it demonstrates that Americans do not expect their lives to be risk-free; they simply rightfully expect that reasonable measures be in place to manage that risk. Second, managing risk works best if safeguards are integrated as an organic part of a sector's environment, and if they are dynamic in adapting to changes in that environment. Third, government plays an essential role in providing incentives and disincentives for people and industries to meet minimum standards. Bluntly stated, security will not happen by itself.

When it comes to critical infrastructure protection, the issue, then, is to engage the private sector to develop standards and create effective mechanisms for their uniform enforcement. This is a task that necessitates a much different kind of institutional framework than setting up a new federal Department of Homeland Security (DHS). What it requires is the creation of a structure that allows the private sector and civil society to participate as equal partners in the process of designing and implementing security for the US homeland.

Conclusion

Admittedly, it will not be easy to muster the political will to admit the post-9/11 error of placing so much emphasis on projecting military might abroad while neglecting efforts to build greater US resilience at home. But now is not a time for timidity. Ordinary Americans and leaders in the private sector must demand that Washington make homeland security generally—and critical infrastructure specifically—a priority. And the entire nation, not just the national security establishment, must be organized for the long struggle against terrorism.

To that end, in January 2005 the Council on Foreign Relations (CFR) initiated a year-long project, informed by a non-partisan working group drawn entirely from the private sector, to assess the extent to which private entities are succeeding at making America safer. The federal government has largely taken a hands-off approach to the private sector, believing that market mechanisms will provide levels of security sufficient to address the modern terrorist threat. This belief has proven to be unfounded. The federal government must abandon its passive role and lead a truly collaborative effort to protect our national assets and leverage private-sector capabilities in defense of the homeland. The conclusions and recommendations below have been drawn from the input of the working group and from the CFR special report "The Neglected Defense." Some of these steps will be the work of Congress, others the purview of the executive branch, still others the responsibility of the private sector, but they all share a common goal—to better secure the homeland.

Recommendations[3]

The federal government needs to urgently undertake steps to ensure that critical infrastructures are better protected and that preparedness, response, and recovery efforts are ready to fully leverage all available assets, including those owned by the private sector. In order to do this, Washington must use a full range of policy tools to engender true public/private partnership in pursuit of homeland security. The federal government must exert greater leadership; establish national priorities; strengthen DHS; provide better threat information; aid in the development of security best practices and standards; provide incentives for greater private-sector security investment; establish liability protections; integrate private assets and capabilities into preparedness, response, and recovery; support the creation of stockpiles or surge capacity for certain critical supplies; and recognize security efforts and innovations that have occurred in the private sector. The following ten recommendations detail these recommendations and their potential benefits.

1. Federal Policy Paradigm

Change the federal policy paradigm. The federal government must be an equal partner in securing critical infrastructures and be a leader, not a follower.

Washington needs to recognize that the current policy paradigm for critical infrastructure protection is flawed because it assumes that the market will provide adequate incentives for security investments, and assigns only a limited support role to the federal government. Security is a public good, and as such, the market will not provide sufficient incentives. The private sector wants and needs the public sector to provide active leadership and coordinated and sustained engagement in crafting policies, identifying and enforcing common security standards, and providing economic incentives for embracing those standards.

2. National Prioritization of Critical Infrastructure

Complete the national prioritization of critical infrastructure, but do not let the goal of completion delay immediate efforts to improve security where known security gaps exist.

Because it is unlikely that DHS will be able to complete the prioritization of critical infrastructure and develop a national protective plan by the end of 2006,

---

3   Excerpted from Flynn and Prieto, 2006.

Congress should commission a rapid-turnaround study to be performed by the National Academy of Sciences with the assistance of a top-tier private-sector management consulting firm. Such a study would prioritize sectors by risk, and would also seek to rank-order protective measures recommended in earlier work by the National Academies based on cost–benefit studies and other analytical methods. These evaluations should be conducted both within each major sector and across sectors so as to identify important interdependencies. Once this prioritization has been completed, it should be used to guide the federal allocation of resources, to keep track of federal and private-sector protective efforts, and to determine how such efforts have improved the United States' homeland security posture.

While a prioritization of critical infrastructure is essential as a tool for long-term planning and accountability, completion of that effort should not be allowed to delay undertaking protective measures immediately in sectors that are known to pose significant risk.

3. Changes in the Department of Homeland Security

Strengthen the quality and experience of DHS, and establish a personnel exchange program with the private sector to help make DHS a more effective partner to the private sector.

DHS has been struggling to fulfill its homeland security mission, in no small part because of difficulties in creating a stable, experienced, and technically knowledgeable professional cadre of managers. DHS is relying on personnel from its component agencies, detailees from other agencies, and private contractors to provide most of the civil service backbone to fill the new positions created at its headquarters. DHS's legacy agencies have been raided to fill DHS management ranks, and too much of DHS's essential policy and strategy work is being outsourced to contractors. For personnel seconded from other federal agencies, their primary organizational loyalty remains with the parent agency, to which they are likely to return. This has led to a troublingly high turnover rate among DHS management personnel. Making matters worse, DHS is struggling to attract the most qualified personnel because it is not viewed as a rewarding place to work. Personnel issues disrupt DHS's capacity to manage long-term initiatives. If this situation continues, DHS will remain an unacceptably weak federal department for a decade or more.

Congress should provide for appropriate billets for permanent senior civil service government employees modeled on the Office of the Secretary of Defense. It should provide the Secretary of Homeland Security with maximum ability to attract and retain seasoned personnel, and DHS should actively recruit candidates with private-sector experience or deep knowledge of industry. As part of that effort, DHS should establish a personnel exchange program between the private sector and DHS. Such a program would allow industry experts and managers to take a leave-of-absence from their companies to serve in government, while DHS employees focused on infrastructure protection, information sharing, and response and recovery could spend time out of government working in the operations of a private enterprise. A prestigious, high-visibility public-private exchange program of this nature could help build mutual understanding and greater trust between the federal homeland security agencies and the private sector. The program could be modeled on programs at the Federal Reserve Banks, where private-sector personnel, with the support of their employers, apply for highly competitive opportunities to serve in the Fed for one to two years.

4. Information Sharing

Move beyond simply talking about information sharing, and hold government officials accountable for doing it.

The government must follow through on numerous recommendations that have been made since 9/11 to improve information sharing with the private sector (Ralyea and Seifert, 2004, 22–5; Government Accountability Office, 2004; ISAC Council, 2004a, 2004b). To build productive information-sharing relationships, government and the private sector should establish standing and formal trusted-information-sharing and analysis processes. The government should explore ways to better integrate industry into the full government intelligence cycle—requirements, tasking, analysis, reporting, and dissemination—both as a consumer and a potential provider of information. The government should increase the ability of the private sector to receive data directly from the most reliable threat and vulnerability sources. There should be a comprehensive and coordinated national plan to facilitate critical infrastructure protection information sharing that clearly delineates roles and responsibilities, defines interim objectives and milestones, sets timeframes for achieving objectives, and establishes performance measures. The White House and Congress need to hold the relevant agency heads accountable for carrying out this vital agenda.

5. Standards and Regulations

Work with industry to establish security standards, and implement regulations where necessary and in areas where industry has requested them.

The federal government should develop security best practices and standards in concert with industry, especially in sectors where industries are advocating greater government involvement (chemicals, maritime transportation) and in industries where interdependencies in fragmented markets (electrical power generation, surface transport, and food sectors) make it appropriate. To the extent that the government develops and seeks to enforce best practices and standards, such practices should be tested within commercial environments before they are applied broadly.

Several measures will be essential to the success of such a program. First, Congress must redress the general lack of regulatory authority granted to the Department of Homeland Security. While the Homeland Security Act gave DHS broad security responsibilities, it largely failed to grant DHS authority to regulate and enforce security (see Section 877, *Homeland Security Act*, 2002). Second, DHS efforts to work with industry to develop standards will be greatly improved by strengthening the private-sector experience and industry-specific knowledge of DHS employees. This can be achieved by pursuing the personnel, recruitment, and human capital exchange programs discussed in the third recommendation. Finally, it is always more effective to embed adequate security protocols in critical infrastructure during the design and construction phases. Therefore, the federal government should promote more secure and resilient infrastructure nationally by making federal funding for new infrastructure or upgrades to existing infrastructure contingent on the adoption of security standards.

6. Tax Incentives

Use targeted tax incentives to promote investments in security and resiliency in the highest-risk industries.

The federal government should use tax incentives to promote private-sector investments in security and resiliency that would not otherwise be undertaken. For example, tax credits could be made available to companies that make investments to improve chemical security, since the voluntary investments being made by chemical manufacturers are acknowledged to be insufficient. Tax credits could also be made available to support private-sector efforts to build redundancy into supply chains and other delivery systems that are critical to the functioning of the US economy, including electric power transmission and the delivery of oil, gas, food, and water. Historically, supply chains and other delivery systems have been designed to be low-cost and efficient. Federal tax policies could enable companies to invest greater amounts in the redundancy and recoverability of such systems, making the American economy and society more resilient in the face of terrorist attacks.

Additionally, tax credits could be provided that encourage companies to acquire terrorism insurance. Tax credits for insurance premiums could help increase insurance coverage in sectors such as chemicals, energy, and transport, which pose some of the most critical infrastructure risks, but which have the lowest rates of terrorism-insurance adoption (Marsh and McLennan Companies, 2005).

Eligibility for security-related tax breaks obviously should be aligned with federal critical infrastructure priorities and an assessment of each proposal's viability. Additionally, tax credits could be made available only for a limited number of years, and on a declining-scale basis, to speed the adoption of security efforts in the near term.

7. Federal Liability Protections

Make companies that undertake security improvements eligible for federal liability protection.

A lack of liability protections acts as a disincentive for companies to pursue security measures. This is because purely voluntary protective efforts can expose a company to claims that they were aware of their vulnerabilities but were negligent in taking *sufficient* measures to address them. In the aftermath of a terrorist attack, owners and operators of critical infrastructure should be shielded from lawsuits if they made good-faith efforts to abide by agreed-upon security protocols, even if these efforts still prove insufficient to prevent an attack by determined terrorists. Similar to the Safety Act, which limits liability for manufacturers of homeland security products, Congress should provide appropriate liability protections for companies that meet or exceed baseline security measures established by the federal government for eligible critical infrastructure sectors. At the same time, the federal government should improve its implementation of the Safety Act by shortening the time it takes for companies to qualify homeland security technologies for liability protection (Starks, 2005).

8. Practice Makes Perfect

Substantially increase the number of tabletop and field exercises for responding to catastrophic events, and integrate private-sector companies both into those exercises and into regionally based emergency planning processes.

One of the most helpful ways to identify gaps within existing plans, develop improved protocols, and generate political and private-sector buy-in to address security shortcomings is to conduct comprehensive training exercises. The private sector possesses extraordinary logistics capabilities to swiftly direct transportation assets, people, and goods where they are most needed. Through their around-the-clock operations centers, senior managers in many large corporations often have the ability to collect critical information at or near the scene of major incidents when local sources of official information may not be available. Homeland security planners should not wait until disaster strikes before efforts are made to tap the latent capabilities that the private sector can bring to the table.

The Department of Homeland Security should work with the Department of Defense to design annual exercises to test these capabilities, held in every region of the country. An emphasis should be placed on high-consequence events that affect multiple critical sectors concurrently. The congressionally mandated TOPOFF exercise should be stepped up from a bi-annual event to an annual exercise, and should be used to ensure that the nation has the ability to simultaneously manage two concurrent major catastrophic events, including terrorist attacks and natural disasters. The exercises should fully integrate the participation of the private sector, identifying private-sector targets, assets, and capabilities ahead of time and integrating them into these exercises. This should lead, over time, to the deeper integration of the private sector into national and regional response and recovery plans.

9. Supplies and Capabilities for Responding to Terrorist Attacks

Identify specialized supplies and capabilities that will be in short supply following certain types of terrorist incidents and other high-consequence events. Develop plans with the private sector to ensure the availability of these specialized supplies and capabilities.

The federal government should identify certain specialized supplies and capabilities—vaccines, ventilators, hospital surge capacity, laboratory capacity, decontamination equipment, electric transformers—that are likely to be critically important but in short supply in the aftermath of various terrorist attacks or other high-consequence events, such as a pandemic flu outbreak or a natural disaster. The government should work actively with the private sector to stockpile these supplies, or it should work to enhance the private sector's capacity to provide them rapidly when there is no viable commercial market (House Select Committee on Homeland Security, 2004; Dade, 2004).[4] To better prepare for mass-casualty events and other major medical emergencies, the National Academies' Institute of Medicine should be provided with funding to convene an expert working group charged with identifying these supplies and capabilities and estimating the cost to the government of purchasing them or building the spare capacity to supply them on a rapid basis. In addition, the government should build on lessons learned from various pilot public-private partnerships to integrate private-sector assets, know-how, and personnel into ensuring that scarce critical supplies and capabilities are available when needed.

10. Federal Awards Program

Establish a federal awards program that recognizes private-sector efforts and innovation in homeland security.

A federal awards program should be established that recognizes the innovation, efforts, and contributions of the private sector toward improving homeland security. A model for this is the prestigious Baldridge National Quality Awards program, a public-private partnership established to recognize excellence in corporate practices. The awards should particularly focus on critical infrastructure protection, information sharing, and response and recovery. The award criteria should be weighted toward industry efforts to improve the security of their own assets; to increase security collaboration within and across sectors; and to increase homeland security collaboration with federal, state, and local governments and NGOs. An awards program would appropriately provide public recognition for the patriotism, goodwill, and creativity of private companies. The publicity associated with the program would also provide a means to highlight valuable and innovative efforts that might otherwise go unnoticed, thereby encouraging their adoption by other companies and sectors. Firms would likely respond well to the opportunity to publicize and market their security achievements.

References

Auersald, P., Branscomb, L., La Port, T. and Erwan, M. (2006), *Seeds of Disaster, Roots of Response: How Private Action Can Reduce Public Vulnerability* (New York: Cambridge University Press).
Benjamin, D. and Simon, S. (2005), *The Next Attack: The Failure of the War on Terror and a Strategy for Getting it Right* (New York: Times Books).

---

4   Both sources advocate significant federal investments in the private sector's capacity to develop more rapidly responses to unforeseen viruses: "The goal of a new 'bug-to-drug' paradigm would be to discover and distribute new antidotes in a few years or even months rather than decades. The system must be nimble and affordable. And it must involve the cooperation and expertise of a wide range of entities, from government agencies to private industry and academia" (quoted in Dade, 2004).

Bush, G.W. (2004), "President Bush Celebrates Independence Day," West Virginia Capitol Grounds, Charleston, West Virginia (4 July); at <http://www.whitehouse.gov/news/releases/2004/07/20040704.html>

Cheney, R. (2005), Remarks by the Vice President at the 123rd Coast Guard Academy Commencement, New London, Connecticut (19 May); at <http://www.whitehouse.gov/news/releases/2004/05/20040519-5.html>

Clarke, R., et al. (2004), *Defeating the Jihadists: A Blueprint for Action* (New York: Century Foundation Task Force Report).

Council on Competitiveness (2002), *Creating Opportunity Out of Adversity*, Proceedings of the National Symposium on Competitiveness and Security.

Dade, J. (2004), "Biodefense Wake Up Call," *Washington Times* (18 October).

Flynn, S. (2005), Testimony before the US Senate Committee on Homeland Security and Governmental Affairs hearing on "The Security of America's Chemical Facilities," 109 Cong., 1st sess. (27 April).

Flynn, S. and Prieto, D. (2006), *Neglected Defense: Mobilizing the Private Sector to Support Homeland Security* (New York: Council on Foreign Relations).

Glasser, S. (2005), "U.S. Figures Show Sharp Global Rise In Terrorism; State Dept. Will Not Put Data in Report," *The Washington Post* (27 April).

Government Accountability Office (2004), "Critical Infrastructure Protection: Establishing Effective Information Sharing with Infrastructure Sectors," testimony, GAO-04-699T (21 April) and GAO-04-780.

Homeland Security Act of 2002 (2002), 107th Congress, 2nd Session; at <http://files.findlaw.com/news.findlaw.com/hdocs/docs/terrorism/hsa2002.pdf>

House Select Committee on Homeland Security (2004), "Beyond Anthrax: Confronting the Future Biological Weapons Threat" (May); at <http://knxas1.hsdl.org/homesec/docs/legis/nps03-051304-14.pdf>

ISAC Council (2004a), "A Functional Model for Critical Infrastructure Information Sharing and Analysis: Maturing and Expanding Efforts," White Paper (31 January).

ISAC Council (2004b), "Government–Private Sector Relations," White Paper (31 January).

Marsh and McLennan Companies (2005), "Marketwatch: Terrorism Insurance 2005; Industry Focus: Chemicals"; at <http://solutions.marsh.com/TRIA/documents/Marshs_Marketwatch_Terrorism_-_Chemicals_Industry.pdf>

National Strategy for Homeland Security (2002) (Washington, DC: The White House); at <http://www.whitehouse.gov/homeland/book/index.html>

"Official: Voice on Tape is bin Laden's" (2002), CNN (13 November); at <http://archives.cnn.com/2002/WORLD/meast/11/12/binladen.statement/>

Ralyea, H. and Seifert, J. (2004), *Information Sharing for Homeland Security: A Brief Overview*, Report RL32597 (Washington, DC: Library of Congress/Congressional Research Service).

Starks, T. (2005), "Best Laid Plans: Effort to Lure Homeland Businesses with Liability Protection Falls Far Short of Goals," *Congressional Quarterly* (7 January).

US Department of State (2005), *Country Reports on Terrorism* (Washington, DC: US Department of State, Office of the Coordinator on Counterterrorism) (27 April); at <http://www.state.gov/s/ct/rls/45321.htm>

Glossary

1267 Committee: A committee established by the United Nations Security Council in 1999 with the adoption of UNSC Resolution 1267, its purpose was to oversee the implementation of sanctions against Taliban-controlled Afghanistan for its support of Osama bin Laden. Also known as the Al Qaeda and Taliban Sanctions Committee.

Al Qaeda: In Arabic meaning "The Foundation" or "The Base," Al Qaeda is an international terrorist network headed by Osama bin Laden whose objective is to violently expunge foreign influence from Muslim regimes and promote a return to the Caliphate.

Bureau of Industry and Security (BIS): A part of the US Department of Commerce. Among other mandates, BIS regulates with whom states trade and regulates the products that are traded. Its mission is to advance US national security, foreign policy, and economic objectives by ensuring an effective export control and treaty compliance system and promoting continued US strategic technology leadership.

Chapter VII: Section of the UN Charter dealing with actions relating to threats to the peace, breaches of the peace, and acts of aggression.

Collateral damage: A euphemism for unintended and inadvertent casualties and destruction inflicted on civilians during military operations.

Counter-Terrorism Committee (CTC): A 15-member committee established by UN Resolution 1373 which aims to increase the capability of member states to fight terrorism. The Counter-Terrorism Committee Executive Directorate (CTED) was later established to further enhance the United Nations' ability to monitor the implementation of Resolution 1373.

Customs-Trade Partnership against Terrorism (C-TPAT): C-TPAT is an initiative introduced by US Customs and Border Protection in collaboration with carriers, brokers, and warehouse operators to improve security of ports.

Diaspora: Religious, ethnic, or national peoples living outside of what has come to be considered their traditional homelands. Originally, the term specifically described Jews dispersed by the Babylonians or Romans living in scattered communities outside Judea.

Extraterritorial sanctions: A measure employed by a country that seeks to affect the conduct of foreign persons outside of its national jurisdiction.

Fatwa: A ruling by a *mufti*, or religious lawyer, on a specific issue; the ruling can either be accepted or rejected by the Islamic community.

Fedayeen: Literally, "he who sacrifices himself." The name came into usage among early Palestinian refugees who organized themselves in armed bands in the Sinai and Gaza Strip to combat Zionist settlers in Palestine; it is now used by several other groups.

Financial Action Task Force (FATF): An inter-governmental body established by the G-7 member states, the European Commission, and eight other countries, whose purpose is the development and promotion of national and international policies to combat money laundering and terrorist financing.

Foreign Assistance Act: Passed in 1961, this act reorganized US foreign assistance programs, separating military and non-military aid and resulting in the creation of the US Agency for International Development (USAID).

Foreign Terrorist Organization (FTO): A designation made regarding foreign groups by the US Secretary of State. Members of groups designated as FTOs are forbidden from entering or holding funds in the United States. It is also a crime for a person in the US or under the jurisdiction of the US to provide material support or resources to a designated FTO.

Government Accountability Office (GAO): An agency that works for the US Congress to study the programs and expenditures of the federal government. Up until July 2004, it was known as the General Accounting Office.

Hamas: The largest and most influential Palestinian militant movement, it combines a campaign of resistance to Israeli occupation of Palestinian territories with social service programs. In 2006, the party won the majority in the Palestinian Authority's general legislative elections.

Hawala: A remittance system that serves as an alternative or parallel to the formal banking system. The components of *hawala* that distinguish it from other systems of money transfer are trust and the extensive use of connections, such as family relationships or regional or ethnic affiliations. Unlike traditional banking, *hawala* makes minimal or no use of any sort of negotiable instrument. Transfers of money take place based on communications between members of a network of *hawaladars*, or *hawala* dealers.

Hezbollah: A major fundamentalist Shi'ite resistance movement in Lebanon formed after the 1982 Israeli invasion. The name translates as "Party of God."

Imam: In general use, an imam is a Muslim leader of congregational prayers; as such, it implies no ordination or special spiritual powers beyond sufficient education to carry out this function. It is also used figuratively by many Sunni Muslims to mean the leader of the Islamic community. However, for Shi'ites the term is more specific. Ali, the cousin and son-in-law of the Prophet Mohammed, is considered to be the first imam; the term is also used to designate Ali's male descendants.

Improvised Explosive Devices (IEDs): A "homemade" explosive device that is designed to cause death or injury. Used by insurgents to great effect in the current war in Iraq and elsewhere.

International Emergency Economic Powers Act (IEEPA): US federal law that allows the President of the United States to identify any extraordinary threat that originates outside the US and to confiscate property, prohibit and block transactions, as well as freeze assets belonging to the identified group in response.

Islamist: Term used to describe radical Muslim groups that hold that Islam is not only a religion, but should be the only political and legal system that governs the economic, social, and judicial mechanisms of the nation-state according to its interpretation of *Sharia*, or Islamic Law. In common usage, it has come to be used interchangeably with "Islamic fundamentalism."

Jihad: This term has often been translated as "holy war," a concept that emerged in Europe in the eleventh century to refer to the Crusades, and which has no equivalent in Islam. Jihad derives from the Arabic root of "striving." Another, better translation would be "striving in the cause of God." There are two aspects of jihad: the greater jihad, the struggle to overcome carnal desires and evil inclinations; and the lesser jihad, the armed defense of Islam against aggressors. The term "jihad" has been used by different armed groups in their violent confrontations with the West; famously, Osama bin Laden called for a jihad in his *fatwa* against Americans, using the term to refer to a "just war" against an oppressor.

Liberation Tigers of Tamil Eelam (LTTE): A politico-military organization that has been waging a secessionist campaign against the Sri Lankan government since the 1970s in order to secure a separate state for the Tamil majority regions in the north and east of Sri Lanka. Also known as the Tamil Tigers.

Light Weapons: A category of arms that includes heavy machine guns; hand-held, under-barrel, and mounted grenade launchers; portable anti-tank and anti-aircraft guns; recoilless rifles; portable launchers of anti-tank and anti-aircraft missile systems; and mortars of a caliber less than 100mm.

Manchester Manual: A manual found on a computer seized in the 2000 arrest of a suspected terrorist in Manchester, UK. It includes instructions on counterfeiting and forgery, security measures for undercover activities, and strategies in the case of arrest and indictment. The manual has since been described by the FBI as an Al Qaeda training manual; versions of it have been discovered in Afghanistan.

Man-portable air defense systems (MANPADS): Man-portable air defense systems are shoulder-launched surface-to-air missiles. Possession, export, and trafficking in such weapons are typically tightly controlled due to the threat they pose to civil aviation, and there has been considerable concern about their use as terrorist weapons.

Money Laundering: The practice of engaging in specific financial transactions in order to conceal the identity, source, and/or destination of money. It is a main operation of the underground economy (black market), particularly of drug and arms traffickers. It is seen as a major source of funding for terror activity, and has been combated in the international community with varying degrees of vigor since 11 September 2001.

Mujahedin (or mujahedeen): The term derives from the Arabic *mujahidin*, plural of *mujahid*, literally meaning "he who wages jihad." The term was applied to Muslims fighting the Red Army during the anti-Soviet jihad in Afghanistan (1979–89), and has been translated as "Holy Warriors." Today it is used to describe Islamic guerrilla fighters, especially in the Middle East.

Mujahedin-e Khalq (MEK): The MEK is a Marxist Islamic group that was initially formed to challenge the Shah's authoritarian government in Iran but was expelled from the country in the early 1980s. Starting in the late 1980s, its primary support came from the former Iraqi government of Saddam Hussein. The MEK currently advocates the overthrow of the Iranian government, and that it be replaced with leaders from the ranks of the MEK.

Muslim Brotherhood: Founded in Egypt in 1928, this confraternity is considered the matrix of all modern Islamist movements of Sunni obedience. Present all over the world, the Muslim Brotherhood promotes a fundamentalist interpretation of Islam.

Narco-terrorism: Use of terror tactics by narco-traffickers and drug lords to protect their illegal businesses. It also describes the alliance between drug lords and armed terrorist organizations. Both have interests in destabilizing governments and breaking down the established social order.

Office of Weapons Removal and Abatement (WRA): Part of the US State Department's Bureau of Political–Military Affairs, this office is responsible for curbing the illicit proliferation of conventional weapons of war (such as light automatic weapons and rocket propelled grenades) and removing and destroying others (such as persistent landmines and abandoned stocks of munitions) that continue to pose a hazard after the cessation of armed conflict.

Offshore Financial Centers (OFCs): Locations that permit the provision of financial services by banks and other agents to non-residents.

Organization for Security and Cooperation in Europe (OSCE): With 56 member states drawn from Europe, Central Asia, and the Americas, the OSCE is the world's largest regional security organization, bringing comprehensive and cooperative security to the OSCE region.

Patriot Act: Formally known as the "Uniting and Strengthening America by Providing Appropriate Tools Required to Intercept and Obstruct Terrorism Act," or USA PATRIOT Act, the Patriot Act was passed by the US Congress after the 9/11 attacks on the World Trade Center and the Pentagon, to enhance the investigatory tools available to law enforcement agencies in the United States. It includes the controversial elimination of a number of barriers to national security-related investigations.

Revolutionary Armed Forces of Colombia (FARC): Colombia's largest, richest, and most powerful rebel guerilla group. Created in 1966, the group has Marxist and peasant origins, and is now dominated by narco-terrorist activities.

SAFETY (Support Anti-terrorism by Fostering Effective Technologies) Act: As part of the Homeland Security Act of 2002, the US Congress enacted this measure to provide risk management and litigation management protections for sellers of qualified anti-terrorism technologies and others in the supply and distribution chain.

Salafism: A movement in Sunni Islam distinct from Wahhabism that holds the words and actions of the Prophet and his successors to be the pure practice of Islam. The movement looks back to early Islam in order to rediscover a new or modern interpretation of Islam. *Salaf* can be translated as "predecessors," and followers consider the Qur'an and the *Sunnah* (or the way Prophet Mohammed lived his life) to be their unique points of reference.

SCADA: Acronym for Supervisory Control and Data Acquisition. SCADA systems are often employed in chemical plants, dams, waste water treatment plants, electricity generation facilities, and other sensitive infrastructures, allowing for remote control and monitoring.

Sharia: The Holy Law of Islam that embodies the legal, moral, political, and economic discourse in Muslim societies. *Sharia* is comprised of the teachings of the Qu'ran, the *hadiths* (or words of the Prophet), the *ijma* (the consensus of Islamic scholars), the *qiyas* (a system of analogies that apply precedents established by the holy texts to problems not covered by them), and *fatwas* (non-binding rulings by Islamic scholars issued to the Islamic community).

Shi'ism: The second largest sect of Islam, Shi'ism was created when Ali, the Prophet Mohammed's cousin and son-in-law, refused to submit to Caliph Mu'awiyya, the founder of the Sunni dynasty. Ali's supporters split from the Sunni and became Shi'ites in the first great schism within Islam. "Twelver Shi'ites" follow the doctrine of the Mahdi, or "Hidden Imam," who has left this world but will return at the end of time to spread justice across the earth.

Specially Designated Terrorist (SDT): Any person who is determined by the US Secretary of the Treasury to be a specially designated terrorist under notices or regulations issued by the Office of Foreign Assets Control (OFAC). The OFAC administers and enforces economic and trade sanctions based on US foreign policy and national security goals against targeted foreign countries, terrorists, international narcotics traffickers, and those engaged in activities related to the proliferation of weapons of mass destruction.

Sunnism: The orthodox and largest sect of Islam. It means "those who adhere to the *Sunnah*," or way of the Prophet. After Mohammed's death, those followers who supported a traditional method of election based on community agreement became known as Sunnis; those who supported Ali as Mohammed's successor became known as Shi'ites.

SWIFT (Society for Worldwide Interbank Financial Telecommunication): Based in Belgium, SWIFT is an industry-owned cooperative that supplies secure, standardized messaging services and interface software to nearly 8,000 financial institutions in 206 countries and territories. After 9/11, the Bush Administration started a clandestine program to sift through SWIFT data to uncover suspicious financial transactions.

Taliban: A Muslim fundamentalist group known for its strict interpretation of Islamic law that controlled Afghanistan's government from 1996 until the US-led invasion in 2001. The group has since re-emerged in Afghanistan as an insurgent power.

Tawhid: Translated as "God is Oneness," this belief is the foundation of Islam and signifies that Allah is indivisible, unique, and indefinable.

Wahhabism: Name used outside of Saudi Arabia to designate the official interpretation of Islam in Saudi Arabia. The faith is a puritanical concept of *tawhid* ("God is Oneness") that was preached by Mohammad ibn Abd al Wahhab, whence his Muslim opponents derived the name. The royal family of Qatar and most indigenous Qataris are Wahhabis.

Wassenaar Arrangement: Formally known as the "Wassenaar Arrangement on Export Controls for Conventional Arms and Dual-Use Goods and Technologies," it was established in 1996 to contribute to regional and international security and stability by promoting transparency and greater responsibility in transfers of conventional arms and dual-use goods and technologies, thus preventing destabilizing accumulations. The 40 member states seek, through their national policies, to ensure that transfers of these items do not contribute to the development or enhancement of military capabilities which undermine these goals, and are not diverted to support such capabilities. It is administered by a secretariat in Vienna.

Zakat: Obligatory alms tax, which constitutes one of the Five Pillars of Islam.

Index

Note: Figures are indicated by bold type page numbers.